Margaret Ford was born in Blackburn in 1926 and grew up there between the wars. She moved away after marrying in 1947 and today lives near Carnforth.

A Daughter's Choice

MARGARET FORD
WITH JACQUIE BUTTRISS

PAN BOOKS

First published 2019 by Pan Books
an imprint of Pan Macmillan
20 New Wharf Road, London N1 9RR
Associated companies throughout the world
www.panmacmillan.com

ISBN 978-1-5098-9192-4

1 3 5 7 9 8 6 4 2

A CIP catalogue record for this book is available from the British Library.

Typeset by Palimpsest Book Production Ltd, Falkirk, Stirlingshire
Printed and bound by CPI Group (UK) Ltd, Croydon, CR0 4YY

Visit www.panmacmillan.com to read more about all our books
and to buy them. You will also find features, author interviews and
news of any author events, and you can sign up for e-newsletters
so that you're always first to hear about our new releases.

A.M.D.G.

With everlasting love for my mother, Ray, Les and Jim

Contents

Prologue

The pavement was hidden under a sparkling white blanket of snow as I stepped out of the front door of our house on Robinson Street for my long-awaited wedding day. Uncle John, who had reluctantly agreed to walk me down the aisle, sat in the back seat of the hired car, waiting for me. I took a deep breath and got in next to him. We sat in silence as we drove through the snow and the slush to St Alban's Church, watching the glittering rooftops and trees go by.

I should be happy and smiling, I thought, but instead I was full of anxiety that things would not go to plan: would tension bubble up between our families? Would my older brother Bobby try to stop the wedding? Or even worse, would Joe find a way to ruin everything? At that moment, it seemed to me that the whole world was against us having the perfect day we'd dreamed of.

Perhaps I'd had too long to think. Maybe I wasn't ready. Conflicting thoughts raced around my brain. By the time we reached the entrance to the church, as I saw him standing there, stamping his feet in the snow, waiting for me with a wide grin on his face, I felt overwhelmed by doubts . . . I couldn't do it.

'Drive away please,' I said suddenly.

'Are you sure, miss?' the driver replied.

'I need to get away.'

Uncle John gave me a sideways look, but he didn't say a word – just tutted and turned back, staring straight ahead.

As we reversed out of the drive I watched my fiancé's smile drop, replaced with a look of baffled dismay, then shock. How could I do this to him? But wouldn't it be worse to subject him to a shattered dream? And it wasn't just about him. I knew he loved me completely, but what if I didn't love him enough? What if I lost my independence? I could see a future stretch ahead of me that I wasn't sure I wanted . . .

1

Playing with Otters

1926–1929

Born blue, the baby was slapped and swung round
in the air by her ankles till she cried.

I was that baby. I started life loudly amidst the silenced
mills of Blackburn following the General Strike of May
1926. I was born in our two-up, two-down terraced house
in Goldhey Street, Little Harwood and was weaned on
Oxo. These were hard times for working families in
Blackburn, but, although we were cash-poor, both sets of
grandparents made sure we always had enough to eat.

Our house was on top of a hill, about fifteen minutes'
walk from the centre of the city and not far from where
my mother's parents lived. Grandad Harrison was a master
builder and had his own building company, with a large
yard near to their home. They lived in a detached house
near Daisyfield Station, about two hundred yards from
Goldhey Street.

Grandad had bought our house for my parents when
they got married, so we occasionally stayed there, but

most of the time we lived at the Tanners' Arms in Dinckley, a village about six miles away from central Blackburn. The Tanners' was a popular pub which was owned and run by my father's parents, Grandma and Grandpa Holden, with the help of my father, Horace, and his brother, Uncle Eddie. They both worked full-time because Grandpa Holden also had another job as a mills inspector, touring all the local cotton mills to check they didn't break any laws. He was a stern man with dark, greying whiskers, a moustache and a bushy beard. He wouldn't tolerate any bad behaviour.

His wife, my grandma, was just as stern. I once heard one of their customers calling her 'a cantankerous woman'. She always wore long, dark clothes and was fierce in her mission for cleanliness. She had a temper and I remember her snapping at my mother if she didn't do something the way she wanted it. She was often cross with her sons too. Uncle Eddie was never quick enough for her, and Father was too generous when he measured out the drinks. Everyone had to jump to, or there'd be trouble.

Although all seven of us lived together on the first floor of the pub, it was a large building and I didn't spend much time with my Holden grandparents. I shared a room upstairs with my brother Bobby who was five years older than me. Downstairs was all to do with the pub. In the main room, there was a big open fireplace and a long bar with a wooden top that had to be polished every day. I think that was my father's favourite place, drinking with his friends at the bar. Along the back was a row of wooden barrels with low taps on them.

One day, as a toddler, I was sitting on the stone slabs of the floor behind the bar and I turned on one of the taps. The brown liquid poured out all over me and I screamed because I couldn't stop it. I was sitting in a spreading pool of ale, crying my eyes out, when Uncle Eddie rushed across and turned the tap off, then roughly lifted me up and bundled me upstairs.

'You must never do that again,' he scolded as he handed me over to my mother. I didn't like Uncle Eddie much as he wasn't very kind or friendly. I don't think he liked me either. He ignored me most of the time.

The bar area led to two smaller rooms filled with curved-back chairs around tables, each with a heavy ashtray. There was also a kitchen on the ground floor. Most of the customers were local agricultural workers, passers-by or travellers during the week, but at weekends, high days and holidays people from Blackburn came in their droves to the countryside for a day out, especially in good weather.

The Tanners' Arms was surrounded by acres of open fields and farmland. Veevers Farm, across the road, had land that stretched out in all directions with a long walk from the road to the large stone farmhouse. It was a wonderful place to grow up.

Grandpa Holden also used to keep animals, like pigeons and hens, on some ground outside. At the time I thought they were pets but we sometimes used to eat pigeon pie and I never thought to ask where the filling came from! I only realized one Sunday, when Grandad wrung a chicken's neck so that we could cook and eat it for lunch. I had watched this chicken and her friends running carefree around their pen in our garden just an hour before. Now the hen squawked and screeched in her death throes. I was horrified, but none of the grown-ups comforted me. This was not a demonstrative family. Only Bobby put his arm round me, which cheered me up.

Apart from the chicken incident, I have only happy recollections of my early childhood, not then knowing or even sensing the frictional undercurrents that existed across my extended family.

My two earliest memories were of being with my gentle mother, Alice – a pretty young woman with thick chestnut curls, a round face and a thin waist. The first was at our Goldhey Street house, where Mother was always more relaxed. Perhaps that's why we went there, away from the pub, just the two of us. I was sitting on her knee in her rocking chair in the living room, rocking to and fro in front of the coal fire in the hearth just as the klaxon was sounding for the mill workers to go home. I watched the flames leap in the fire and I remember the cosy, warm feeling I had, feeling safe in her company. The other was on a bright, sunny day when she took me half a mile down the lane from the Tanners' to the river Ribble in my big pram.

When we reached her favourite spot, she lifted me out of the pram and held my hand as I toddled down to the water's edge and sat on the patch of sand that she called 'Little Blackpool'. While she sat next to me and did her crocheting, I splashed about with my stubby fingers in the puddles on the sand. Slowly, a baby otter approached and dared to come out of the water, followed by his more timid siblings. I remember watching them as they played with each other, turning and tumbling on the sand around my legs as if they trusted me. I think the brave one let me touch him. Mother laughed with me at their antics. I've loved otters ever since. It's just as well that I knew nothing then about the annual Boxing Day gathering of otter hounds and their masters, along that very stretch of the river. I was always happiest with my mother. Unlike Father and some of the other grown-ups, she was never raucous or unpredictable, angry or upset when it was just the two of us – always calm and happy.

During the day at the Tanners', everyone in the family had their jobs and Bobby was at school, so I was very happy to be left to my own devices. Looking back, I expect the adults were happy to get me out from under their feet. It might seem strange now, but in those days nobody worried about young children playing unsupervised in the countryside, which seemed so safe. I became a very independent child and loved making up my own games to keep myself occupied.

Outside the pub, the farmer from Veevers Farm stood his milk-kits every morning, on two platforms at the side of the building, one higher than the other. I sat and waited to watch them being collected by a man driving his horse and wagon. This carthorse was a gentle giant, with its long fetlocks and glossy mane – it gave a friendly whinny whenever it saw me.

Across the road from the Tanners' was a small, rectangular red postbox on a wooden pole, next to a grassy mound.

There was very little traffic passing down the road then
– just the odd, lumbering horse-drawn cart or pushbike,
as very few people had motor cars yet in Blackburn – so
it was safe to let me play out there. In fact, it was an
exciting occasion if ever we did see a motor car, and
everyone would go outside to have a look.

Every morning, after breakfast, I used to wander across
the road to the postbox, and scramble up the grassy
mound. Then I could grab hold of a branch that jutted
out of the overgrown hedge to pull myself up to reach
the slit. I spent many happy hours carefully picking grasses
and gathering stones, roots, pebbles, twigs, nuts – anything
I could find – from around the Tanners'. I started to build
a pile of them on top of the bank, so that I could have a
lovely time posting them all through the slit of the postbox
until I had filled it right up to the top.

Having finished this task, I would potter off a few yards
down the road to talk to the horse that lived in the field.
He always came to the fence as soon as I arrived and
listened intently to whatever story I told him that day,
while he patiently munched on the tufts of long grass in
my hand, plucked from the verge on my side of the fence.

After I'd filled up the postbox for three days in a row,
it began to cause some alarm at the Tanners'.

'Somebody has blocked up the postbox!' complained
one rather large lady who popped into the pub with her
letters in her hand. 'Who could have done such a thing?'

'Don't ask me,' was my grandpa's curt reply, though I
think he might have guessed the small vandal's identity.
'Just put your letters up on the bar for now and I'll tell

the postman to call in for them.' As I continued with my mischief, he put a table outside where people could leave their post. Then, at the right time, he would go out and bring all the letters and parcels in to put on the bar, ready for the postman's visit. Well, anyone who came inside would stay for a drink, wouldn't they?

So, each day, the postman pedalled up to the Tanners' to collect the letters . . . and stayed for a pint to 'wet his whistle'. Sometimes he stayed for two!

It wasn't long before the local policeman, patrolling on his clattering bike, took to popping in as well. It was always at about the same time, just to make sure everything was all right . . . and to have a drink while he was there. Some days he stayed so long that the inspector came to join him! When I was old enough to think about it, I realized I must have done my family a favour by filling up that postbox so efficiently.

The Tanners' Arms was quite an old building, probably Victorian. It had no flush lavatories or hot water. Consequently, we had outside latrines and chamber pots that were emptied into 'tubs' with carrying handles at each side. At the end of each day, after I'd gone to bed, Father and Uncle Eddie had to empty them somewhere outside. I never knew where. It was only when I was older that I realized why we so often ate mushrooms for breakfast!

Down the side of the Tanners' there was a long, narrow tea room, which was a glass-fronted extension. It had a lovely garden where people brought their children to have free lemonade and play, while the adults sat on old school benches and paid for their drinks. Even when I was very small, I always joined in the fun and games, though many of the children were older than me.

Beside the tea room there were lots of sheds and the area of ground where my grandfather kept his hens, pigeons and doves. There was one smelly shed I was forbidden to go into. One day I asked my mother why.

'That's where they make gas for the lights,' she explained. 'So it's dangerous. You haven't to go anywhere near it.' For once, I did as I was told.

As an independent three-year-old, I continued to seek out new adventures. One very hot day, whilst Mother and I were at our Goldhey Street house, with all the windows and doors open to let the air through, I couldn't resist the chance to have a little wander, as I often did at the Tanners'. As soon as Mother noticed I was missing, she went round to all our neighbours, looking for me. They came out to help search the street, gardens and alleyways, whilst Alice Fish, from the shop over the road, ran down to the police station.

'They're sending a policeman out to help us find Margaret,' Alice told my mother. 'They said for you to stay at home, in case she turns up again.'

Mother must have been very worried about me, waiting at home for news. But I was having a whale of a time . . . until our friendly local policeman looked over the school railings half an hour later and recognized me sitting in the middle of a circle of children in the playground, as they took turns to roll a ball to me. He tried to pick me up, but I struggled and kicked and screamed.

'Let me go,' I wailed, tears running down my cheeks. 'Go away!'

So in the end he had to go and ask my mother to come and fetch me. When she arrived, she walked across and took my hand.

'Come home now, Margaret,' she said in as calm a voice as she could, highly relieved, no doubt. But I was completely oblivious to all the worry and upheaval I had caused. Despite her anxiety, she was such an easy-going person, kind and considerate to everybody, that she didn't tell me off that afternoon. In fact, I don't ever remember her telling me off for anything. Thinking back now, I know I was quite a handful for my mother to manage. I often led her a merry dance, but she was as stoical as a saint.

I was glad my father wasn't there that day. He would have been furious!

One day, I can remember my mother dressing me up in a pale-blue outfit, trimmed with white fur. 'Your father wants to take you on an outing,' she smiled brightly, in an attempt to give me confidence. But I was not so sure, as I was not close to my father and feared his temper. Now I realize Mother must have had her qualms about this 'outing' too, particularly as my father had never taken me anywhere alone without the rest of the family. I wasn't excited about the trip but he did make a fuss of me sometimes, giving me sweets and once buying me a doll.

So off we went. I don't know where we went or what we did, except for a vague memory of walking across Blackburn and going into a big house with a wide doorway, up the stairs, and being left in a room on my own. It was a small, pretty bedroom and I lay down on the pink candlewick bedspread. It was so comfy that I must have fallen asleep. After a little while, Father woke me up and we walked to another noisier building, where he left me sitting outside while he went in. Much later in the afternoon, my father arrived back home without me.

My mother frantically asked him where I was but he was so drunk he couldn't remember where he'd left me. Exasperated with him and worried about me, she had to send for the police again. He was probably too drunk to care. This time the search was much wider, as Father couldn't even remember where he'd been. There were a lot of pubs in Blackburn, so I could have been anywhere. I suppose I was always such a happy child that I must have amused myself in some way while I was waiting for him – playing with stones or making patterns with leaves, maybe.

All I remember is a kind policeman coming to find me, sitting on the bench where I suppose Father had left me, outside one of the pubs. I don't think I would have been tempted to wander away in a strange place. The policeman took me back to our house in Goldhey Street, where my mother rushed up to me, bent down and looked at my face. 'Are you all right?' she asked, stroking my tangled hair with relief.

I nodded. I was fine. Knowing me, I probably wondered what all the fuss was about. Mother made me something for tea and then helped me wash and put me to bed. I don't know what happened between the grown-ups after that. However, I do know that Mother was 'not pleased', as she told me years later, when relating the tale to me.

As I grew older, my mother started to talk to me about her past. She used to tell me how, as a young girl of about fifteen, at the end of the First World War, she used to bake cakes or shortbreads and take them in a basket down to the railway station at Daisyfield. There she distributed them to the returning wounded soldiers, some of whom had been prisoners of war.

'They were all bloodied and dirty from the trenches,' she explained.

One of those men was my father. Horace Holden was only fifteen when he joined up in the Sherwood Foresters Regiment during the First World War, and just sixteen when he was wounded in France and taken as a prisoner to Germany.

When he returned home to Blackburn, skin and bone from being a prisoner of war, he and my mother met at the railway station and started courting. She soon fell pregnant and in 1920 they were forced by both sets of parents to marry. He was nineteen and Mother was seventeen. He took a job in a cotton factory – it was a terrible place to work but he had no choice as he now had a wife to keep and my brother Bobby was on the way. Fortunately, two or three years later, his father was able to give him a better job, working in the Tanners' Arms. By the time I came along, five years after Bobby, we lived in at the Tanners' most of the time. I suppose it was easier that way.

I didn't usually go into the pub part of the Tanners' in the evening when it was very busy, but I often walked through at quieter moments in the morning or afternoon.

There were two or three regular drinkers I came to recognize, who used to smile or wave if they saw me. One of these was a lovely man called David Furness. Mother told me he had a large house overlooking the river Ribble but he spent most of his days at the Tanners'. He always had a skiver bag with him – a small bag, made of the finest leather. He laid it on the table, next to his pint, while he talked with his mates. Or sometimes he sat on his own.

One day, when he sat alone, I asked him what was in his bag.

'Why don't you look and see?' he grinned and pulled a chair round for me to sit on.

I clambered up and knelt on the chair, so that I could reach his bag. He opened the tab for me and I looked inside.

'What is it?' I asked.

'Empty it out and see,' he suggested.

So I gently poured the contents out onto the tabletop. 'Oooh,' I exclaimed as I saw the gold coins glinting in the sunlight from the window. 'Is it money?'

'Yes, in a way,' he agreed. 'But it's old money.'

I pulled the coins across the table so that I could see them better.

'They're gold sovereigns,' he said.

I turned one over to see both sides. Pointing at the head engraved on its surface, I asked him, 'Is this you?'

He laughed kindly. 'No, it's the king. He's better-looking than me.'

Whenever I saw him in the pub after that, he always let me play with his sovereigns. I would pile them up carefully to make a tower, or place them side by side in a row, making a pattern with them on the table. My mother even gave me some paper and a crayon so that I could make rubbings of them to keep in my room.

Like most small children, as I approached school age my life was exciting and carefree. I had no idea that frictions between my mother's staunchly Protestant family and my father's equally devout Roman Catholic family had existed even before they got married. In those days, Catholics were not allowed to enter a Protestant church or marry a non-Catholic, so my parents had to go to a registry office. Both sets of grandparents were very wary and critical of each other's religion. But that wasn't all. The animosity between them was much more to do with the circumstances of my parents' marriage, as my mother had fallen pregnant so young and out of wedlock.

As a young girl I was ignorant of these troubles so their sometimes strange interactions with each other just made me laugh. Grandma Holden used to peg a large sheet on the washing line at the Tanners'. I thought it was so the two sets of grandparents couldn't see each other across the fields. I found this funny, especially when Grandad Harrison got out his telescope while I was at their newly built bungalow in Salesbury and looked through it in the garden to annoy them at the Tanners'. Later my mother told me that the real reason for the sheet was to signal when we left the Tanners' to walk over to my Harrison grandparents' bungalow, so that they knew we were on the way. But I liked my version of the story better! Grandma and Grandpa Holden were older, stricter and mostly ignored me but Grandma and Grandad Harrison always welcomed me into their home and loved to watch me playing in their garden. I knew who I preferred.

There were growing tensions, too, of a different kind, between my mother and father. After my mother's frustrated reaction on the day my father got drunk and came home without me, things never really felt the same. Though they did try to shelter me from all that most of the time. I know now that there must have been a lot of pressures on their marriage, having been made to wed so young, when they had hardly had time to form a true relationship. I never witnessed any arguments between them but sometimes heard raised voices when I was tucked up in bed at night. One such night, in our Goldhey Street house, there was a knock on the door and I heard my cousin Billy's voice.

'I was passing a pub just as Uncle Horace came out,' he explained to my mother. 'He looked as if he'd drunk too much, so I thought I'd better bring him home, or there'd be no knowing what he'd 'a done next.'

I heard my mother thanking Billy in a tired voice as my father stumbled into the house and shouted gibberish back at him. That wasn't the last time Billy brought him home.

2

Family Frictions

1930

As my fourth birthday came and went, Father's mood and his drinking didn't seem to be getting any better. One morning, we were all sitting round the table in our Goldhey Street house – Father, Mother, Bobby and me, eating our breakfast. I can't remember who was talking, but suddenly Father made a rude noise. It made me burst into a fit of giggles. Mother gulped as Father's face turned red with anger.

I suppose I should have seen the signs and stopped there, but I was too young to pre-empt the consequences.

'You trumped,' I said in my innocence.

This enraged him even further. He shoved back his chair, scraping the quarry-tiled floor, thumped his fist on the old wooden table and stood up, towering over us. We all fell silent, unsure what he would do next.

'Don't you dare use rude words against me!' he shouted, pointing his finger at me, his eyes bulging with anger. He grabbed his belt, undid the buckle and pulled it off, winding part of it round his hand. As he took a step towards me I heard Mother cry out.

'You can't hit little girls!' She looked alarmed and upset. I'd never seen her show this kind of emotion before. Suddenly I was afraid.

'Right,' barked Father, turning to my nine-year-old brother, Bobby. 'I'll punish you instead.' Father took hold of his ear and propelled him outside into the yard, where he thrashed him with several lashes of his belt, till his anger ran out.

I cried and cried, but Mother held me back, gently but firmly. Finally Father let Bobby go, so he stumbled back inside and, with his hand on his sore back, he gave me a wink.

'It's all right,' he said, trying to reassure me. From that moment, I feared my father's unpredictability, especially his anger, and avoided him whenever I could. It took a long time for me to get over what had happened that day, but Bobby and I bonded more closely than ever as a result.

My father's drinking pals started coming to the Tanners' every weekend. He didn't believe in taking money from them . . . and he had a lot of 'friends', so it was free drinks all round. I used to stay away from the bar area when it was busy, so I never got to know any of them personally. I could often hear how loud and rowdy they were, though.

Grandpa and Grandma Holden, landlords of the pub, started to worry about the growing number of 'friends' arriving every week, so thought up a solution to avoid losing so much drinks money. They arranged for us to go away at weekends, when the weather wasn't too cold. We used to take the train either to Southport, Blackpool or

Morecambe, where we stayed in boarding houses. To keep the cost down, we used to take some food with us and the landlady would cook it for our tea.

I always liked those family weekends by the sea – Mother, Father, Bobby and me. Mother, Bobby and I played on the beaches, visited the piers, watched Punch and Judy shows and went for walks. Father would sometimes tag along but mostly went off in search of the pubs.

We used to take the train back on Sunday evenings, sometimes after dark. One moonless night, on our way back from Blackpool, Father had had quite a bit to drink. It was a long walk back to the Tanners' from Langho Station, along York Lane, which was unlit. About halfway along, Father suddenly tripped over a cow lying in the middle of the road. He said a funny word which I'd never heard before. Wanting to show off that I'd learned this new phrase I repeated it again and again as I skipped along. Suddenly, his temper flared and he motioned for me to come and stand in front of him. 'Don't you dare use a word like that!' he scolded. Surprised and hurt, I kept walking at a distance from him. Mother came and took my hand gently and I knew to keep quiet the rest of the way home.

I enjoyed our trips, but I was always glad to get back to the Tanners' on a Sunday evening. Even I could tell that things seemed to be changing, though. Instead of going to the pub, my father started playing cards for money with his friends at the kitchen table in our Goldhey Street house. Mother was 'not pleased', as she told me later, and I tried to keep out of their way as much as possible. So, if it was fine weather, I would go and play out on the street with the other children while Bobby kept a close eye on me. If Father had an evening off from the pub, I would usually be in bed asleep by half past six when his 'friends' came, though I often woke to hear male voices talking or laughing. Mother also had to stay out of their way, so she went into the front room, furthest away from the kitchen, and did some sewing or knitting. She seemed rather subdued around my father and his 'friends', but was always careful to hide her true feelings when I was in the room. I'm sure she must have shed tears when she was on her own. She certainly had a lot to cry about.

As tensions grew at home, my big brother, Bobby, used to go and help out at Veevers Farm over the road from the Tanners' after school and in the holidays, to avoid my father. He helped the farmer and his wife all through the year in their big creameries, stirring the vats to separate the cream, then the curds from the whey to make cheese. Through the winter he helped to feed the cattle in the barns and in the summer he collected the eggs laid by their free-range hens and joined the vegetable and fruit pickers. He loved it at the farm and spent all his time there, which is why I didn't see him much during the day. Every evening, though, without fail, he told me a bedtime story in the room we shared or sang me to sleep.

Bobby's favourite time, and mine too, was haymaking. That summer, he asked me if I would like to come with him to help.

I didn't hesitate. 'Yes please.' I idolized Bobby, so I felt proud that he wanted to show me the things he did at his favourite place. He took me across the road from the pub and I said hello to the friendly farmer and his wife, who always waved at me when they saw me in the lane. Their children were grown-up, so they seemed genuinely pleased to see me.

As they did at this time every year, the merry haymakers had come over from Ireland to work at the farm. I loved their laughter, their lilting accents and the Irish songs they sang as they worked. I remember giggling one lunchtime as I watched them eating slithery white tripe with their fingers. After lunch one of them lifted me right up to the top of the hay wagon for a ride, trundling along on the uneven ground with the prickly hay scratching the backs of my legs – I can almost feel it now. But I laughed and laughed at their antics, which I'm sure they put on especially for me. They let me join in their songs too, like the last bit of the chorus to 'Molly Malone' – I used to love singing 'Alive, alive oh!' That made them all laugh. Those were wonderful, fun-filled, carefree days – some of the best of my childhood.

Just after I turned five, my mother's brother, Uncle George, suddenly took me to stay in Blackpool with his wife's family, who lived there. Maybe it was to give Mother a break. He was the most successful of Grandma and Grandad Harrison's three children, as he helped Grandad to run the building business and was also an alderman in Blackburn Town Council. His wife Evelyn was often poorly, but she seemed better than usual on this holiday, perhaps because we were staying with her parents in the seaside air.

My mother had given me some spending money for the first time ever, so, on my first day there, I decided to buy some small presents to take home for everyone. There was a shop across the road from their house, so I went there to choose what to buy, paid and carefully took everything back to my room, where I put them in my own little case. It's amazing how clear that time is to me now. I can recall every detail – the colour of my leather suitcase, a patch where it had been mended underneath and a scuffed corner; the flowery cotton dress I was wearing, made by my mother.

Auntie Evelyn's sister Norma also came to stay at her parents' house for that week. She was very pretty, I remember, and her boyfriend Connor was Irish. The weather was so sunny on that second day that we all went to the Pleasure Beach to make the most of it. We had sandwiches and ice cream for lunch and Uncle George bought me some Blackpool rock. But later that day, when we returned from the beach, the happy atmosphere of the morning turned sour. My aunt and uncle told me to go and sit in my room and I knew something was wrong. I felt nobody wanted me there any more.

What I didn't know then was that while Uncle George took me for a stroll to the nearby park with swings, Norma and Connor had told her parents and Auntie Evelyn that she was pregnant. Well, that was a terrible shock for them. It was quickly agreed that, like it or not, Norma and Connor would 'have to' get married. Auntie Evelyn must have told Uncle George when we got back, as he went quiet, no doubt recalling the exact same situation between my parents . . . and the repercussions.

Sensing the tense atmosphere around the house, I got out my case from under the bed and packed my few possessions in it. Then I tiptoed down the stairs and out of the back door without anyone hearing me. My plan was to walk home to Blackburn. I didn't know how far it was or how long it would take, but I was quite confident I would find the way.

Of course, it wasn't long before someone noticed I was missing, and Uncle George came after me. He soon spotted me, a small child carrying a case and striding along on my own. He took me back to the house, but it was no longer a happy stay in Blackpool. I couldn't wait to get home.

A few months later, Norma and Connor's baby boy was born. Sadly, Norma died in childbirth. The family were devastated, particularly Auntie Evelyn and Uncle George. Regardless of their connection to the new baby, they snubbed Connor because of the stigma of unmarried pregnancy and his Catholic religion. Norma's parents really felt it was Connor's fault their daughter had died, so he was left to bring up his son alone. We never saw the new baby boy.

While Bobby escaped to Veevers Farm, I used to love going to my maternal grandparents' house in the countryside at Salesbury, about an hour's walk from the Tanners'. I went to see them at every possible opportunity. They were much easier to be with than my father's parents. I loved their house, a spacious bungalow built by Grandad's workmen, all beautifully decorated and furnished. The rural area that surrounded it was perfect for long walks through the woods and I would bake biscuits or play card games with Grandma when it was wet. I loved them. I thought the world of them. But I didn't love Grandad's silence punishment.

I don't know what I'd done to deserve it, but I do remember that, every Sunday afternoon, after tea, I had to sit on the chair in front of the clock on the mantelpiece and not move or speak for a whole hour. I wonder now whether perhaps they just wanted a rest. I tried to sit still and watch the minute hand as it hardly moved at all. I began to count the seconds in my head, up to sixty each time, and then see if I was right – had the hand moved a minute? I was frightened I might cough or sneeze – would that count? And what if I had an itchy foot? It was a terrible trial for a small, energetic child like me. After a while I stopped watching the clock and started making up stories in my head. When the hour was over, Grandad used to give me a shiny new penny. I wouldn't do that to a child. But, after that, whenever I couldn't get to sleep, I started counting seconds and minutes . . . and soon nodded off.

As I've said, this was not a family who openly showed affection. Neither side gave me hugs or kisses. The only time I can recall my mother being affectionate was when she cuddled me in her rocking chair when I was a toddler.

I don't remember it happening again. Regardless, Bobby always looked out for me and cheered me up if I hurt myself, and Mother was always making me clothes and taking me for walks, so I knew I was loved. They just chose to show it in different ways. With my father spending less and less time with us and my parents not being close, the idea of adults hugging or kissing each other never occurred to me. But one morning, while I was staying at Grandma and Grandad Harrison's house, Grandma was cleaning out the fireplace. She was on her knees in front of the grate and Grandad was ready to go out. I came into the room and stopped still as I saw him bend down to kiss her. I thought that was marvellous, absolutely wonderful. I was awestruck. I have never forgotten that moment. It was the only time I ever saw anyone in my family kiss.

Grandma and Grandad Harrison had three children: Mother, George and Elsie. We saw Uncle George every week and sometimes his wife Auntie Evelyn, when she was well enough. Mother's sister, Auntie Elsie, never married and lived with Grandma and Grandad throughout my childhood, though I didn't see much of her, except when she wanted me to help clean her shoes.

My father's parents were, coincidentally, born with the same surname, Holden, and came from Hurst Green, quite close to the river where my mother would take me and I would play with the otters. Father was the youngest of their four sons – Percy, John, Eddie and Horace, my father, but we only regularly saw Uncle Eddie, who lived and worked at the Tanners'. He was not the friendly sort and kept to himself because he was shy.

The other two brothers led more separate lives. Uncle John and his family lived in Little Harwood, close to our Goldhey Street house, and he was the manager of Bastfield Mill in Blackburn. He was always busy with work and lived a grander life than we did. He had a wife, Auntie Frances, and two children, older than me, but I hardly ever saw them. Father's other brother was Percy, who lived in London with his wife and his daughter Iris. I only ever remember meeting her once, when she came to stay at the Goldhey Street house and we went to the swimming baths.

Apart from religious differences, money was the cause of all the problems on both sides of my family. Grandad Harrison made a lot of money from his successful building business, but he was very careful with it, which would later cause rifts within the family. For Grandpa Holden, things were more of a struggle. He had to do his extra mills inspector job to keep the Tanners' going, so there was only just enough to go round.

Mother often used to tell me about Grandma Holden's brother Richard, who was my great-uncle. He started out home-brewing beer in his kitchen for himself and friends. As it grew in popularity they started to sell it from behind the bar at the Tanners'. Then other pubs in the area wanted it too. Very soon he expanded his little kitchen industry into a thriving business – the Nova Scotia New Brewery, well loved across the whole of Blackburn. The business was so successful that he made a lot of money and sold his company for a fortune to Lion Brewery on Coniston Road in 1920. As a Roman Catholic, he was a great supporter of the Church, but he also wanted to benefit his family with his new wealth. However, a bitter falling out with his sister, my stern 'cantankerous' Grandma, jeopardized his plan.

'Uncle Richard was so cross,' Mother told me, 'that he went red in the face. He said he had come to see her to give her and the family some of his money, but now he would give it away to where it would be more greatly appreciated.'

Mother paused as she recalled the scene. 'And do you know what Grandma said?'

'No,' I replied in wonder, hearing all this for the first time. 'What did she say?'

'She turned on him and shouted: "You can keep your money. I don't want it. I wouldn't have it even if I was penniless." Then she stormed out of the room and they never spoke to each other again.'

This was one of the first times in my life that I was party to such family gossip. Knowing Grandma Holden's reputation, and having seen her occasional fits of anger, I believed it all. A small part of me had to admire her too, for sticking up for herself, even though it left our family without a share of Great-Uncle Richard's wealth.

Mother pursed her lips. She seemed quietly aggrieved about it, particularly when money was always short in our household.

So Great-Uncle Richard gave all his profits away to the Blackburn Royal Infirmary, to pay for new wards to be built and more beds to be put into use. He also gave money to a few small charities and to the Catholic Church, who bestowed on him the honorary title of 'Papal Knight'. Shortly after this, he fell gravely ill and the nuns made good use of their enhanced facilities to nurse him through his final days.

It was generally understood that young children didn't go to funerals or burials, so on the day of Great-Uncle Richard's service – a Catholic Requiem Mass – Mother, Father, Bobby and the rest of the Holdens went to the church, while Auntie Frances took me for a walk instead, picking bluebells in Sale Wheel Woods. Later that day, as Auntie Frances and I joined everyone gathered in the Tanners' for Great-Uncle Richard's wake, I eavesdropped on snippets of conversation from under the tables.

'Do you know?' began one rather frumpy woman to a more elegant relative: 'Richard wrote in his will that he wants to have a solid stone slab, with a marble statue on top of it.' She paused for a quick breath. 'Would you believe it?'

'Well, that will keep him down all right!' said the other with a high-pitched laugh.

What a family!

A few weeks after the wake, Mother became ill with rheumatic fever. She had to go to the Infirmary for some treatment and children weren't allowed to visit. She was a patient there for quite a long time and I missed her every day. I worried about her too. What if she never came back? When Bobby was at school, nobody really bothered about me, but when he came home he did his best to cheer me up. Eight weeks later, Mother was allowed out and I was very glad to have her back home again.

'Was it horrid in the infirmary?' I asked.

'No. I felt quite at home there,' she told Bobby and me with a smile. 'The ward was full of beds with Great-Uncle Richard's name on the end of them, including mine.' She paused, with a look of surprise. 'And nearly everyone knew who he was.'

3

Gandhi in Blackburn

1931–1934

Not long after Mother came back home from the Infirmary, just after my fifth birthday, Grandpa Holden died suddenly. It was a great shock for the whole family. What would happen to the Tanners' Arms? While the solicitors tried to sort out what to do, Father and Uncle Eddie took over the day-to-day running of the pub. They rubbed along somehow, though they were never close as brothers and neither of them was much good at the management side of things. They must have felt uncertain about their future but they carried on as best as they could.

Grandma Holden could have taken over – she was bossy enough. But, only days after Grandpa Holden's funeral, Grandma Holden fell ill and was confined to her bed upstairs in the Tanners'. Mother took over the nursing of her difficult mother-in-law with enormous patience and care.

'You must eat,' scolded Mother, as kindly as she could.

Grandma just shook her head, with her lips firmly sealed.

'You won't get better unless you eat something nourishing,' persisted Mother. 'Is there anything you would like, anything at all?'

Grandma paused to think, then came out with a surprising answer.

'Oysters.'

'Really?' My mother patted Grandma's wrinkly hand.

Grandma nodded and added, in a weak voice: 'I always loved oysters.'

'Then oysters it shall be,' nodded Mother.

'Thank you.' A big smile lit up Grandma's weary face as she lay back to rest.

Somebody must have given Mother some money, as she bought a piece of the finest silk from the market. I remember watching her cut the material into squares before sewing two together with tiny stitches to make little pouches, with one side open on each. I couldn't understand why she'd made them. When they were finished, she took me with her to Langho Station, where we caught the train to Blackburn, then on to the fishmonger's stall at the big, bustling indoor market to buy a bag of oysters. As Mother paid, I looked around with wonder at all the colourful stalls, selling everything from fresh fruit to clothing. The different sounds and smells muddled together – I'd never been to a place like it! When we got back home to the Tanners', Mother removed one of the oysters from its shell, put it into a home-made pouch and gently placed it in Grandma's mouth for her to suck on. It seemed such a strange thing to do.

I can still picture the look on Grandma's face – a smile

of bliss at the delicious taste as she sucked the silk bag
to savour the sensation and nourish her thin, weakened
body with this very special delicacy. The protein from the
oyster juice was what her body needed to keep her going
a little longer.

As Grandma sucked on her oysters, she beckoned me
and pointed weakly at a special little cupboard she had
in the corner of her room, with silk curtains drawn across
the glazed part of the door. I had noticed it before, but
never knew what was in it. I would never have dared to
look inside.

'Go and see,' whispered Grandma.

I went over to the cupboard, opened the door and
looked inside, to find a large, decorated box. I turned to
Grandma to see if this was what she meant.

She nodded her head with a slight smile of encouragement, so I lifted the big, heavy box out of the cupboard
and put it down on a nearby rug. I was still a bit hesitant
as I had never seen a gentle side to Grandma Holden
before. Perhaps it was because she was ill. She watched
as I opened the lid to see the most astonishing collection
of golden jewellery and precious stones sparkling in the
light from the half-curtained window.

'You can play with them if you like,' she said. Every
day from then on, while Mother cared for Grandma, I
played with these special jewels. There was an array of
necklaces, rings and brooches, each embedded with shiny,
colourful stones. I would inspect and arrange them into
patterns on the rug before trying them on as if I was going
to a grown-ups' party. It never occurred to me that they

were valuable. They might as well have been penny-stall trinkets to me.

Grandma soon became too ill to speak and slept all the time. A few weeks after Grandad had died, I was sent out of Grandma's room while Father and Uncle Eddie came to sit beside her bed. It was just in time as she took her last breath.

Both Grandma and Grandpa Holden were buried in a private graveyard in the grounds of Stonyhurst College, alongside their parents and ancestors, just a mile from where they were both born.

After their deaths, everything seemed to change. While their belongings were distributed among the family and the inheritance was paid, it became clear that not everyone was happy. One day, arguments suddenly erupted between my father and his brothers. Accusations and raised voices were flying to and fro between the grown-ups in the bar area about 'messy dealings' and anger at the fact that the Tanners' had been left to Father and Eddie only. It wasn't a happy atmosphere for a child. Mother took me out of the way upstairs while all the shouting was going on and sat with me until Bobby came home. By the evening, things were simmering down and it was quiet again. Bobby read me the story of The Three Billy Goats Gruff and tucked me into bed. But as I lay down under the covers, I worried what would happen next.

It was just Uncle Eddie, Father, Mother, Bobby and me at the Tanners' Arms now. Without my grandparents it didn't feel right, and Mother was expected to cook, clean, mend clothes and tidy for all of us while helping with customers too. Before long, she fell ill again. This time I was told it was a very serious illness and I overheard Uncle Eddie telling Bobby: 'Your mother's rheumatic fever has returned and this time it's affected her heart.'

'Oh,' said Bobby in a shocked voice.

I was worried when I heard it was her heart. What if she didn't come back this time?

She was taken back to the Blackburn Royal Infirmary for about three months and I missed her terribly. When she came home, she had to stay in bed for several weeks. I was still worried about her. Would she die, like Grandma? I was so relieved to have her back at the Tanners' that I helped to look after her. I brought her a drink of water every morning and helped Bobby to make her meals each day. I took my favourite books into her room for her to read and I sang her some of the children's hymns we learned at church. She was still very weak but her face lit up whenever I came to spend time with her.

She did slowly start to get better but was far too fragile to take on the chores around the pub any more.

Instead, Uncle Eddie decided to take on a pretty young woman called Jenny from St Alban's Church to live in at the Tanners' and be our cleaner, cook, housekeeper and childminder. I didn't take to her at all.

Well, she started out all right, doing a few chores, but she soon set her sights on Uncle Eddie. Even I could see that. Consequently, she did precious little cleaning, housekeeping or childminding. Especially not the child-minding. I think I just looked after myself, as I had done most of the time since I was a toddler.

Jenny wheedled Uncle Eddie round and made merry with him. They got married and drank together so much that it didn't take them long to drink the pub dry. Customers stopped coming and there was no money to pay the bills or restock the pub. Eventually they had no choice but to sell up and find somewhere else to live.

Mother had recovered and was up out of bed just as the pub had to be sold. This left us without a home and my father without a livelihood. Luckily we were able to move back into our house on Goldhey Street, but Father still needed an income. So Grandad Harrison stepped in. He offered Father a job in his building company and, regardless of the animosity between them, Father didn't have much choice, so he took the job.

Following the sale of the Tanners', Father's friends continued to come round to our house to play cards for money every weekend. Father started building up debts, which he failed to tell Mother about.

'The insurance man called yesterday,' she said to Father at breakfast one Saturday morning. I was about to ask what an insurance man was, but I hesitated when I saw Father's stormy expression.

He mumbled something under his breath and carried on eating.

'He says we owe him three months' payments.'

'Who needs insurance?' he replied, avoiding her gaze.

'They're all money-grabbers. We're healthy enough. Let's keep it that way.'

Mother pursed her lips and looked away, keeping her thoughts to herself, probably because she didn't want to worry Bobby and me. But I could tell she was anxious.

We finished our breakfast and carried the plates through. Bobby started washing up and I dried, while Father clattered the chairs as he rearranged them.

The door was open a crack, wide enough for us to hear Mother's quiet voice.

'Are your friends coming this morning?'

'Yes, of course,' he snapped. 'What of it?'

She said nothing more, but joined us in the kitchen to put things away. She had her back to us, but as she turned to reach for something I caught a glimpse of her sad face. It looked as if she was close to tears.

Fortunately for Father, when the Tanners' Arms was sold there was a share of the remaining money left for him. He was able to pay off his gambling debts, much to Mother's relief. He then made the decision to sell our Goldhey Street home. I had some wonderful memories of living on the street, particularly of the times Mother and I had spent there in each other's company, so I was sad to leave it.

Father bought a slightly bigger house on the much busier Whalley Old Road, only five minutes' walk away from Goldhey Street. We all settled in there quite quickly and things seemed better for a while. Mother didn't have to worry so much about Father's debts and he was happier too.

'Now, we've got out of that house your father gave us,' he said to Mother. 'We're living in our own home at last.' So they were both more relaxed . . . for a while.

One sunny September day, not long after we'd moved into the new house, my mother took me to see my godmother, Auntie Maggie, who lived nearby and had a sweet shop. I loved going to see her because she always gave me a scoop of her delicious home-made ice cream – a great treat, and while I ate that I could look at all the different jars of sweets on the shelf behind the counter. My favourites were aniseed balls and spearmint balls, both twenty for a penny or ten for a ha'penny, or you could have them mixed. I liked humbugs too, and chocolate bonbons. Her window was always beautifully arranged with sweets of all colours, including marzipan ovals, little Pontefract cakes, sherbet dips, liquorice sticks and coconut ices. Sometimes she would let me choose a few of each in a little bag to take home and I made them last as long as I could, which usually wasn't very long at all! Because it was so warm that day, I took my ice cream outside to eat, just as a group of people were approaching down the middle of Florence Street. This was unusual as it was a quiet road, but I didn't take much notice at first.

As they came closer, I saw that in the centre of this group of men, mostly in suits and some of them writing in notebooks, there was a small, skinny old man, draped in what looked like a white sheet. I'd never seen anyone like that before, so I watched as they came closer. At first, it looked as if he didn't have anything on his feet, but then I realized he had sandals on, with his toes poking out. He looked as if he must be very poor. I didn't really understand what was going on, but Mother and Auntie Maggie came out of the shop and stood with me to see what was happening.

The whole group walked on past, turned the corner and went off towards Bastfield Mill, on the corner of Church Hill, where Uncle John was the manager. Could they be going there?

That evening I heard Mother telling Father about it: 'We saw a little man wearing a sheet and sandals walking down Florence Street when we went to Maggie's shop today.'

Father looked up from his newspaper.

'On his own?'

'No, he was surrounded by several men and some of them were taking notes. I suppose they wrote down what he was saying to them.'

'He must be very poor,' I interrupted, 'if he has to wear a sheet!'

Mother smiled but Father tutted and ignored me.

'Which way were they going?'

'They turned the corner towards Bastfield Mill. Isn't that strange?'

'Not really,' said Father.

'What do you mean? Who could it be?' asked Mother.

'It says here,' he said, pointing at the front page of the morning paper. 'It says that Mahatma Gandhi was due to visit Blackburn and Darwen today, visiting mills, because of the Lancashire mill workers' letter to him. Gandhi is a very important man in India and he sticks up for the poor all over the world. He has come especially to respond to their letter.'

'What is the letter about?'

'Telling Gandhi about the damage India's embargo on imports of cotton from England is doing to our mills, especially to the workers being laid off because of it.'

I didn't know what the words 'imports' or 'embargo' meant, but I liked the sound of them, so I tried to remember to ask Bobby later.

'So that was Mahatma Gandhi?'

'Yes, I expect he was on his way to visit John's mill. What an honour.'

'Yes, it must be. You'll have to ask him about it.'

As I went off to play, I kept repeating that name: 'Mahatma Gandhi'. It sounded so funny to me!

That September also marked a milestone for me – my first day at school. I was very excited. Ever since I had gone wandering that day as a toddler and the policeman had found me in a school playground, I had longed to be part of all that.

I was five years old when I proudly waved goodbye to my mother that first morning as I set off with Bobby to St Alban's School in Birley Street. I was starting at the mixed infants' school, while Bobby, aged ten, was in the top class of the junior school, on the same site. We were divided into separate classes and playgrounds, one for boys and another for girls. From that very first day, I was in my element at St Alban's and made lots of friends.

I quickly found I loved learning too. From that moment, school was always a happy place for me.

A couple of months later, on Bonfire Night, my father was upstairs for a long time with Mother and another lady. Then he came down the stairs to see us.

'You've got a little brother,' he said, with a weary smile.

I couldn't believe it at first. Of course, I had no idea how babies came about. I grinned at Father, then turned to Bobby, who looked less surprised than me, but very pleased all the same.

'Another boy, eh?' he said to Father.

'Yes. Isn't that grand?'

The birth of my little brother Jeffrey was an exciting event and I loved him from the first time I saw him, when we were allowed upstairs to meet him that evening. Baby Jeffrey helped us feel more like a family again, for a while at least. I would play with him every day when I came home from school, so I didn't take much notice of the underlying friction that continued between my parents. Only a few days after Jeffrey was born Father's friends came round and money became an issue again. Mother would give him a look when Father handed over the housekeeping money.

'It's short this week,' she said.

'Well, it's all I've got left,' he replied, then turned his back and marched out of the house, slamming the door behind him.

Mother looked at the back of that door, hiding her face from us.

I know now that the missing money went on Father's gambling habit, but I don't believe I thought much about it that day. Times were hard for most people and there was a lot of poverty in Blackburn, as I suppose there was everywhere else too. I don't remember ever going hungry myself, but I did know people who were, including other children in my class.

Mother was always knitting, crocheting, sewing or mending clothes for us. Sometimes, neighbours and friends who liked her designs and knew her expertise as a seamstress would ask her to make an outfit for them, or perhaps to mend or darn something. She was also very good at making new outfits out of old clothes, perhaps a blouse from a torn summer dress, or shorts from trousers. She could turn cuffs and collars with ease. These commissions gave her a little extra income, on top of Father's wages, to put towards the housekeeping bills. Though money was tight, that helped us get by.

As the school term progressed, I grew in confidence and made a wide circle of friends. St Alban's School had a cobbled playground on a slope. All the older girls used to skip in the playground, so I watched how they did it and picked up a rope abandoned by the wall to try and do it myself. After several days of effort and a lot of tangles round my ankles I eventually learned to skip. This was a big milestone for me. Gradually my friends learned to skip as well and one of them brought a long length of rope to school so that we could have our own group skipping games. The only trouble was that two of us at a time had to miss out on the fun, and swinging the heavy rope round was hard work, which I hated.

Mother used to put an apple in my satchel every day. I would eat it at morning break. One of the 'Cottage Home' girls came up to me one breaktime and asked if I could 'stump' her and she would take my turn at 'twisting' or swinging one end of the rope, in return for my apple. I was very happy with that arrangement.

So I gave her my apple and watched as she devoured it, core, pips and all. I could see she was hungry, so it seemed a fair exchange.

What we called 'stumping' was more like a bribe, I suppose, looking back on it now. But I didn't see anything wrong with it at the time, as we both benefited. In fact, it still doesn't seem wrong to me; two children swapping for each other's gain. But I do feel bad that this girl was obviously not fed well enough at the children's home and I never thought to tell anybody about it.

Father was building up debts again and Mother protested in her own, silent way. If she ever voiced her complaints I didn't hear them. The atmosphere was becoming very tense again in our house, so Bobby often took me out with him, especially on Sundays, when the card-players came.

Bobby had the responsibility of going down to Grandma and Grandad Harrison's every Sunday afternoon to give their hen cabins a thorough clean-out, so he often took eighteen-month-old Jeffrey and me with him. Grandad was a lovely man, but a strong character who liked the boys best. Grandma was always gentle and kind. She used to take me for walks along the lanes, telling me the names of flowers and pointing out the different birds' songs, while Bobby worked. When it was time to learn the times tables at school, I told Bobby, so every time we went down to see Grandma and Grandad Harrison, I practised them. It was quite a long way to their house in Salesbury from Little Harwood – over three miles, so we used to catch the tram to Wilpshire, and then we walked the rest of the way, down the hill to their house. Bobby would carry Jeffrey while I skipped along, chanting whichever of the tables I was learning as I went.

Jeffrey seemed to find it funny, laughing a lot while watching me from his perch in Bobby's arms. I told him that when it was his turn, I would teach him the same way, though I don't suppose he understood what I was saying. It was an easy way to learn and I practised all my tables that way. They are still as fresh now as they were then.

Father's growing debts soon meant we had to move house again. This time he sold our Whalley Old Road house to Uncle Eddie and his awful wife Jenny and bought a smaller one in Whalley New Road for us to live in, so that he could pay back the money he owed. This meant we were living on a shoestring, with Mother often counting out her pennies, but once again it felt happier there for a while.

Grandma and Grandad Harrison used to come every Saturday for tea, so Father would go out after lunch for the rest of the day.

'Right, I'm off,' he called out as he slammed the door.

Mother rarely reacted, though I'm sure his attitude must have affected her. Father and her parents used to avoid each other as much as they could, but it was always a happy, relaxed day when they came to visit.

They used to bring with them a big ham for Mother to cook, that would last us a few days afterwards, and a whole basket of eggs, vegetables and cheese from their hens, their garden and a local farm. Their generosity helped Mother to keep food on the table.

When I had just turned eight, Bobby was injured when a motorbike ran into him as he walked along the pavement to school and knocked him over. After a couple of days in hospital he came home and Mother nursed him, but then she fell ill with another recurrence of rheumatic fever. With the doctor worried about her heart, the decision was made for Bobby, Jeffrey and me to spend some time away from her to aid her recovery. Bobby was taken down to Salesbury for Grandma Harrison to look after him while his injuries healed, and Jeffrey, still a toddler, was taken in by Mother's brother, Uncle George, and his wife Auntie Evelyn.

I suppose I didn't need as much looking after, and the school holidays had just started, so I was sent to stay with an Irish family who lived near Liverpool. I can't remember how long I stayed, but these people were very kind and made a lot of fuss over me. While I was there, they took me and their two children, of similar ages to me, on a special outing in their car to the opening of the new

Mersey Tunnel. It was 15 July 1934, and there was a lot of cheering when the ribbon was cut. After the opening ceremony, I think we were one of the first cars to drive right through the tunnel from Liverpool to Birkenhead . . . and back again. It was all very exciting.

It does seem strange as I think back now. The thing is, I had never seen these people before or since and cannot work out who they were. I do know they were Catholics and they took me to Mass on Sunday mornings, so I assume they must have been friends of my father's family. I never did find out, but they were lovely people and were kind enough to treat me as one of their own when our family was in need.

4

Kidnapped!

1935–1936

By the time I got back home to Little Harwood, my father's money problems had loomed large again. He had carried on with his card-playing friends in our absence, no doubt drinking with them as well. Money was so tight we had to sell up once again and move to a rented house back in Whalley Old Road, this time with a shop attached. I don't know what Father did with any money he had left over from the house sale, but I'm sure Mother never saw any of it. He was still working for Grandad Harrison, building new houses, but I don't know where his wages went either.

With the few things Mother already had, or could make quickly, such as baby clothes, cushions and gifts, she started up the shop, whilst also minding Jeffrey, who was then three or four years old and quite a handful.

With virtually no money, Mother could not buy in enough stock to set up a shop properly, so she tried to expand her dressmaking business, designing and making clothing on commission. She was a talented seamstress and designer, but in those days there was very little money about in Blackburn for such luxuries, so she took in mending as well. Sadly, business was only spasmodic and she didn't have enough time to do all her sewing and knitting while looking after Jeffrey, so the income barely paid the bills.

There was also another problem. Right from when we moved to the new rented house, my parents stopped talking to each other. It was a strange atmosphere. It made us all feel uncomfortable, as if something might happen at any time. It was always better when Father was out – which was most of the time – as Mother could relax for a while, though her sadness spread to Bobby and me as well. But things were about to change.

We suddenly started to have a lot of visits from a woman with bleached blonde hair who seemed to be a friend of Father's. She would arrive at different times throughout the day and was always wafting around our house and shop in a red dressing gown, smoking. I don't think Mother liked her and they hardly said a word to each other. I felt confused about the whole situation and nobody told me anything, not even Bobby. I think he must have known the truth, but he was very protective of me. I was like a mushroom – always kept in the dark. I just tried to ignore it and carry on as if nothing was happening.

A strange thing happened one Saturday afternoon, just after Father and the blonde had gone out and my Harrison grandparents were due to arrive for tea. I must have been playing in my bedroom and I opened my door to catch sight of my mother emerging from the bathroom, trying

to disperse a mist of smoke clinging around and behind
her. The smell was the same as the blonde's smell when
she smoked her cigarettes. Was Mother secretly smoking?
I could hardly believe it. But when I thought about this,
I worried about the stress she was under. I wondered
whether smoking would maybe calm her down. Perhaps
she had smoked before and was trying to keep it a secret.
I'd never seen her do this before.

One morning, when I went to clean my teeth before
school, I noticed a grey pumice stone next to my nail
brush. I'd never seen it before, so I knew it must be the
blonde's. Was she living here? By now, it must have been
two or three months after she first came to our house,
and I didn't like her. I don't think she liked me either, as
she never once talked to me and I had to spend all my
time in my room, outside or at friends' houses. Bobby
would go out with his own friends and Mother kept out
of the way with Jeffrey. We all seemed to be living separate lives during this period.

I used to go to bed at half past six. Bobby would come
up to my room and read stories to me – always about
flying. His favourite book was called *Flying Aces*, about
Baron somebody and other famous pilots from the Great
War. Bobby was so keen on aeroplanes that the porch and
the front room, where he slept on a pull-out bed, were
full of model aeroplanes, hanging from the ceilings. He
was always explaining them to me – what models they
were and what they were used for. Some nights he used
to tell me funny stories – jokey things, but never anything
rude. Occasionally, for a change, he would sing to me to

send me to sleep. The song I liked him singing best was
'Drink to Me Only with Thine Eyes'.

One night, after Bobby finished reading to me, he put
out the light and left. I was halfway to sleep when there
was a sudden explosion of noise from downstairs. I
remember a lot of shouting and banging about. I got out
of bed and tiptoed out onto the landing, but somebody,
I think maybe Bobby, told me to go back to bed and stay
there, so I did. I never found out what happened that
night, but it sounded like a fight and the next day my
father had broken ribs. I wasn't allowed to watch the
nurse putting bandages on him, round his chest, but I
could hear the awful fuss he was making about the pain.

A few days later, my father disappeared. In the morning
he was there with his lady friend at the breakfast table,
but when I got back from school he had gone. At first, I
took no notice. I thought he would just come back again
later that day. But he didn't. A few days later, while having
breakfast with my mother and Jeffrey, I plucked up the
courage and asked her about it.

'Where is Father?'

'He's gone off with the blonde,' said my mother.
'Together with all the money from selling our old house.'
She pursed her lips with a firm expression, which suggested
that I should not ask her any more, so I didn't.

I could only remember him going away once before
and that was on a business trip to Jersey, for Grandad
Harrison. So this sudden disappearance with the blonde
did seem unusual. Though, thinking about it now, the
blonde might have gone with him on that trip . . .

That night, when Bobby came to tuck me up, I asked him about it.

'Do you know that Father has gone off with the blonde?'

'Yes, Mother told me.'

'Where has he gone?'

'I don't know where,' he said. 'But I reckon it's good riddance.'

I was shocked. 'But why did he leave us?'

'You mustn't worry your pretty head about it,' was his only answer. 'Now tell me about what you did at school today.'

And that was that. Nobody told me anything else about it. I never saw Father much when he did live with us anyway, so I didn't really miss him. In fact, the tension seemed to have left with him. Mother was more relaxed than I'd seen her for a long time, despite her immediate money worries. I was old enough now just to get on with my life, both at school and with my friends. I tried not to think about what had happened at home. The landlord allowed us all to stay, as long as we paid the rent. This proved almost impossible for my mother, with so little income from the shop. Jeffrey would be starting school soon, giving her more time to work, so being the positive person she was, she soldiered on for a while, but it was a struggle to earn enough to make ends meet.

Despite her best efforts, Mother had no choice but to give up the shop. The rent for the house with the shop included was too high for her to manage, so we moved again and took on the rent of a more affordable small two-up, two-down terraced house, just nearby in Robinson Street. There she could continue making things for people privately, as she had often done in the past.

Even with less rent to find, she had three of us to provide for and virtually no income apart from the odd seamstress job, so it was tough for her. She had never had a job since she met my father, and of course she had Jeffrey still at home to look after for a few more weeks before school started.

Bobby was now fourteen, so he decided to be the man of the house and left school to work for Grandad Harrison, as an apprentice carpenter. Though relatively meagre, his weekly wage made all the difference for Mother. At last she could pay the rent and all the household bills without having to juggle one against the other. There was precious little left over, but Bobby's contribution removed a lot of her anxiety for the first time in years. Finally, we all felt happier in our new home.

Luckily, despite all the house moves, we had always been within walking distance of St Alban's School, so I was able to remain with my old friends.

I had quite a walk to get to school each day and home again at lunchtime, then back for the afternoon before my return journey at the end of the school day. On the coldest winter days, when the ground was covered in snow, Mother used to give me a basin of food, covered with a lid, for my lunch. All I had to do was to ask the caretaker if I could heat it up on his stove. Fortunately, he was a very kind man with lots of grandchildren and he always said yes. I loved his cosy little cubbyhole and warming myself by the stove. I mainly walked down a long road called Cob Wall, which ran along a high wall around the buildings and grounds of the Convent of Notre Dame, the best girls' school in the area. I was in awe of the girls and their smart uniforms when I saw them in the streets. Being a Catholic, I would have loved to go to the convent when I was older, but I knew it was an impossible dream. For a start, you had to be very clever to get in there, and I also knew we couldn't afford it.

One of my best friends at school, Winnie Binnington, used to walk part of the way home with me. Like many people in Blackburn in those days, Winnie always wore clogs. I suppose they were more hard-wearing than shoes. One day I was curious.

'What does it feel like to wear clogs?' I asked.

'Quite comfortable really,' she replied. 'Do you want to try them on?'

'Ooh, yes please.'

We were about the same size, so we swapped. She wore my shoes and I wore her clogs. They were much more comfortable than I thought, but it took me a few minutes to get used to them. Then I discovered something. I found that if I walked in a certain way, I could strike sparks off the flagstones beside the road. This was an exciting discovery and I loved doing it, so we often exchanged footwear after that. But I had to make sure that I changed back into my own shoes before I reached Robinson Street, as the first time I did it, Mother was surprisingly upset.

'I know a lot of people wear clogs in Blackburn,

including some of your lovely friends, but I don't want *you* to wear them,' she explained. 'We may not have much money, but my days of working in the cotton mills were long ago, before you were born, and I don't want to be reminded of them.' She paused. 'Now, Uncle John is a highly respected mill manager and of course Grandpa Holden was an inspector of mills, not to mention Uncle George being an alderman, so I don't want you looking like a little mill girl, wearing clogs.'

'But . . .'

'I don't like you wearing Winnie's clogs where anyone will see you,' she continued. 'Please don't wear them home again.'

'Yes, Mother.' I was quite shocked – I had never before heard her speak so vehemently.

One very hot afternoon, as I was returning to school after lunch, I noticed little bubbles, hundreds of them, rising up from between the tarred wooden cobbles that made up the road surface of Cob Wall. These bubbles were gas rising from the tar, which was melting in the warmth of the sunshine. I stopped, mesmerized, to watch them rising from the cracks. I just couldn't resist the temptation to pop some of them. As soon as I stepped on one or two, another five would appear in their place. Well, once I'd started, I couldn't stop. It was compulsive. I just had to pop every bubble. I stepped from one to another and another . . . hearing the sticky 'pop' as I stamped each bubble out. It was such fun, almost like a dance.

I was enjoying myself so much and was so intent on

popping every single bubble, that I completely lost track of time. It was only when I heard the voices and laughter of my friends approaching that I looked up and realized it was the end of the school day.

'What are you doing, Margaret?' asked Winnie.

'Popping bubbles,' I said. 'What are you doing here? What time is it?'

'It's home time,' replied Theresa. 'Have you been out here all afternoon?'

'I suppose so,' I replied, suddenly feeling guilty. 'Did anyone notice I was missing?' I asked, hoping they hadn't.

'Yes, the teacher asked where you were.'

'Am I in trouble?'

'Well, you might be,' said a quite serious friend, Agnes, with a worried face. 'But Melanie said she thought you had a headache this morning . . .'

'Oh, that was kind of her.' I knew in a way it was wrong, but I was pleased she liked me enough to stick up for me.

'The teacher might write a letter to your mother,' suggested another friend.

'Oh dear,' I sighed. 'I suppose I'd better tell her, then, just in case. I expect I'll be in trouble whatever I do!'

When I got home, I told Mother what had happened. I thought she would be cross, and she was. But she had a hint of a smile as she told me off. I wondered if maybe she had done something like that herself when she was at school. I was dying to ask her, but I didn't dare.

Sure enough, I did get into trouble at school the next day. I had to own up about why I had missed the whole afternoon and had to stay in at breaktimes that day to make up for the lessons I'd missed. Still, it was worth it.

A few months later, when the weather had turned cold and there were council workmen replacing some of the worn wooden blocks on Cob Wall that I had been jumping on, I saw a pile of the old ones that had been rejected and took a few of them, as many as I could carry, home to put on our fire. We burned one of those tarred blocks on our fire each evening for the next few days and they made a wonderful smell throughout the house.

The following year, on a beautiful spring day, the four of us were walking home from school in a dawdling sort of way, chatting and laughing. We came to the point where I had to walk on in a different direction from Winnie, Theresa and Agnes, so we stopped and chatted some more before I said goodbye and continued following Cob Wall. Only a hundred yards on, I was walking past some houses when a man came out of an alleyway and grabbed me – a big, ugly man with a beer belly and tattoos all up his arms.

'Help!' I yelled. 'Let me go,' I shrieked, as he held my arm in a vice-like grip. I tried to shake him off, but I had no chance against his strength. His face was set as he dragged me, kicking and screaming, down the alleyway and into a double garage in the 'backs' – a narrow roadway along the back of the houses. I kept hollering as loudly as I could, till he growled at me to stop. I was so frightened that I did. Why had he grabbed me? I didn't have any money. He plonked me down to sit on a large and

very rusty Nuttall's Mintoes tin. There was a horrible
smell – all oily and something else I didn't recognize,
probably paraffin or petrol, but it was very strong. I was
so scared that I didn't dare move. I started to cry.

'Shut up!' he bellowed at me.

'I can't,' I sobbed. It wasn't so much because I was
frightened for myself, though I was, but mainly because
I was wearing my mother's favourite scarf and she didn't
know I had borrowed it. It was pale blue, with darker
blue spots. But now it was all creased and dirty, the blue
so dark that the spots didn't show.

Suddenly, there was a huge commotion of shouting
outside and people kicking the garage doors. I froze with
fear. Were these more men who were going to come in
and hurt me? I realized I was in danger and couldn't see
any way to escape.

My kidnapper's jowly face turned bright red with fury.
The racket outside continued a little longer and the wooden
garage door was nearly splitting at the joints with all that
kicking and battering. I could hear adults' voices now, as
well as children, and someone called my name.

Finally, the hinges gave way and the doors burst inwards,
followed by my three friends, who had seen what happened,
and a lot of adults who lived near the garages. They had
heard my friends' shouts and joined the fray. I was moment-
arily surprised to see that one of them was my godfather,
George Watson – my father's cousin. But I didn't stop to
wonder how he came to be there. I just ran straight outside
and breathed in the fresh air, with my friends gathered
round me, as if protecting me. They were so kind. Everyone

was. As I left, there were some men still wrestling with my assailant and pinning him down, but I don't know what happened after that – whether anyone called the police or reported him. I suppose they probably did, but I don't remember being interviewed about it, or anything like that. Still concerned for me, my friends accompanied me back home, by which time I had calmed down a lot and could walk into my house as usual, as if nothing had happened.

When my mother found out about it from our neighbours, she must have told the rest of the family and there was a lot of fuss made, especially by Bobby, who told me to walk home by a different route in future. I was so naive that I had no idea then just how much danger I had been in that day. Thank goodness my lovely friends had witnessed my kidnap and rescued me.

That evening I rinsed out my mother's scarf. I knew how special it was to her as we didn't have a lot of money to buy pretty clothes. It was dry by the next morning and the pattern had come back, so I never had to tell her about that part of the story.

Only weeks after Bobby had started his apprenticeship with Grandad Harrison, I had a bad toothache so had to go and see a dentist for the first time in my life. He took one look in my mouth and sent me to the clinic to have a lower back tooth taken out. I knew the tooth was bad, but dentists cost money and I didn't want to bother Mother with it, just when she'd got straight. But finally the pain was too strong and I had to go.

I remember being asked to sit down in the chair, but I

don't recall being given any anaesthetic or pain relief. The dental surgeon started poking about in my mouth and every time he touched the rogue tooth I felt a sudden sharp pain. I flinched several times and once or twice cried out, as he tried to get a grip on the tooth. Finally, he put something on it and twisted it. Parts of the tooth came out in the tool and he used tweezers to pull out a few more.

Outside in the street, my school friend Winnie was walking past the clinic with her mother when they heard a piercing scream. 'That's Margaret,' she said to her mother. 'I'm sure it's her.' And it was.

I couldn't take any more, so I jumped off the dentist's chair, ran screaming through the waiting room, which must have caused some consternation, out of the door and straight home. I could feel with my tongue that I still had jagged shards of tooth sticking out and a sort of string hanging from it.

My mother was cross and wanted to go back with me, but I downright refused. I didn't want anybody to touch my tooth. Not long after, Bobby came home from work and he was furious, but I still refused to see any dentist to put it right, so he helped me work the tooth fragments free, little by little, over the following days. And whatever the string thing was, it was stuck fast, so I just chewed at it on and off all through the week and finally it fell away. I later discovered the 'string' had been a nerve – no wonder it hurt so much.

This episode put me off going to the dentist for many years, well into my adult life. I'm very glad that today's dental care is so entirely different and nobody has to suffer like I did that day.

I don't believe we ever got a bill for that tooth disaster, so we continued to scrape by with reasonable comfort . . . until the next big expense.

5

A Pinch of Snuff

1937

I was now in my final year at St Alban's Junior School, enjoying it and doing well, but I wasn't sure where I would go from there. I just hoped I could continue to have the kind of teachers I'd had so far, who would help me to go on learning new things and do my best in every subject. And, no matter what school I went to, I looked forward to keeping the friends I had as well as making new ones.

I was delighted when I was invited to try for a scholarship and I straight away said yes. That year, there were only two scholarships on offer for a free place at the Convent of Notre Dame, and I wanted one of them. I knew it was a very hard school to get into, and we couldn't afford to pay for me to go, so the scholarship would be my only chance. I didn't know whether I was good enough, but I had no qualms about trying my hardest to succeed.

When the time came, the whole of the top class at St Alban's Junior School sat the scholarship exam. I never liked doing tests but I worked my way through the English and maths papers methodically. I don't remember anything that was in the exam, except the final maths question. There was a diagonal line, with a complicated sum to do and instructions showing how I should work it out. But I noticed there were two numbers on the side, when the question said there was only one. I had just enough time left, so I worked it out both ways, first using one number, then the other, with a written explanation that I had done both versions to make sure one would be the answer they wanted. I closed the paper and put my pen down with just one minute to spare.

After that, we all just carried on for our last two terms at St Alban's. Nobody knew when the results would come out, giving the names of the lucky pupils who had won those two scholarships. So, after a couple of weeks, I stopped thinking about it.

On the way to St Alban's, I used to pass a tiny shop every morning on the other side of Cob Wall. One day, out of curiosity, I crossed over to have a look in the window. It was full of all sorts of tins of tobacco, things in tubes, cigarettes and snuffboxes. I'd heard somewhere that people take a pinch of snuff to make them sneeze. An idea formed in my mind. Wouldn't it be a lot of fun to make everyone sneeze in class? I only had a term or so left at St Alban's, so I went into the shop and asked how much snuff I could buy for a penny.

The shopkeeper laughed. 'What do you want snuff for?' he asked.

'As a joke,' I explained. 'To make the people in my class sneeze.'

He grinned. 'Well, how much money have you got?'

I put my hand in my gymslip pocket, took out the penny and placed it on his counter.

'That will do.' He obviously liked my idea, as he measured a teaspoonful of snuff onto a piece of white paper, then twisted it. 'There you are, love,' he said with a grin. 'I hope you have some fun with it.'

I placed it in my pocket and carried on to school. In the top class, our teacher was Miss Baldwin. She was lovely and enjoyed a laugh, so I told my best friends, Winnie, Theresa and Agnes, what I was going to do. They all liked the idea and, once we got to the bit of the lesson when we were doing some writing, I opened the twist of white paper in my lap, took a tiny bit, put it to my nose and sniffed. Then I passed it on. Within seconds I started sneezing, and so did the girl next to me. Before long the whole class was sneezing. Miss Baldwin was sympathetic when I sneezed, but her expression soon changed to confusion at the uproar of sneezing and laughter all round the room. We had tears rolling down our cheeks.

Gradually the sneezing subsided and Miss Baldwin regained our attention, so the lesson continued as normal. I always wondered whether she guessed what had set us all off. But the thing that really hurt me was that she didn't even ask who started it!

The weekend after this escapade, my mother received an official-looking letter in an embossed envelope with a typed address through the post. I watched her as she opened it and then read it through with a straight face.

Was this the one? She reread it, making me impatient to know.

'Who is it from?' I asked, as casually as I could manage. But she must have known I had guessed as I never usually took any interest in her letters.

'See for yourself,' she replied, showing me the letter heading. She was unable to conceal a hint of a smile, yet also had some slight hesitancy as she handed me the letter.

It was from the Convent of Notre Dame and, with trepidation, I started to read the first paragraph. Straight away it said I had been awarded the only scholarship for the convent this year. It was written by Sister Josephine, the headmistress, and asked Mother to pass on her congratulations to me for doing so well in the exam. I could hardly believe it. She even said they were looking forward to having me in their school. I was thrilled.

'Well done, Margaret,' said Mother, with her usual measured response. 'It says you scored nearly top marks in the scholarship exam.'

'I'm so excited,' I said with a grin. I felt like my insides were doing cartwheels. 'I expect I only got it because I did two alternative answers to the last question.' I paused, trying to take it in, after the long wait. 'I can't quite believe it. Isn't it wonderful?'

'Yes, it is very good,' she said. 'Clever girl. You have worked hard and you deserve it,' she continued. There was a pause while she read through the other sheets of paper that came with the letter.

'What is that all about?' I asked.

'The first page is the dates of school terms for the year

and the special days for religious closures, so that's fine,' she said, going through the letter. 'The second page is about the class you will be in and what you are to do on the first day of term. The third is about the uniform and other things you will need.' I noticed her smile disappearing as she quickly scanned the long list. 'The uniform is all supposed to be bought from a particular shop – Johnny Forbes.' She gulped. 'Or if I want to make your summer dress for next year, the material for that is only stocked by Porritts, so I expect that won't be cheap.' She paused. 'And all your stationery has to be bought at Seed and Gabbutts. Well, I expect we can buy some of it cheaper at the market.' Mother's smile had turned to a worried frown as she shuffled to the last page, about extra activities, which again had to be paid for.

From such initial excitement, I now doubted whether I would even be able to take up this precious scholarship. How strict would the nuns be about the uniform? Did I have to have all of it?

'I don't care about the activities,' I reassured her. 'But do you think we can afford to buy the uniform?'

'I don't know,' she replied with a shrug, then attempted a slight smile. 'But we'll go and find out the prices and I expect I can make some of it.' She paused. 'Don't worry, Margaret, I will do everything I can to try and make it possible.' I suddenly felt like Cinderella. Would I be able to go to the ball? And if I did, would I have to go home early?

Up to now, I hadn't considered any potential obstacles that might get in the way of my ambition, but now I knew these strict requirements could change everything.

I fervently crossed my fingers, prayed like mad and hoped for a miracle.

It was a Saturday, so Mother suggested that after lunch we should at least go to the uniform shop and look at the clothes and their prices. I sent up a few prayers that afternoon as we walked towards Johnny Forbes, the school outfitters.

I looked at the uniforms in the window – all very smart and expensive-looking. I was almost shaking with nerves. My mother opened the door and strode confidently in. I followed her through the doorway and was immediately hit by a strong smell. At first I couldn't work out what it was, then Mother leant over me to whisper, 'Mothballs.'

I couldn't help wondering: did all the convent girls smell like that? I hoped not.

Inside Johnny Forbes's shop, there were rails of uniforms for all the local senior schools, all with different colours and designs. I was sure that everyone in Blackburn must be able to recognize the uniform of the Convent of Notre Dame. We certainly did. Mother led the way over to the display in the middle of the shop, while I hung back, fearing the worst.

I held my breath as Mother picked up the first item – a dark-green gymslip. She didn't flinch as I had feared, but took a careful look at the fabric and the way it was made. Watched by the shop assistant, she then had a quick look at the price, as if that was of secondary importance. Next she picked up some of the other items of uniform, studying each in turn. She left the green blazer till last and asked me to try it on. 'How does it feel?' asked Mother.

'A bit stiff,' I answered.

'It would soften with wear,' she said.

I noticed that she said 'would', so maybe the cost wasn't an impossible demand. How could Mother afford any of this, even with Bobby's contributions? I was downcast. But then she did an unexpected thing. She picked up a school tie, dark green with pale-blue and yellow stripes, and took it to the polished wooden counter.

'I'll take this now,' she said. 'How much?' I knew she had already looked at the price, so I assumed she must have brought enough money with her. She took a note and some coins from her purse and handed it over. The assistant wrapped the tie in tissue paper and Mother gave it to me to carry as she led the way out of the shop.

I was puzzled by her purchase of the tie. Did that mean I could take up the convent scholarship? On the way home I plucked up courage and asked her.

'Why did you buy the tie?'

'Because it's made of a specially woven fabric, so it would be difficult for me to copy if I made it.'

'So does that mean I can go to the convent?'

'I hope so,' she said with a smile. 'But only if I can save up enough money to buy the material and make all the rest of your uniform; well, most of it, anyway.'

'How long will that take?'

'I don't know, but I'll do my best. I've got a few months before you need it, so I hope I'll get it done in time.' She paused. 'Now let's get back home and rescue Bobby from looking after Jeffrey.'

I was full of joy for days after that. I would have liked

to give my mother a hug, to show her how relieved and grateful I was, but we didn't hug in my family.

Over the years, my mother had learned to be very thrifty. That week, she walked into town and scoured the indoor and outdoor markets to see if she could find affordable materials. She saw just the right colour of dark-green wool at a knock-down price, bought it and straight away started knitting me a cardigan for school. She also put a deposit on a length of dark-green worsted to make my gymslip, adding a bit more each week till it was hers. She unpicked an old cream shirt of Bobby's to make into a school shirt for me, and we already had the tie, so I began to feel a little more confident that I might indeed be able to take up my scholarship place at the convent. I couldn't wait!

We had now settled well in our rented house in Robinson Street. It was a stone-clad terraced house in a row of thirteen, all joined together. It had iron railings in front, the same as all the ones in the row, a gate, a small front garden with a path and two steps up to the front door. It was a nice house, with sash windows. I've no idea how old it was. Quite likely Victorian or Edwardian. Inside, there was a vestibule going down. On the right when you came in through the front door was the front room, where Mother slept with Jeffrey on fold-down beds. Then down the tiled passage was the sitting room, with a lovely coal fire in the fireplace that warmed the walls all around and made the house cosy. The fire had a stand over it to boil a kettle or pan on.

The kitchen and the scullery beyond it were built out on the back of the house. We thought it was a good kitchen, with a new gas stove and a dresser. But, of course, it would be almost unrecognizable as a kitchen these days.

Beyond the scullery, we had a yard, surrounded by a wall, with our outside lavatory and a back gate that linked us to the 'backs', a narrow passageway between our neighbours' houses and the back gates of those on the next street.

Upstairs, there were two bedrooms. Mine was on the right and Bobby's was on the left, both with their own wardrobes. Straight ahead was the bathroom, with plenty of hot water from the sitting-room fire's back boiler. But it had no lavatory. The only one we had was outside in the back yard, so if you needed to go in the night, you had to brave all weathers in the dark to use it. Woe betide you if you needed it on a freezing night, when the water in it had turned to ice.

We had flower-patterned wallpaper on all the walls. The sitting room had a big leaded-light window. To the left of the fireplace was Mother's rocking chair, and a large, comfy fireside chair on the right. The mantelpiece was wooden, covered with ornaments, with a big mirror over the top.

My bedroom was my favourite place. It was a pretty room, quite big for one person, with chintzy curtains and bedcover and a rug beside my bed. I put lots of pictures up on my wall, so Mother called it 'the gallery'. Whenever any of my friends came round, she would tell them: 'Margaret is up in the gallery.'

At that time, Robinson Street was a road that petered out into a path at one end, so it was like a cul-de-sac, and children used to play outside in the street. It wasn't tarmacked or anything like that. The ground was just black and gritty. We played games like hopscotch and sack races. The coalman gave us a pile of sacks and we took one each to step inside and pull up to have races in. I always tried to be first and to pick the cleanest sack.

Across the road from the houses, on what seemed like spare land, were 'Howarth's Pens', with rails and wire fencing all round. Lots of chickens were kept here, out in the open in the daytime and in their huts overnight. Imagine, all the thirteen houses in Robinson Street had open land opposite them to look out on. The other two-thirds of the land had nothing on it at all, so we used to go over there and play. At one end, there was a gate to the Conservative Club, with a bowling green alongside it.

Mother's brother, Uncle George, was a town councillor and alderman for the Conservatives and one day he took me inside the Club building and showed me round. First, he showed me the Mayor's portrait in the hall.

'Haven't you been the Mayor?' I asked him.

'No, I'm afraid not. I was asked, several times, but Auntie Evelyn is not a well woman and she doesn't want me to leave her on her own in the evenings.'

I remember there was a grand staircase, with old men's portraits on the wall all the way up, including a large one of Uncle George. The upstairs landing led to a posh ball-room where they held their Conservative parties and dances.

I liked Robinson Street. It was a lively and safe place to live, with friendly neighbours and lots of space to play with my friends. After all the moves we'd made, and all the previous family troubles, this was a calm and secure house. It felt like a proper home.

For a reason I never understood, it was important to have our doorstep donkey-stoned. This was my job every day before school. Looking back on it now, it was really just keeping up with the neighbours. Everybody seemed to take great pride in what the fronts of their houses looked like, so each household felt the need to outshine every other . . . as if the world would fall apart if they missed a day. I thought it was a crazy thing to do.

'Why do we have to do this?' I once asked my mother.

'Because it looks nice,' she replied. And that was that.

The 'donkey stone' was a hard, rectangular greyish-yellow block, like a small brick, that we used to scrub the stone steps.

'Who started all this?' I asked.

'Oh, I think it was in the cotton mills, in Blackburn and all the other towns that had mills. I think it was to stop the stone steps in the mills from being slippery. It probably has the same effect on our steps.'

'Do I really have to do it every day?'

'Yes,' was her curt reply.

So each morning I went out with the donkey stone and some water to scrub and scour the two stone steps up to the front door till they were almost sparkling clean and a light shade of yellow. When I'd done it, I stood back and had a good look to make sure I hadn't missed a bit. I was usually quite proud of how well I'd done them, particularly as you could see the contrast with the boards round the steps. But not content with doing just the minimum, I often went round to our yard and donkey-stoned the back doorstep too, and all around the drains. Was that one-upmanship? Or maybe just me being a perfectionist.

Finally it was July 1937 and time to leave St Alban's Junior School behind. I had always enjoyed my time there and I knew I would go on seeing my friends, but I was especially sad to say goodbye to my favourite teacher. I loved Miss Baldwin. She was a very good teacher, and, oh! . . . that green hat with a feather! Unforgettable.

6

New Challenges

1937–1938

The summer holidays flew by, and as September began my mother had just managed to finish knitting and sewing all the uniform she thought I would need. She carefully laid out the various items on the eve of my starting at the Convent of Notre Dame. I was proud that she had done all that work for me, but a little worried that I had no blazer, since that was supposed to be an essential item. However, she had made a very good copy of the dark-green coat and saved up to buy me a new bonnet-style hat. Some more of the items had to be bought, such as the five pairs of shoes (outdoor, indoor, gym, sports and formal) and the essential 'extras' too.

I got up early on the first day and started to get dressed. Three days a week we were to wear a dark-green dress with white collar and cuffs. The other two were gym or sports days, and this was one of them. First my regulation dark-green knickers (which had to be bought from Marks & Spencer), my new liberty bodice, my crisp cotton shirt and then my home-made gymslip. Bobby had taught me how to fasten my tie, so I did that without much trouble. Then I put on my knitted green cardigan and finally my dark-brown stockings, which had to be attached to a suspender belt, worn round my waist.

Standing in front of the mirror to see how I looked, I couldn't help but feel proud. I had seen some of the convent girls walking to and from school in their smart uniforms. Mine didn't look quite the same, but nearly, and with my home-made but beautifully tailored green coat and my shiny brown leather lace-up shoes on, nobody would know. I was just so happy to be going on this new adventure that I thought it would do. Indeed, I knew it would have to do.

I gladly set off on that first morning, with Mother, Bobby and Jeffrey waving me off from the doorstep, wearing my satchel and clutching the expensive art portfolio Mother had had to buy for me. As I neared the school, I was conscious of not having a blazer to wear, but it was a warm day and I hoped nobody would notice.

I had reread the first day instructions the evening before and my first job on entering the school building was to unlace my outdoor shoes, place them in a locker by the entrance and put on my softer indoor shoes. Everyone else also took their blazers off and hung them on their allotted pegs, so now I felt less conspicuous. There was a nun who greeted all the new girls in the hallway and she pointed us down a corridor.

I soon found the right classroom, went in and sat down in a space next to a girl who smiled at me. All the other girls were new like me. And, like me, they all looked nervous but also curious; eager to begin our first day at the convent. I think I was rather more apprehensive than the others, who were all wearing their posh and proper uniforms.

A smiling nun entered the room, followed by a little terrier dog on a lead. This was a nice touch as it made many of us feel more at home. He was a lovely dog, friendly and well trained.

'I am Sister Magdalene and I shall be your form mistress for this year. Your class is called Lower III German and we will meet here every morning for the register, before you go to your lessons. First today, after the register, we will go to the hall to meet our headmistress, Sister Josephine.'

As we soon discovered, Sister Josephine was an imposing woman. She must have been over six feet tall. We stood in our straight rows across the polished wooden floor as she spoke to us about the history of the school. But I didn't hear much of it that day, as I was mesmerized by her height. To me, close to the front, it was like looking up a tree trunk. She terrified me.

Back in our classroom, Sister Magdalene told us which houses we would each be in. I was put in Ward House. This was specifically for when we were playing sports or competing for something. The girls in each house played against the other houses.

By the end of that first day, I had found my way around most of the school and learned the rules the nuns told us – don't run in the corridors, no hair loose below the collar, hems below the knees, only brown shoes, no loud voices (except for the teachers) and, most important of all, it seemed: when you see a nun, always stand still and curtsey. We all had to practise the right kind of curtsey, which caused some merriment and broke the ice. By home time, I had already got to know several other girls and a few of them walked part of the way home with me. My school life from then on was timed by the ringing of bells.

The twin-gabled stone frontage of the Convent of Notre Dame was an imposing building. Inside, I thought it was beautiful. The walls of the corridor to the chapel were covered in tiny, multicoloured pieces of ceramic tile, with a predominantly blue effect. I loved walking along it, running my finger lightly over the fragments. The chapel itself had such a calm, peaceful feel too. But if I was late for the morning service and ended up sitting near the altar, I sometimes had to leave because of the powerful aroma from the incense. On one occasion the fumes knocked me out – it was quite dramatic. Then there was the embarrassment when I came to, lying on the hard floor, with nuns and pupils gathered round me, looking anxious. But it conveniently got me out of prayers, because one of the nuns took me to a quiet room with soft chairs where she gave me a thin slice of buttered bread, then sat and talked to me.

Over those first few days, I settled into the different routines. There were new subjects to learn about and new ways to learn. Most of the teaching involved listening to the teacher, reading from books and a certain amount of rote-learning. But in some lessons we were also encouraged to think for ourselves. The convent homework of essays and equations was more interesting than the spellings and sums I used to have at St Alban's, and we knew that high standards were expected of us all.

There were thirty-two pupils in my class and several of them came from abroad, so we had lovely long school holidays. The teachers themselves were inspiring, kind and always willing to help.

Miss McAvoy taught maths and geography – my favourite. I loved learning about other countries and I was always asking questions, quite often to get a laugh from my friends. But she always had a sort of smile for me. Of course, I was always near the top for arithmetic, though I could never see the point of algebra or geometry.

One day I asked her: 'Miss McAvoy?'

'Yes, Margaret.'

'Can you tell me,' I asked as politely as I could. 'What use will algebra and geometry be to me when I grow up?'

She paused, and for a moment I feared she might be cross, but then her expression softened and she smiled.

'This is a school of social etiquette,' she explained, decisively.

A fat lot of good that would be to me, I thought, but I had enough social etiquette not to say it.

Miss Finnegan taught us French and German. I loved French, but German was too guttural and full of declensions. Besides, my mother told me about the awful things going on in Germany at that time, so I didn't really want to learn it. Being in a 'German' form, we had to say prayers in German at the beginning of every lesson, so, with Latin as well, at least I can pray in four languages! But I still prefer French.

There was a story going around the convent that Sister Mary Brendan, our needlework (or 'knickers') teacher, was a titled lady. Apparently she came from an aristocratic family, and she did sometimes act as if she was from another world. She was obsessed with cleanliness, especially hands, so she was always dashing off to wash them.

Miss Wren, the art mistress, was quite a large lady. She could be strict, if necessary, but I think she just tolerated me as, although I was no good at art, I did try.

Miss Binks taught gym and games and I adored every minute with her. We all had to learn the old ballroom dances. I suppose that was part of our social etiquette training, but I loved it. The tall girls had to be boys and they had to ask us 'petite' girls to dance. At the end of each term we had a dance afternoon and wore party dresses. Mother, of course, excelled herself and made me a beautiful dress with a blue silk top and layers of net for the skirt, scattered with butterflies. Everyone crowded round me to admire this dress. Philomena McDermot, a close friend of mine, loved it so much that I gave it to her. She was thrilled.

As well as Philomena, I made several good friends and, from the start, I was very happy there. Every day in the convent's chapel, I thanked God for helping me to win that scholarship.

One day in the second or third week, my form teacher, Sister Magdalene, asked me to stay behind after school and have a chat with her. I hoped I hadn't done anything wrong. There were so many rules that I was almost sure to have broken one or two already. But it wasn't anything bad. Apparently she was speaking to each of us in turn, to make sure we had settled in all right.

'Now, Margaret, how have you enjoyed your first few weeks here?'

'I love it,' I said with obvious enthusiasm. 'I love everything about it.'

'Good. I can already see that you are doing very well . . . in most of your subjects.'

'Except in art?' I grinned. 'I can't draw for sixpence.'

'Not everyone can be a talented artist,' she reassured me with an understanding smile.

'I enjoy all the other lessons,' I said eagerly. 'I always want to know new things.'

'That's excellent, Margaret,' she said with a smile. 'Keep it up and you could go far with your studies.' She paused. 'Now off you go home. I don't want your mother worrying about you being late.'

I felt like dancing all the way back to Robinson Street, but I knew my responsibility as a pupil at the Convent of Notre Dame was to be demure and behave in a modest way, to keep the school's good name. We had been told this every day since I arrived, so I just walked as fast as I could, to get home and tell Mother what Sister Magdalene had said.

Every day, just like at St Alban's, I walked home for lunch and back again. The convent was very close to Robinson Street and school lunches were expensive, so it made more sense for me to eat at home. It had the additional advantage that I then wasn't free to take up any of the extra activities, like art club or piano lessons. They all had to be paid for and I knew we couldn't possibly afford it. I was useless at art and couldn't sing a note, so I didn't mind missing all that.

To my great relief, no one ever mentioned my home-made uniform during those first few weeks. A few of my fellow students may have made comments when I was out of earshot, but, if they did, I wasn't aware of them. I would have ignored them anyway.

As the dark, cold evenings drew in and there was less light to play outside, I started doing handiwork and making things. One of my jobs was to cut up Mother's old dress-making patterns into squares and thread them on a string that we hung up and used in the outside lavatory as toilet paper. As I did this boring task, while five-year-old Jeffrey played with a toy train by the fire, I had an idea.

'Come here, Jeffrey,' I said, in what I hoped was an encouraging voice. 'I want to show you something.'

Not wanting to miss out, Jeffrey came over and sat on the chair next to me.

'What is it?'

'We all have jobs in this house,' I began. 'Now that you're getting bigger, would you like to have a job too?' I asked him.

'Yes, please.'

'It's a very important job,' I explained. 'Because you have to learn to use scissors safely, and I'm going to teach you how.' So I showed him, then gave him the scissors to try. They were our smallest scissors, but it still took a couple of days before he could use them properly. Then I showed him how to cut squares and soon he was building up a pile of his own. One less job for me!

After tea one evening, Mother said to me: 'I'm going to teach you how to do corkwork.'

'What's that?' I asked. 'I've never heard of it.'

'I'll show you,' she explained. 'First you need this special bobbin.'

She handed me a cotton reel with a hole down through the middle of it, and four nails hammered into the top. It didn't look very special to me, but I'd never seen one before, so I watched as Mother took one end of a ball of wool and started to wind it round the nails, using a thick needle to hook the strands over each time. I was fascinated to watch as this started to make a sort of woollen string. She added in other colours as well to make a pattern down the 'string' that turned into more of a snake.

'Can I have a go?' I asked.

'Yes, here you are. Just continue to wind it round like I did and you can make a piece as long as you like.'

So that's what I did. It was quite exciting to watch the pattern change as I chose the order of colours to use. Soon I had a 'snake' that trailed halfway across the sitting-room floor.

'You can stop it there if you like,' she said. 'I'll show you how to finish it off, then you can coil it to make a mat or pot-holder, or even a teapot stand if you like. Later you could think of some other things to make with it.'

So, that first evening, I followed Mother's instructions

and carefully coiled the snake into a tight circle on the table and pinned it, so that I could put in some stitches to keep it coiled flat.

After that, I made lots of things we could use around the house or give as presents, keeping my biggest and best circle of rainbow colours to put on the dressing table in my bedroom.

Bobby was out a lot with his friends, so most evenings it was just Mother and me, sewing or making things together.

I had not seen my father since he had left that night and hardly ever thought about him. One evening though, I became curious.

'What happened to Father?' I asked her. 'Have you seen him since he left?'

'No,' replied Mother with a shrug. 'He's too busy with his blonde.'

'I wonder whether Jeffrey remembers him,' I said.

'I shouldn't think so, love.'

Jeffrey was growing fast now and it was fun to see more of him, to read him stories and to teach him things like the alphabet. He was so excited about his first day at St Alban's Mixed Infants' School, following in the footsteps of both Bobby and me.

While living in Robinson Street we'd taken in a stray cat called Gerry, who loved sunning himself in the street. One Saturday, Mother took Jeffrey with her and went to the local shops. Meanwhile, I was playing across the road with some of my friends, when something made me look back towards the house. I saw Gerry lying down near our front gate as usual, and I was about to turn back when I noticed something odd. It looked like there was a movement by his tail. I didn't know what it was so I edged closer for a better look. What I saw really frightened me. It looked like another animal – maybe a rat. What was it doing to Gerry?

I rushed round the corner to the little grocer's shop, where I found my mother talking with one of her friends at the counter.

'Mother!' I yelled as I burst into the shop. 'Come quickly. You've got to come.' I was out of breath from running.

My mother looked alarmed. 'Why, what's the matter? Is there something wrong? Is someone hurt?'

'It's Gerry. Please, you have to come. The rat is eating Gerry. It's eating his tail.'

Mother and Jeffrey ran back with me to see. I was frightened that we might be too late, that the cat wouldn't survive. But he was still there. As we approached and could see more clearly what it was, Mother's expression changed from anxious to smiling.

'That cat is good at keeping secrets,' she said with a laugh in her voice. 'So Gerry isn't Gerry. She's Geraldine, and she's had kittens!'

'Oh,' I gasped in confusion. 'So it wasn't a rat?'

'No. It was probably the first kitten.'

'I didn't know,' I said, confused.

'No, I didn't know either. I thought he was getting fat, so I cut down his food ration – and now, this.' She laughed again.

But what I meant was that I really didn't understand. I didn't know about kittens or any kinds of babies. Nobody ever told me anything, so I had no idea how they came to be or how they were born. I wasn't even allowed to watch.

Geraldine had four kittens that day, all tiny and cute. But that was the first and last I saw of them. I never knew where they went or what happened to them, and I didn't dare ask. But we kept Gerry and carried on calling her by her familiar name, as that's what we were all used to.

So, despite almost having witnessed the kittens' birth, I still knew nothing. I don't think any of my friends did either. It wasn't that, as children, we were missing anything. We just didn't know what there was to miss. We were all in the same position. Nobody ever explained anything.

The first time I saw Raymond Nash he was wearing shorts and riding a shiny red bike down Robinson Street and back again. He had medium-brown straight hair, a strong jaw and looked quite sporty. Raymond was thirteen, a year older than me, and almost a neighbour, living at the bottom of Coniston Road. I was friends with a lot of the local children, most of them boys, but Raymond was special. We just liked all the same things. His father was the manager of the main butcher's shop across from Blackburn Market. Ray would help out at a local butcher's in Rydal Road after school, and I'd see him in a striped apron delivering meat on the shop bike to houses all over Little Harwood.

We were a happy group of children, playing together

in the street or in the 'rec', the recreation ground down the road. There wasn't much on it, just some patchy grass and a small play area, with a see-saw for the little ones, which Jeffrey loved, roundabouts, a slide, swings of different sizes, some bars to climb, and ropes, knotted at the bottom, to climb or swing on. Through the summer the council employed a man to watch over the playground, to make sure children stayed safe.

For going to the rec, which I did nearly every day after school, Mother would never let me wear a frock. I always wore shorts. I lived in shorts and jumpers. And I was never allowed to wear my school shoes, so I had to change as soon as I got in, before she would let me out to play.

Ray and I were always the adventurous ones – especially me. My favourite thing was to swing on the ropes. As soon as I climbed halfway up a rope, the watchman would wag his finger at me and tell me off.

'Don't climb so high,' he used to shout at me. 'Or there's going to be an accident!' I always pretended not to hear him as I climbed right up to the top.

'Hold on tight, Margaret,' shouted Ray, the steadying influence to my impulsive nature, sounding just a little concerned.

Then I'd come down a bit, grab the next-door rope and start to swing. The girls used to move out of the way, whilst the boys stood in a circle under the rope as I swung round over their heads. I used to love playing on the bars too. It was good practice for the gym at school, and I was the only one who could pull myself over the top bar.

*

These were some of the happiest times in my childhood, both at home and at school, and, with no notion yet of what might occur beyond our little world, I looked forward to every day, having fun with the people I loved.

7

A Royal Visit

1938

We were sitting in class on the morning of 16 May 1938 when Sister Magdalene gave us some exciting news.

'As some of you may already know, King George and Queen Mary will be coming on a royal visit to Blackburn tomorrow. And the whole of the school has been invited to come out together and line one of the streets along which they will pass.'

There was a collective gasp around the classroom.

'So we are relying on every girl in the school to look her best, in full, pressed uniform with blazers over your summer dresses and immaculate panama hats. I'm afraid that anyone not in full uniform will not be able to join the reception line. Those properly attired and neat will have the privilege of seeing and maybe even meeting the king and queen themselves.'

I thought she was going to look straight at me when she said we needed to be in full uniform, but she was sympathetic enough not to show me up in that way and I was very grateful.

At breaktime that morning, the whole playground was buzzing with excitement . . . all except for me. I didn't have either a blazer or a panama hat – both far too expensive. So presumably that meant I couldn't see the king and queen. What could I do? I thought it all through over and over again during lessons, but couldn't see a way to take part, so I was very subdued for the rest of the day. I did consider hanging back at the end of school and asking at the school office if there was any spare uniform, but I didn't. I was too proud to explain my plight to any of the staff.

I came from a good family, a well-established Blackburn family, with both sets of grandparents running successful businesses, one of them also a mills inspector; two uncles were mill managers and another a councillor, plus a great-uncle was a Papal Knight who had endowed various institutions in the town. Mother might have fallen on hard times through no fault of her own, but she never dropped her standards and brought us all up very well.

However, none of this helped me when it came to the question of whether I would be able to go and see the king and queen. Philomena was worrying for me too.

'I wish I had a spare panama hat,' she said, as we started to walk home after school. 'But I haven't.'

'I'd need a blazer as well,' I reminded her.

'Not necessarily,' she replied. 'You're quite small, so if we squeezed you in at the back nobody would see you weren't wearing a blazer . . .'

'Hmm,' I mumbled. 'That's not a bad idea. Do you think we could pull it off?'

'Yes, I do . . . if you had the panama hat. That's all that would need to show.'

'Thank you,' I said. 'It's a brilliant idea and I'm going to think about it.'

That night, after tea, I played with Jeffrey and put him to bed, then went to my bedroom to read . . . and think.

When I got up in the morning, I knew what I had to do.

'Mother, did you know that the king and queen are coming to Blackburn today?'

'Yes, Alice told me.'

'Well, all the convent girls have been invited to line part of their route.'

'How exciting for you,' she said, pouring milk into Jeffrey's glass.

'Yes, it would be, but I need to beg or borrow a panama hat or I won't be allowed to be there. So, Philomena thought up a good idea.'

'What's that?'

'Do you have any spare change at all? I've got about a shilling left of what Grandad gave me for my birthday. If I can scrape together enough money and run down to Johnny Forbes, I can ask if they will lend me a panama, or sell me a damaged one for whatever money I have.'

Mother went straight to the tin where she kept the housekeeping money and gave me another four shillings.

'That's all I can spare,' she said. 'I hope it's enough.'

I ran all the way to Johnny Forbes's shop and stopped outside all breathless, looking in the window while I caught my breath. The shop had just opened and was empty of customers, so I walked in and spoke to the man at the counter – the same one we'd seen the previous summer.

'I can't afford a brand-new panama hat for the convent,' I began, in a rush. 'And I can't go and line the royal visit route with all the other girls if I don't have one. I've brought all our spare housekeeping money – five shillings. I know it won't be enough to buy a new one, but I wondered whether maybe you have a damaged or stained panama hat that you can't sell? Would five shillings be enough?'

I was breathless again now, but more out of nerves than anything else.

'We don't have any faulty stock,' said the man, in a snooty voice. 'So we won't have an unsaleable panama hat.'

'Are you sure?'

'Yes.'

'Couldn't you even go and look? Please.'

'It wouldn't be any use.'

I could feel the tears coming, so I ran out of the shop. But I didn't want to leave altogether. This was my only chance, so I knew I had to swallow my pride and go back in. I stood by the display of convent uniform and tried on the new panama hat on the stand. The man disappeared into an area behind the counter and I stayed put, hoping against hope that he might come back with something.

Sure enough, five minutes and a lot of rustling later, he reappeared, holding a panama with the convent's colours on it.

'Here we are,' he said with a smile. 'I can see you really

want to see the king and queen, so I've found you a reject that I wouldn't be able to sell in the shop. Look.' He held it out for me to see. 'It has a few darker pieces of straw, so you can have it for five shillings.'

'Oh, yes please!' I could have kissed him. I saw that the faults were hardly noticeable, unless you looked really close up. I handed over the money and looked at the clock on the wall. The girls would all be assembling at the school about now, so I had to rush.

'Thank you, thank you, thank you,' I yelled as I raced out of the shop. Breaking all the rules about behaving decorously in public, I all but flew to the convent, where I joined the girls in my form, wearing my hat and the green coat that Mother had made. I stood well away from the nuns, walking behind some taller girls, and, in the rush, they didn't notice my lack of blazer. When we reached our places on the royal route, we shuffled into place. True to her word, Philomena stood right in front of me so that only my head and my panama hat were showing over her shoulder.

Sister Magdalene walked along our part of the line, stopped in front of Philomena and looked over her shoulder at me. She fixed her eyes on the hat for a moment, then back at my face with a smile and a nod of approval.

As we stood waiting, someone distributed red roses, one to each of us – red for Lancashire – so we all had one to wave when the royal cavalcade drove down our street on the way to the town hall, where our head prefect had a space in the specially erected stand outside.

The king and queen were in an open-topped car, moving

slowly along as they waved to the onlookers at either side. When they reached us, they both looked and smiled in our direction. I felt so proud to be there.

It was the most exciting event in my life up to then. I couldn't believe it was real. Our school magazine later said we *made quite a stir with our light-green dresses, dark-green blazers and panamas, each carrying a rose.* If only they'd known!

At regular intervals in the convent, we had to have 'inspections'. They were nothing to do with our learning or our safety, but they had everything to do with the convent's strict rules about uniform. (Here we go again!)

Every morning, as we arrived at school and took our outdoor shoes off, we had to line them up with all our other pairs for a prefect to check that we had the right number and type of shoes, in good order.

When it came to the end of my first year at the convent, this worried me a lot. My feet were growing too fast! I had the right number and styles of shoes, but some of them were too small for me, so I had to push and squeeze my feet into them, with increasing discomfort. I knew that by the beginning of the new term in September, I might not be able to get them on at all.

I also realized that I couldn't ask Mother for so many pairs of new shoes so soon. She had enough trouble affording more than one thing at a time. Five pairs at once would be an impossibility – especially as the convent decreed that four out of the five could only be bought at Johnny Forbes, who charged accordingly. The only exception was our outdoor shoes, which had to be bought from a proper shoe shop. So I decided to ask, as soon as we had broken up, for just one new pair to replace my outdoor shoes, which were the tightest. Mother gulped, but immediately started saving what she could, so that by the end of August she had enough money and we went to have my feet measured, ready to buy the appropriate size, with room to last.

'Wait a minute,' said Mother. 'I've just realized. Your feet are now the same size as Grandma's and I think she has a pair of brown shoes she hardly ever wears. Let's ask her first if you can wear her shoes for school.'

'All right,' I agreed, my heart sinking a bit as I hoped they were not too old-fashioned.

'I suppose all your other shoes are too small as well?' asked Mother as we walked back home.

I nodded. 'Yes, they're getting a bit tight, but not quite as bad.'

'All right, I'll have to take on some more work,' she sighed. 'But don't worry. Now that Jeffrey is nearly six, you could look after him some days while you're on your school holidays. You can take him to Grandma and Grandad's to visit, one day a week. That way I'll be able to do more dressmaking during the day and I'll save up gradually so that we can buy one pair at a time.'

'Thank you, Mother. That will be fine.'

I would have done almost anything to help Mother buy my shoes, but Jeffrey turned out to be more of a handful on the tram to Grandma and Grandad's house than I expected. He made faces at other passengers and climbed over the seat to stroke a very hairy dog before pinching an apple from an old lady's basket when she wasn't looking. I felt awful about that and had to apologize for him. Fortunately I'd stopped him taking a bite out of it.

'Don't worry,' she said with a twinkle in her eye. Then she handed it back to me. 'Here, love. I've got plenty. Let him have this one.'

'Thank you,' I said, and I made Jeffrey thank her too.

The trouble was, he was such a bright child that he was inquisitive about everything. On one trip he even asked the tram driver how old he was. I was always apologizing for him, but people were very kind in those days.

On the last part of the journey, walking to their house, I used to get him skipping along down the hill while I taught him to chant the times tables, just as Bobby had taught me. He was younger than I had been and wasn't doing the tables at school yet, but he was clever enough to pick them up, starting with the easiest ones: two, five and ten.

At the convent, we had our hair length checked every now and then, to make sure any girl with hair touching her shoulders tied it back. Mine was short enough, but always curling round my hat. I tried to tuck it away underneath, but it kept popping out again. One particular nun, Sister Bernadette, didn't like that.

'There's one way to make sure your hair will stay put, Margaret,' she said, getting out her wire brush and using it vigorously. With my hair, I knew this wasn't a wise thing to do. The whole class watched as she brushed and brushed. Finally she stood back to examine the results – only to realize that my hair was now extremely frizzy and standing on end. The other girls could hardly suppress their laughter!

The length of our gymslip skirts were also regularly checked. The sight of Sister Magdalene with her long wooden ruler would fill me with dread. Each pupil had to kneel down on the floor, while she measured to make sure that our gymslips were no shorter than our knees. In the summer our dress hems also had to be below our knees, and as soon as I saw that ruler I used to start pulling my dress down as far as I could. It had worked so far, but for how much longer? At the last inspection at the end of my first year, I only just passed.

'Margaret, I think you'll have to tell your mother that you'll soon be needing some new uniform.'

I nodded, feeling forlorn, but determined not to show it. 'Yes, Sister Magdalene.' But I didn't tell my mother, not till I really had to. She was already saving up for my new shoes, after all.

Sunday was always a busy day for me as I went to Mass at St Alban's Church. I was a Roman Catholic, like all the Holdens, and having spent my early childhood living mostly at the Tanners' Arms with my Catholic grandparents, Sunday morning Mass was a way of life for me. My mother never came with us to church, as she was from a strongly C. of E. background; hence the past animosity between the two families.

I know my father was not the best example of what a

Roman Catholic should be, but praying in the chapel at the convent, and watching the nuns every day, my faith developed and grew. Gradually I passed it on to Jeffrey as well. I'd take him with me to Sunday morning Mass, then we caught the tram and walked the rest of the way down to Grandma and Grandad Harrison's house. As well as visiting them, my weekly task, unpaid, was to clean all of Auntie Elsie's shoes. Elsie was my mother's younger sister, who had never married and still lived with Grandma and Grandad. She had shoes of many colours and I had to clean them all for her. I don't know why she didn't clean them herself.

We stayed for a lovely roast lunch, then took the tram back home to Blackburn. Bobby didn't come with us because he was now a dedicated member of the local model aeroplane club. Every Sunday afternoon they would all go to the flying field, which was on the farm at the side of the New Inn pub, or in one of their barns if it rained. One weekend at breakfast time, Bobby had an idea.

'You're good at arithmetic, Margaret. We need an official timekeeper at the flying field. Why don't you come with me one Sunday and see what it's like?'

I adored my big brother Bobby, so the fact that he thought I could do something like that for him and his friends was a tremendous boost to my self-esteem.

'Yes please. I'd love to come and keep the times.'

So, from then on, I went to join him and his pals every Sunday afternoon. I loved it. At the end of my first session, Ernie Aspinall gave me the title of 'official timekeeper' and enrolled me as the only female in their club. Every week, the boys brought along the model aircraft they had made. Each of them in turn wound up their plane with rubber bands, set it off and I timed its flight.

One rainy Sunday afternoon in 1938, when we were messing around in the barn, the boys seemed to notice that I was growing up. It was quite funny really, as they started to be polite and actually talk to me.

Most of the model aircraft were quite small, but once someone brought along a petrol model with a six-foot wingspan. Off it went, soaring into the air like an eagle . . . but it flew so well and so far that we quickly lost track of it. Later in the afternoon, we discovered that it had flown off towards Accrington, where the military defence chaps spotted it and, knowing that an international conflict was looming, and suspecting it might be an alien spy plane, followed it with their binoculars, but it crashed before they could shoot it down.

The plane had to be accounted for and collected from its crash site in a farmer's field. Bobby, Ernie and the other boys were working late on the Monday, so Bobby's great pal Gordon Fudge brought his tandem and I agreed to go with him. I had always liked Gordon, although he was six years older than me. He was tall, with curly reddish hair and a friendly smile. He worked at the tea warehouse in Blackburn and used to bring me stickers off the crates from India, Ceylon and other countries. Gordon was born and brought up in Scotland, but his grandmother lived in Blackburn, so he had moved south to keep her company. He must have been such a help to her.

We set off at teatime and arrived half an hour later at the farm, where we were taken to the site of the crash. There, in a forlorn heap on the ground, was the suspect model-kit plane. Only its nose and parts of the wings were recognizable. Everything else had fallen apart.

We loaded all the smaller pieces into the large basket on the front and the panniers at the back and got back on the tandem. If I hadn't been so anxious not to drop or damage anything, I would have seen the funny side of it – Gordon pedalling away as hard as he could to carry both our weights as well as the smashed-up plane, with me sitting on the back seat, trying desperately to hold on to all the larger parts, all the way back to Blackburn.

Despite the five-year difference in our ages, that was when Bobby started to see me as not just a child to protect, but also a part of his world, if only for a relatively short time.

That year, 1938, I spent most of the summer holidays outside playing with my friends, particularly Ray, who always used to call for me. He was good fun. We laughed at the same things, so when the rest of the group weren't there, we would just go for walks or bike rides together, and we got to know each other's parents quite well, so they were happy for us to visit each other's houses when it rained. In fact, Ray was at our house so often that Mother was quite amused.

'He's like another son,' she said with a laugh.

Ray was a dab hand at most of the dice games, like 'Snakes and Ladders', that we always played with Jeffrey.

One day Ray brought round a brand-new board game called 'Monopoly' and Mother joined us to play, helping five-year-old Jeffrey to 'buy' houses. Ray also loved card games and he even taught Jeffrey to play poker, just for fun of course, though I'm not sure what Mother thought of that.

These were good times and, still only twelve, I was hardly aware that Britain's relationship with Hitler's Germany was fractious and that a war was becoming more and more likely. Unlike my parents, I had never lived through a war, so I had little idea how that might change our lives. For now, I let it all simmer in the background while I enjoyed the rest of my summer break.

8

'Look, Duck and Vanish'

1938–1939

Five empty lockers, with names removed; five empty spaces in the classroom. Most of us had come back to school chattering nineteen to the dozen, but now our voices were hushed. What could have happened? Our new form teacher, Miss Wilson, came in and, before we had the chance even to speculate about this mystery, she gently broke it to us:

'Good morning, girls, and welcome back for the new school year.' She paused, taking a deep breath. 'As you can see, we have some empty desks. I'm very sad to have to tell you that five of your friends have died during the summer holidays. I'm afraid I don't know any more, but I'm sure you will want to remember them all in your prayers.'

One of the girls, Anastasia Long, was quite small and was not very good at games, but excelled in her other subjects. Another was Eileen Parkinson, who was very, very good at drawing. They were both lovely girls and I couldn't believe they were gone. It was a subdued atmosphere that first day of term as we all went to the chapel to pray for their souls. Most of us had not previously experienced the death of someone we knew in our own age group, someone who was part of our everyday life.

I was now in Upper III German and continued to do well – usually near the top of the class, especially in arithmetic. But I was also the class joker. I loved acting and was in all the plays we put on, including *A Midsummer Night's Dream*. With so much going on, this term seemed to go by quickly, now that it was my second year at the convent.

Walking to and from school each day I passed Plane Street, where there was a row of shops. One of them was Sellers' Butcher's, where a boy called Clarence Charnley worked. Most people called him Clarry and he was three years older than me.

It seemed that Clarry was well aware of me going to school, backwards and forwards each day. I was only twelve, but I must have looked older, despite the uniform. Four times a day I went past that shop and it felt as if Clarry was always standing outside, waiting for me to walk by. Initially, he just smiled at me, but then he started to whistle, wave and call out to me every time. I used to put my head down and walk swiftly past, trying to ignore him, but with a small smile on my face.

As I eased myself back into school rules and routines after our carefree summer, my brother Bobby and his pal Gordon Fudge joined the Civil Air Guard at weekends so that they could learn to fly. Every Saturday morning, they cycled the twenty-five miles to Squires Gate airfield near Blackpool, making the same journey back again in the evening. Before long, both of them applied to join the RAF. Gordon gained his wings, but his medical found him slightly deaf in one ear and the RAF turned him down. Poor Gordon. I did feel sorry for him as it must have been quite a stigma at that time, especially since Bobby passed the medical, and was in training to gain his wings. He was soon accepted by the RAF.

Bobby had completed five years of his carpentry apprenticeship, so just before he turned eighteen he joined up. He was extremely excited at the thought of becoming an RAF pilot but his happiness was short-lived, as they refused him pilot training. When he asked his commanding officer why, he was told that it would take only six weeks to train him as an RAF pilot, whereas it takes five years or more to train a carpenter. They were desperately in need of fully trained carpenters to build and repair their wooden Mosquito aircraft and he was already well on the way to having the relevant qualifications.

Once he was reconciled to his initial disappointment, Bobby made some new friends, in particular one called Arthur Isherwood, who was training to be an aerial photographer. The RAF certainly kept my brother busy from the outset and he made good use of the excellent carpentry skills he had learned in Grandad Harrison's workshop and building sites. He was always away from home now, either at his base or working on airfields around the country. I worried about him and I know Mother did too, in case anything should happen to him. I missed him terribly. It was a miserable time. My father had left us and now I had lost my big brother as well. But Bobby was very good, as he continued to send part of his RAF pay to Mother every month and wrote letters to both of us. The letters he sent to me were full of questions about what I had been doing and instructions on what I shouldn't be doing, such as not going out except with Mother or to school or church. It was as if he had put me in a tin when he left and he didn't want me to get out of it till he got home again. I knew it was because he loved me, but I didn't tell him half of what I did. Bobby came home on leave whenever he could, often with a toy for Jeffrey and a bracelet or other special present for me. We were all glad to have him home each time, but it was difficult for me as, now I was older, he just wanted to follow me around all the time, keeping an eye on me.

As the new year of 1939 dawned, tensions were rising in political circles, if the headlines on newspaper sellers' boards were anything to go by. Many of the younger working men were being put on the army's reserve lists, and some began to enlist in the forces, to train in earnest. Several of the men of Blackburn, conscious of the talk of a coming war, got together at weekends or during the evenings to start training, just in case. Every now and then, on fine days, we used to see these middle-aged men marching up and down the streets or lanes practising drills, old brooms on their shoulders, always with at least one of them woefully out of step. They called themselves the Local Defence Volunteers.

It looked quite comical to Ray and me as we sat on a wall and watched them passing by, whilst others with enormous tubas, French horns and drums played them on, seriously out of tune. We giggled at their uncoordinated efforts, but I don't think the prospect of war troubled us much at that stage, if at all. We couldn't imagine it would ever really happen.

More worrying for me was my shrinking convent uniform – I was growing too fast! So, to help Mother out with our finances, I decided it was time for me to take on some part-time jobs. On Friday nights, I went round collecting payments for a dentist. I recognized the irony of that, having had such trouble with my teeth when I was younger, but I quite liked the job as I could chat to people.

On Saturday afternoons I'd taken a job covering buttons for the 'Holidays' stall in the market hall in the centre of Blackburn. It was run by two glamorous sisters, selling haberdashery such as ribbons, threads, buttons and zips. My task was to sit at the stall and cover buttons to order. Customers would bring me a piece of their dress material and ask me to make buttons out of it. I had a little gadget that helped me punch the fabric over each of the little metal discs and they looked lovely when I'd finished. It was just the one afternoon each week and for that I was paid five shillings, which was half a week's wages for some people, so I did very well. The market hall was always so full of life, with its little cafes, high-class groceries and butchers.

*

In the summer of 1939, during Blackburn's Wakes Week, when the mills and factories were closed for their annual maintenance, Bobby and his pal Arthur had a week's leave, so he paid for Mother, her friend Alice, Jeffrey and me to join the two of them for a week's holiday in Blackpool. It was excellent timing, as it turned out. We stayed at a good boarding-house and the friendly land-lady was happy for us to buy our own food, which she cooked for us. We had done the same thing in previous childhood visits, to keep the costs down. It had rained a lot in Blackpool for the two weeks before our visit, but the week we were there it was dry every day, so we took Jeffrey on the beach and he had a ride on a donkey for the first time. Knowing this might be the last carefree holiday we could all have for a while, we made the most of the time together. War was becoming almost inevitable now.

As soon as we were back home again, Mother was suddenly in demand. This time not as a dressmaker, but rather a blackout-curtain maker. We had various neigh-bours' and friends' bales of blackout material stacked all over the house, ready for Mother to make up into curtains to fit their windows snugly.

Nobody knew quite when the war might happen, but the talk was non-stop and there seemed little doubt that it would, so the government was urging all citizens to be prepared. We were allocated rolls of gummed brown paper to tape up our windows with diagonals or criss-cross lines making diamond or square shapes, so that if a bomb fell nearby, it might not shatter the glass and injure anyone.

Well, that was the idea, anyway, but I couldn't see how a few strips of thin brown paper could block out the lethal power of an exploding bomb.

It was rather worrying in a way, but I was such an optimist that I really didn't think it would affect us in Blackburn. Mother must have been anxious, however, even though she didn't show it. I once overheard her talking about the coming war with one of her friends. They were discussing what might happen if the Germans came over to Blackburn and tried to take their daughters away. I didn't like the sound of that!

By late August the Local Defence Volunteers were out every day practising their marching, and generally making a nuisance of themselves.

'Look at their medals,' I said to Ray as we stopped to watch them in the square. 'Some of them must have fought in the First World War.'

'Yes, and some of them are so old, they were probably in the Boer War too!'

We watched them getting in a bit of a muddle, doing some sort of manoeuvre.

'Do you know what my father calls the Local Defence Volunteers?' he asked.

'No, what does he call them?'

'Well, their initials are L.D.V., so he and his friends call them "Look, Duck and Vanish". Don't you think that's a good name for them?'

'Yes.' We laughed and walked on.

As war loomed, the LDV became the Home Guard,

which Ray's father was in and Ray had just joined as well. Some of them were also training to become air-raid wardens, preparing themselves for the worst so that they could do 'save and rescue' duties. But few of them had been issued with their uniforms yet, or any proper equipment.

On Friday, 1 September, I was walking into town when I passed a newspaper hoarding which said Germany had invaded Poland. I didn't know much about politics, but I knew that was serious.

Later in the day, on my way home, I saw a forlorn group of children with labels around their necks and their gas-mask boxes across their chests, carrying small suitcases. Some of the youngest were holding older siblings' hands and carrying teddy bears. There were a few adults with them, leading them into a big building.

When I got home, I asked Mother if she knew about them.

'They must be evacuees,' she said. 'I think they arrived today at the station and now they have to be found places to stay. When I went to the shop, some of the locals were talking about it. Apparently, most of these children come from Manchester . . . or was it London? They will be given temporary homes in farms and country houses outside Blackburn.'

'Like Grandma and Grandad's?'

'No. Their house is probably too small, with Elsie living in their main spare room.'

'Why not in the town?' I was curious.

'Because Blackburn is a city and the Germans will probably target urban areas, so it might not be much better than where they came from.'

'But we're not even at war yet, are we?'

'No, but Hitler has invaded Poland now . . .'

'Yes, I saw that on the newspaper seller's board this morning.'

'So, it can't be long,' she said quietly, putting on our tea, while I read a book with Jeffrey.

That Sunday morning, 3 September 1939, I took Jeffrey to Mass at St Alban's Church as usual, completely unaware that this day would be different from any other Sunday. I did notice that there seemed to be a few of the regular congregation missing, but that was all . . . till we came out of the church and saw the street full of Home Guard men, including Ray himself and his father, out on parade.

I was amazed. It was the first time I'd seen Ray in that role, alongside some of the other boys from the neighbourhood, and the grown-ups. He looked across and gave me a rueful smile. It was quite amusing really, after all the fun we had made of these would-be soldiers, often called 'Dad's Army'. Now he was one himself.

There was a buzz of conversation and I kept hearing the words, 'war with Germany', 'Hitler' and 'Chamberlain'.

'Why are there so many soldiers?' asked Jeffrey, watching them with evident excitement. 'I want to be a soldier too.'

Before I could say anything, one of the church ladies

standing nearby said: 'I think we must be at war, dear. And you're too young to be a soldier.' And then she turned to me. 'I just heard somebody saying that Neville Chamberlain was on the radio, talking about it.' She paused, looking distracted. 'Perhaps we'd all better go home and find out for ourselves.'

Sure enough, instead of standing and talking for ages outside the church as some of the grown-ups usually did, they moved away very quickly, hurrying off in search of news.

From that day on, almost every time I went into the town, I was stopped by one of the LDV or the Home Guard, checking that I was carrying my gas mask and my identity card. Mother had had to fill in a form about how many lived in our house and the children's ages. Once she'd sent that in, we had our gas masks in their boxes and identity cards delivered to the house, including a small gas mask for Jeffrey. At the beginning, I often got into trouble because I had forgotten to bring them with me wherever I went. I'm sure I wasn't the only one.

Early the next week we had a leaflet through our door about what to do if the sirens went. Both Mother and I read it through, but hoped we wouldn't need it. However, days later, the sirens sounded loudly across Blackburn and we all had to follow the instructions to 'take cover'. This wasn't very helpful, but we knew that under the stairs must be the safest place, so that's where we went, all squeezing into the cupboard and closing the door. We didn't know it was only a practice run, but at least now we'd done it. We'd be ready for a real air-raid warning, if it came.

As we hid under the stairs, I asked Mother, 'Surely the war won't last long? It's a real nuisance, having to leave everything and rush to take shelter.'

'Yes, I was about your age when the Great War started, and we thought that one would be over quickly, but it lasted more than four years,' she explained. I knew she didn't want to worry me, but her voice did sound a little higher than usual. 'And Hitler seems to be an even worse enemy than the Kaiser.'

On the following Saturday, 7 September, we heard that the first air raids had been carried out in Britain. They were in Kent, so a long way from Blackburn, but it showed that the Germans were serious. The war was a reality. I wasn't so concerned for us, but I did worry that our poor fighter pilots might have to put themselves in danger. All I could do was think of Bobby, working on the airfields, and hope he'd be safe.

Throughout that autumn term of 1939, although the war was an ever-present threat, it still seemed distant as not much had happened so far in Blackburn. Personally, I had more pressing concerns at that time – in particular, I was still growing too fast. I only just managed to avoid some of the uniform inspections that term, and had a close shave with others. But by Christmas, I was being told more and more often that I must have a new gymslip, new shoes and all the rest. In fact, I didn't need to be told by the nuns. It was getting hard to do up my shirt buttons, but luckily Mother had enough material to make me another shirt, which she did over the Christmas holidays. Other items were not so easy to replace or conceal. I dreaded the day I would be told to buy new everything . . . or else.

9

New Beginnings

1940

On 6 January 1940, food rationing was introduced for every person in Britain. It started with bacon, butter and sugar. Other foods were gradually added to the list, including meat (the equivalent of just over a pound in weight or half a kilo per person per week), tea, jam, biscuits, cereals, cheese, eggs (one per person per week) and milk. To make the rations go further, powdered egg and powdered milk also became available. Sausages were not rationed at this time, but they began to contain less meat, and bread was used to fill them out. 'National' bread, a filling wholemeal loaf, was freely available but wasn't very nice.

Mother had to nominate the shops she would use to buy each type of food and could only buy our rations there. If they ran out of something, we had to do without. We had a ration book each and the shopkeepers had to cancel each coupon as the item was purchased.

This was all quite strange at first, but soon everybody got used to it. Luckily for us, Grandma and Grandad

Harrison had their own hens, laying plenty of eggs, and we were able to buy or barter for dairy products from neighbouring farms, so, between us, we made sure we had enough healthy food most weeks of the year.

Clothing was rationed on a points system, equal to one whole outfit a year to start with, though it was gradually reduced. That's where Mother's dressmaking skills came into their own.

Despite my contributions, our finances didn't improve much in early 1940. Through that school term, I continued to dread more uniform inspections, but somehow they didn't happen so often. I think because of the war they were a little more lenient, so I got by for a while longer. I desperately wanted to talk to Mother about my concerns, but I didn't want to upset her. Bobby was always away, so I couldn't talk to him, and anyway, he sent as much of his RAF pay home as he could. I dreaded the day the nuns would give me the ultimatum – buy new uniform or else – but I never told Mother how bad I felt.

One Sunday, when we were all at Grandad and Grandma's house for lunch, I was playing a game with Jeffrey on the rug while the grown-ups talked. I wasn't really listening to the conversation, but Mother must have said something and I heard her mention my name so I listened for what would come next. There was a brief silence, then Grandad responded.

'She'll only get married,' he said.

There was another silence and then Grandad changed the subject. I had my back to them, but I was pretty sure that Grandad had said that about me. What did he mean? Maybe I would get married one day, but there were a lot of other things I wanted to do as well.

In bed that night, I couldn't sleep for thinking about it and wondering about my future. What had Mother said to Grandad? Might it have been about money? I would probably never know. But it was Grandad's comment that had stayed in my mind. Was marriage the only thing Grandad expected of me? I loved him dearly and I knew he loved me, but that throwaway remark had upset me. Here I was at the best girls' school in town, with the best teachers and so many opportunities. I loved the convent. When I won that scholarship, it was for all my schooling up to the age of eighteen. But now we had so little money that I had to give all I earned to Mother and there was hardly anything left to buy the necessary extras, especially the books I needed. Only the day before I had taken the few pennies Mother could spare into town to see if I could buy a copy of *Nos Amis Français* that I needed for my French lessons. It had cost two shillings, and that was just one of the books I needed, so it was out of the question to buy it. How would we manage if anything happened to Bobby? I felt like I might be losing something special . . . all my hopes and dreams were crashing to the ground. What if I had to give up school for good? I sobbed myself to sleep.

One Saturday in March 1940, I was mopping my bedroom floor when Mother called me. Her voice sounded urgent so I went to the top of the stairs.

'I want you to go to the phone and speak to Auntie

Elsie. Tell her, "This is the time." She'll know what you mean,' explained Mother.

It didn't make much sense to me, but I knew not to ask questions, so I ran up the road to the phone box and asked the operator for my grandparents' number. Luckily, it was Auntie Elsie who answered, so I told her exactly what Mother had said.

'All right, love,' she said, without a hint of surprise. 'Now you go home and collect Jeffrey, then bring him here to Grandma's. I'll come and join your mother, so we might pass on the way.'

I ran straight home and in through the door, which was never locked during the day.

Mother was in the vestibule, looking a bit flustered.

'Auntie Elsie said I should take Jeffrey down to Grandma's house,' I told her. 'And she is coming here.'

'Good,' nodded Mother. 'Now I've packed you both a bag and here's the tram fare. You're to stay overnight. I want you to play lots of games with Grandma . . . and let her win!'

She briefly waved from the front step, but then a neighbour popped round and ushered her inside. By the time we reached the end of the road, she had gone in. I didn't really think anything of it.

After lunch the next day, we were allowed to go home again, so we skipped and sang our way along the lanes, took the tram to Bastwell and walked the rest of the way back along Plane Street, under Star Bridge and past the memorial clock, to Robinson Street.

When we arrived home, Jeffrey went straight out to

play in the street with his friends, while I went in and called out for Mother to tell her we were back.

'In the living room,' she replied.

I walked through the door to a wonderful surprise. Mother was sitting in her rocking chair by the fire, gently cradling a baby.

'Come and meet your new brother,' said Mother, stroking the baby's tiny hand. 'This is Alan.' She passed him over to me.

'Hello, Alan,' I whispered, full of love and pride, as I took him into my arms. From that moment, I was totally smitten. Looking back on all this now, I hadn't noticed my mother gaining weight. She normally had a tiny waist and was such a skilful dressmaker that she probably concealed her pregnancy well.

I never heard any of our relatives or friends questioning who the father was, though they might have done amongst themselves. Being very naive about such things, I don't think I even knew there had to be a father!

But now I remember that the previous summer, when we'd spent that week in Blackpool with Bobby and Arthur, just before the war started, there was one evening when Mother went out somewhere with her friend Alice. I had taken Jeffrey to the cinema. I knew my mother was not a drinker. However, she always liked peppermint, so I can put two and two together and surmise that Mother and Alice might have met a couple of RAF men – there were plenty of those about in Blackpool, because of the airfield. Perhaps they encouraged her to have a drink or two of peppermint liqueur.

Looking back, the only difference I can recall after that was her withdrawal from going anywhere and her friends coming round more often to spend time with her at our house.

What the real story was I will never know, but I was delighted to have Alan to fuss over. What I wanted more than anything was a real baby to look after . . . and now, here he was. From that moment on, whenever I could, I cared for him, sang to him, bathed him and played with him. I even carried him all the way to his christening at St Alban's Church. I often argued with Mother because I wanted to be the one to look after him – for Alan to be *my* baby, and she couldn't allow that.

Regardless, his addition to the family was a wonderful surprise and I couldn't have been happier about it.

With another mouth to feed and only a few days left of the Easter term, I had to face the truth. Although I dreaded the idea and still hoped for a miracle, I was realistic enough to know that I might have to leave the convent soon. I just couldn't let Mother struggle any more. In a few weeks I would turn fourteen, so I could at least postpone thinking about it till then . . . or that's what I thought.

A few days later, I bumped into one of my local friends, Hilda, who was a couple of years older than me and worked as a secretary at Hodgson and Taylor's Dye Works. We stopped for a chat.

'I think I could get you a job,' she said. 'Where I work. They're looking for somebody bright like you to test the yarns.'

'But I don't have an insurance card,' I told her.

'Don't worry about that. I work in the office, so I can help you get away with it. I'll just put you through without it. Nobody at the Works will ask about that. But you'll have to come and meet my boss. I'll introduce you. He just wants to fill the position, so if he offers it to you, then you'll probably have to start straight away.'

'All right,' I said, with hardly a thought. 'I'm leaving school anyway, so what difference will a couple of weeks make?' I had my practical head on now – no looking back.

I went for an interview with a middle-aged manager, but he didn't ask me much. I can't remember his name, but he seemed like a nice man, with a friendly face, and I knew Hilda was happy there, so when he asked me, 'Will you take the job, starting next Monday?' I gulped, smiled and said 'Yes.'

So that was it. The decision was made. Deep down, I was immensely sad about leaving the convent, but this was an opportunity I could not turn down. It would solve all our money problems. I became quite excited at the thought of it as I walked down the street and in at our front door.

'It's only me,' I called out, as usual, closing the door behind me and walking through to Mother in the kitchen. 'I've got a job.'

'Oh yes?' she said, as if I'd told her I'd brought the washing in. She looked round at me while she carried on stirring. 'Where?'

'At the dye works,' I said. 'It's a full-time job and I'll be earning ten shillings a week.'

'Really?' She sounded surprised. 'When do they want you to start?'

'Monday.'

'What, during the Easter holidays?'

'No, this coming Monday.'

'But . . .' she gasped, 'it's Friday today.'

'Yes, so I won't be going back to school. I would have had to leave at the end of next week anyway, right?'

Mother nodded. 'Yes, I suppose so. But you're still only thirteen.'

'I know, but I'll be fourteen in May, and then I'll be legal, so nobody will worry about a few weeks, will they?'

I never went back to the convent again after that weekend and never told any of my teachers I was leaving. I didn't know then, but the convent always checked up on their pupils, so they did write to Mother to ask where I was a few weeks later and to see if I was all right. She must have replied that I'd had no choice but to leave.

Early on the Monday morning, I started my working life. The company was housed in a big building on the corner of Willow Street and Bay Street, with several different sections. The noise from all the machines hit me as I walked in through the factory entrance. Everyone looked up and smiled at me when I arrived and went through to the winding shop, where the machines thinned the yarn and wound it onto spools. The workforce were mostly young girls close to my age and all seemed very friendly, so that was a good start. Just like at school, I settled in easily.

At the end of my first week, we were all told that Mr

Hodgson, the owner of the dye works, was coming on a visit and he wanted to talk with us on his rounds. I saw a gleaming Rolls-Royce convertible pull up outside and our manager striding out to meet Mr Hodgson and escort him in. I rushed down to meet them with a smile as they entered the building and the manager took Mr Hodgson's hat and coat.

'Hello,' said the very small man with blond hair and a bristly moustache. 'I haven't seen you before. What's your name?'

I told him my name and what job I was doing.

'Yes, and I've noticed what a quick learner you are, Margaret,' said the manager. 'Well done. You've made an excellent start.'

'Thank you,' I said with a smile at them both.

'Haven't we got a job coming up soon for a bright young woman like this?' asked Mr Hodgson, turning to the manager.

'Yes, as a matter of fact, I was only talking to Hilda about that yesterday. She suggested Margaret for the job.' He turned to me. 'Hilda tells me you won a scholarship to the convent and you're very good at maths. Is that right?'

'Yes, it is.' I tried to look a bit modest.

'And writing too?' asked Mr Hodgson.

'Yes, sir.'

'It's a much more challenging job,' continued the manager. 'And Hilda thinks you're just the right person to take it on. What do you think?'

'What job is it?' I asked.

'You'll still be testing the yarns,' replied the manager.

'But also in sole charge of recording all the results and writing reports about them. It's a job with a lot of responsibility, testing and comparing the various yarns' strength and other properties on the machines and then filling in the results on mathematical tables to attach to your reports. Do you think you could do that?'

'Yes,' I said straight away. 'I love working with figures.'

'Good. You will have your own office and . . . let me see . . .'

'What wage are you on now?' interrupted Mr Hodgson, twisting his moustache.

'Ten shillings a week.'

'Oh,' he continued. 'I think we could change that, couldn't we?' he asked the manager, who nodded with a smile.

Mr Hodgson turned back to face me, with a twinkle in his eye. 'Make it fifteen shillings. What do you say?'

'I say yes please!'

Before we left for home, Hilda took me up to show me my new office. I was astonished. It was fabulous – a large, spacious room, beautifully clean and tidy, with huge windows letting in lots of light. I had never imagined I would have my own office, and such a beautiful one, after such a short time . . . and still only thirteen years old!

I went home that evening with a light heart, my first pay packet and a strong temptation to skip up our street, like I did as a small child.

I couldn't wait to tell Mother all about it.

'Well, that's a great turn-up,' she said with a smile. 'I

always knew you were a worker, and a clever one at that. Half again added to your salary, eh? What a difference that will make.'

'Yes, I was very surprised when he told me.'

'Does he know you're under age?'

'I'm not sure.' I hesitated. 'Why? Does it make any difference?'

'I shouldn't think so, now that he values your work.' She went to the mantelpiece and took down an official-looking brown envelope and handed it to me. It was addressed to her and she had already opened it.

I took the letter out of its envelope and started to read.

'What's a summons?' I asked. 'And why do you have to go to court?'

'It's because it's illegal for anyone under fourteen to leave school. And because of your age, it's the parent who has to take the blame. The summons means I have to go to court on that day and explain. Then they will fine me.'

'Really?' I was shocked. 'I had no idea that could happen.' I paused, but she didn't look too worried. 'It's so unfair,' I continued. 'How can they expect you to pay a fine, when the reason for my leaving school early is that we don't have enough money?'

Mother shrugged. 'Well, they can't get blood out of a stone!'

Things began to look up for Mother, the boys and me, now that there were two of us contributing to the house-keeping – no more scrimping to pay the rent, buy fresh food or pay for a bus ride.

Mother carried on with her sewing as well. I don't want to sound vain, but it was true – I was always the best dressed girl in the town. With the war on, other people were buying clothes where they could, but there wasn't much choice and nobody had enough clothing coupons in their ration book, so Mother came to their aid. She was very clever and resourceful, mending as well as dressmaking. Every dress she made was different. I never saw any two customers in a similar style. She even made coats, and it didn't stop there. She treated me to her wonderful creations as well. With a piece of extra material she had she made me a raincoat, with some ruching at the top and a matching bag. Everyone admired what she made and she became even more sought-after as the war went on. No wonder she had so many kind friends, giving us free fruit from Blackburn Market or an extra couple of slices of bacon at no charge and ration-free.

However, I never had stockings. They were very scarce during the war because the military was given priority over the nylon supply, so we all used to paint our legs with something out of a bottle, specially made for that purpose. You could buy the liquid at a chemist or Woolworths. Some people used to do it with tea or coffee. Mine came from a bottle. I can remember one day, when Ray was round at our house; I was going upstairs and he was walking up behind me, when Mother saw us.

'Where are you two going?' she asked.

'Ray is going to draw the seams down my legs.'

'Oh no, he's not!' she said, with the tone of a policeman about to arrest someone.

'But he's good at painting and decorating, so he's the best one at drawing lines,' I explained.

'Not on you,' she insisted. 'If anyone is going to do that for you, it will be me, so give me the crayon and I'll do it now.'

Although fourteen and thirteen respectively, Ray and I were so innocent that we had no idea why Mother was so intent on stopping us going upstairs. The trouble was, we didn't know what we didn't know. Nobody had ever mentioned anything about how babies came to be. They just seemed to arrive in people's families. One weekend, Ray and I were at the rec, sitting and chatting on a bench, watching a mother and her little ones, who were playing on the toddlers' slide. I said something about how sweet they all looked and it went from there.

'I don't understand it,' I murmured.

'What don't you understand?' he asked, with a quizzical smile.

'I'm not sure,' I replied. 'Babies, I suppose . . . I've always wondered. Where do babies come from?' I paused. 'Do you know?'

'Yes.' He nodded. 'One of my pals in the Home Guard told me.'

'What did he say?'

'It's all to do with the atmosphere,' he began. 'The atmosphere in the bedroom has to be a certain temperature for several nights in a row. I've forgotten how many nights.'

'Oh, is that all?'

'I think so.'

We sat in silence while we both tried to puzzle it out. My first thought was for those of my convent friends who were boarders, all sleeping in the same dormitory. What if it was the right temperature for babies and they all had them . . . and I was the only one without? Wouldn't the nuns have a fright? Or even better, what if the nuns were in the same room?

I decided to ask Bobby the next time he came home on leave. But I knew he wouldn't answer a straightforward question – he was too protective of me and still saw me as his innocent little sister. He wasn't far wrong. So I decided to try a different angle, inspired by a book I had on African wildlife.

'Where do baby elephants come from?' I asked him, as we did the washing-up together one evening.

He gave me a quizzical grin. 'From eggs, of course,' he said.

Well, I knew that baby birds came from eggs, but I didn't know animals and humans did too. I also knew Bobby could be a bit of a joker and liked to tease me sometimes, but I couldn't tell if he was teasing me now.

I tried again another day.

'Elephant egg shells must be very hard,' I said. 'How do their babies break out?'

'Don't tell me you're still on about that elephant!' he replied, without giving me an answer.

And that's the way it stayed. I never did get another explanation, so it remained a big mystery.

*

Now that we had enough income to pay all our bills, with a little left over for treats, we could relax a bit more and enjoy occasional outings.

I had always loved going to the pictures as a small child, and now that I had a few pennies to spare, I occasionally treated Mother to a trip to the cinema, leaving seven-year-old Jeffrey and baby Alan with her friend Alice or one of our neighbours. In fact, I only had to pay the first time at the Star Cinema in Little Harwood, because the projectionist was the grandfather of one of my old school friends and he recognized me.

'Hello. It's Margaret, isn't it?' He paused. 'Do you remember me?'

'Oh yes. You're Sheila's grandpa.'

'That's right.' His face lit up, as if he'd had a good idea. 'Did you pay to come in today?'

'Yes.'

'Well, you won't have to pay again. Just say my name at the box office and they'll let you in free.'

'Thank you. That's very kind of you,' I said with a smile, just as my mother had taught me. He was true to his word. From then on that cinema was always free for me and a relative or friend. And even better, once they knew me, an usherette would come and take me and whoever was with me out of the queue for downstairs and up to the best seats in the balcony. So that was lucky – we could splash out on snacks instead.

I was always hungry at the pictures. If I went with Mother we would take some sandwiches with us, or sweets if they were available. If not, my mother always took a brown-paper bag full of cornflakes for us to munch. I don't suppose the people sitting near us were too pleased about that.

The only thing I ever made was a sort of humbug, with dried milk. It was surprisingly good and minty. I'd bake a batch of them and take them to the cinema to share with anyone who wanted one.

Sometimes I used to go to the cinema with Ray, after we'd both finished work. In fact we went to most places together in those days. We liked the same films and we chatted and laughed all the way home afterwards.

I can still remember some of the things we saw. They were nothing like the old silent films. These were 'talkies', mostly black-and-white, of course, like *Goodbye Mr Chips* and *Wuthering Heights*. But the first colour movies were coming out too, and they were wonderful. The two I remember best were both American: *The Wizard of Oz* and *Gone with the Wind*. I loved the costumes in that, as well as the story. But it was such a long film that we were very glad we had brought sandwiches with us that night.

My favourite movie actor was Walter Pidgeon. I loved going to see his films most of all. He always made me cry. I suppose it was because he was the father I had always wanted, the father I wished I had.

10

A Scary Warning

1940

I'd been working for about three months when Bobby came home again on leave.

'Can I come and see you at the dye works today?' he said at breakfast.

'Why do you want to come to my work?' I asked, feeling rather annoyed that I couldn't go anywhere without him checking up on me.

'Just to make sure it's a good sort of place where they treat you right.'

'Well, all right,' I sighed. Much as I loved Bobby being home, I did find him restrictive sometimes, but I was resigned to it.

'When can I come?' he asked.

'Lunchtime,' I suggested. 'You can come straight up to my office. One of the girls will tell you where I am.'

He looked rather pleased . . . and I suddenly realized why.

'Do you know a girl called Nellie?' he asked.

'Do you mean Nellie Forrester?'

'Yes, that's her. Will she be there today?'

'Yes, she works in the winding room. She's a pretty girl,' I added. 'About two or three years older than me. How do you know her?'

'I met her once while she was visiting her brother, who's one of the mechanics at my RAF base,' he explained. 'I'd like to just pop in and say hello.'

So, as promised, Bobby arrived during my lunch break.

'What a big office,' he said, looking around the room. 'You've done well for yourself here, Margaret.'

'Yes, it's not bad, is it?'

By now I'd worked out that Bobby had a crush on Nellie Forrester, so I took him to her machine, where he could casually bump into her, and left them to it. He didn't have long before she had to get back to her yarn-winding, but it was long enough for him to arrange to meet her at the end of her shift and walk her home.

Some of the girls at work became good friends of mine and, all of them being older than me, they used to talk a lot about boyfriends and going to dances. I'd never been to a dance and it sounded like fun, so when Hilda and the Snape sisters, Irene and Edna, asked if I'd like to go with them, I didn't hesitate. Of course, I had to ask, or rather tell, Mother. I was a bit worried about that, so Irene and Edna came with me. Mother had met them a couple of times before and said what nice girls they were.

'Hello, Mrs Holden,' said Irene with a smile. 'We would very much like to take Margaret with us to a dance on Friday night. We'd collect her from the house and take her there. She'd be with us all evening and we'd bring her straight back here as soon as the dance finishes,' she explained.

'What time would that be?' asked Mother.

'Oh, about midnight, I expect.'

Mother turned to look at me. 'Do you want to go?' she asked.

'Yes, I do. I've got enough money to pay to get in and buy a lemon drink. I promise I won't drink anything else.'

'Well, you're a working girl now,' said Mother. 'So if you are paying, you can go.'

I was surprised that she agreed so readily, but she seemed to have confidence in Irene's promise and I knew she didn't want to spoil my evening. She even offered to make a dress for me out of the leftover blackout material.

'At least you know how to dance,' she added. 'That's one good thing the convent taught you.'

'That's true.' In those days, dancing was a big thing, but it was always the ballroom classics, such as the waltz, the quickstep or the foxtrot that were the most popular. I remembered those lessons at the convent when my tall friends had to be the 'boys'. Luckily, I was small, so I was used to taking the girl's part.

There were a few days to go before the dance on the Friday night, so Mother rustled up this beautiful black dress for me – I would never have believed that such a special-looking dress, with a bit of lace at the neck and some sequin trimmings round the waist and hem, could be made out of the same material as our blackout curtains!

She helped me put it on and it fitted perfectly.

'I'll just put in this pin over the zip to stop it falling,' she said. 'Now let's look at you.'

I stood back. She looked me up and down and turned me round, then stepped back. 'You'll do,' she said with a nod. 'You look very nice, Margaret.'

One of the girls called for me and I picked up my dance shoes to go out. 'Don't forget,' Mother called after me. 'Be home by midnight. Don't be late.'

Blackburn had three main dance halls: St George's Hall, the Pal de Dance and – most popular with the girls from the dye works – Tony's New Empress Ballroom, or Tony's for short. I didn't know at that time who Tony Billington was, but I soon found out.

'Hello, Margaret,' said a cheery voice across the entrance hall, and a small round man walked towards me. I recognized him from my time at the convent – I sometimes used to go and call for his daughter Josephine, a year younger than me, to walk to school together in the mornings.

'Hello, love,' he used to call cheerily as I arrived at their gate, before we set off together. They only lived a few streets away in Little Harwood, and his cousin lived a few doors down from our house in Robinson Street.

'Have you paid to get in?' asked Tony.

Thinking he was checking to make sure, I said yes and showed him my ticket. Irene, Edna and Hilda gathered round me protectively.

'Well,' he said with a smile. 'Our Josephine always liked it when you walked to school with her, so you won't have to pay next time you come. Just tell the doorman, "Tony says I can come in for free." Do that every time and you'll never need to pay again. The same with the cloakroom.'

I was amazed at people's generosity. After all, I didn't know him very well, but I always used to smile and say hello. I later found out that he and his wife had been a professional dancing couple.

My friends were impressed. 'You lucky thing,' said Hilda as she led the way up the beautiful wide and shallow curved steps into the dance hall. It was an enormous room, with a column just by the entrance door and triangular seats at its base. There was a huge mirror ball hanging from the high ceiling and uplighters all round the ballroom that sometimes dimmed or brightened. The band were in their place on the stage at the front of the room, smiling at all the girls. The dance floor was shiny polished wood and the rest of the room was carpeted, with a small bar tucked away in the corner. I had a marvellous evening. The band played a mixture of tunes and it was a joy to dance to their music.

Many of the boys at Tony's were in uniform and looked so much more exciting than the ones I knew, who were far too young to join up. I recognized several of the soldiers, sailors and airmen as Bobby's pals. They all came over to talk to me, and some even asked me to dance. I knew that would get back to Bobby and wondered how he might react. He was always overprotective of me. I had liked that when I was young, but now I had turned fourteen and, much as I loved him, I wanted a life of my own.

Suddenly I realized it was time to go home and I would have to dash to get back by midnight. One of the boys offered to escort me, which was kind of him. I checked with Irene and she knew him so she said that would be fine. But she and her dance partner would come with us, in case Mother objected. Not far from Tony's, we were stopped by an LDV volunteer who asked for our identity cards. Luckily I had tucked mine into my pocket before coming out.

'Where's your gas mask?' he asked.

'I couldn't bring it,' I replied. 'Because I had to carry my dance shoes and I couldn't manage both.'

Irene laughed, but he gave her a look as she tried to straighten her face. He insisted on looking at my dance shoes, with a sneer of disapproval. 'Make sure you always carry your gas mask,' he said with suitable emphasis. 'Your dance shoes won't save you from a gas attack.'

We continued on our way, this boy and me chatting as we walked, and he gave me a peck on the cheek as he left me at the front gate.

I was elated with my evening. This was the start of the rest of my life.

From then on, I went dancing at Tony's a lot, and loved to see even the plainest boys made handsome by their uniforms. Hilda, Irene and Edna were often there, so we had a lot of fun. I danced with several of the boys and there was always somebody to walk me home if Ray couldn't be there. He came whenever he could, but some nights he was on duty, practising drills or helping out with the Home Guard. He was happy that some of his or Bobby's old friends walked me home when he wasn't around to do it himself. But Ray and I were best pals and I loved it when he could come with me. Most people assumed we were a pair, and always would be. We assumed it too.

One by one, the boys Bobby's age donned their uniforms and went away on training, a few of them all the way to Canada, before joining the action. Many of them were posted overseas, mostly to Europe, but some much further away. Those who were based near home would come back on leave whenever they could. They were always renewing acquaintances for a few days, before they disappeared again.

It was June or July 1940 when one of the RAF boys, Ernie Aspinall, who had been a member of the model aeroplane club, came back to Blackburn on his last leave before joining the bombing raids across Europe. I bumped into him at Tony's where we sat and chatted light-heartedly for quite a while, reminiscing about the old days. We laughed at the memory of me and Gordon on the tandem, carrying home bits of the wrecked model plane that was nearly shot down in Accrington.

'Those were happy days, weren't they?' he said. But then he turned a little more serious. 'Do you remember how excited you were when I told you I was going to be an RAF pilot?' he asked. 'I think you assumed I would be piloting Spitfires.'

'Yes,' I replied.

'I don't want you to be disappointed, Margaret,' he continued. 'But I'm going to pilot bombers.'

I tried not to show it, but I was disappointed. Being a Spitfire pilot sounded so much more glamorous.

'They asked me to be on the bigger planes,' he told me, 'because they consider me to be steadier than most, which is what they need for taking charge of a crew, rather than flying a fighter.'

'Well, that's quite a compliment, isn't it?' I said. 'They obviously have faith in you.'

'Thanks.' He smiled with a look of relief that I had taken it well.

Within days, Ernie was flying on his first operation of what later became known as the Battle of Britain. Not long after, I had a letter from Bobby. He started by telling me about his imminent posting to the Sudan. But when I turned to the second page, it changed:

I'm sorry to tell you some sad news, Margaret. Ernie flew on a raid the night he saw you, after he got back to the base. He and his crew, and several other planes, went off to bomb German cities. A few hours later, our bombers started to come back. I watched and counted them as they landed, but there was no sign of Ernie's plane. The next morning we heard the plane had been shot down with the loss of all lives. Ernie didn't make it. But it may help you to remember that he was doing what he wanted to do. Ernie always loved planes, ever since those happy days with our model aircraft in the club.

That was a terrible shock – the first of our friends to be killed in action. Now the war was not just about handsome uniforms. This war was real. It had come close to home. It was deadly. I looked again at Bobby's words, stunned . . . but then the tears came, welling up and trickling down my cheeks. I was miserable for days afterwards.

It was a warm summer's evening, the sun just going down, when Ray and I came out of the Palace Cinema on Blackburn Boulevard. Across the road was a familiar figure, Clarence Charnley, the butcher's boy who used to wave at me, now dressed in a smart blue uniform.

'Oh, there's Clarry. He's in the navy!' I said as I ran across to see him. The boys in blue were always my favourites, and I was particularly fond of Clarry. I wanted to talk to him and find out more about his training, whether he'd got a ship yet and when he would have to leave for active service.

'Hold on,' I told him. 'I'll just go and tell Ray.' Then I ran back to Ray, whose face was a picture!

'I've got to walk home with Clarry,' I said. 'He's in the navy and I expect he'll be leaving soon.' We were such close friends, Ray and I that I didn't think he'd mind, but he did. I could tell he was upset but I ignored it. I felt bad about that afterwards.

So I left Ray and walked away with Clarry. We walked and we talked. He told me about his naval posting and wanted to know about what I'd been up to.

'Where have you been all these months?' he asked. 'I've

missed seeing you with your short skirt and your cheeky smile.' Well, I didn't think I had ever been cheeky, but it was fun being teased like that, by an older man – all of eighteen years old.

I told Clarry about having to leave the convent. 'And I got a good job with good pay and my own office.'

'That's a turn-up,' he said with a grin. 'So now you could stand me a fish-and-chip supper!'

'Not yet,' I replied, mirroring his smile. 'I've got to help Mother out with the housekeeping and I want to try and save up too.'

'Very sensible,' nodded Clarry. He stopped me and took a good look at me. 'You're a pretty girl, Margaret,' he said. 'You'll have all the boys after you, like bees to a honeypot.'

I wasn't sure what to say to that so, as usual, I made light of it. 'I've got three brothers,' I said with a smile. 'So I'm used to boys.'

'Hmm.' Clarry paused, just as we reached my front steps. 'That's not quite what I meant.'

Well, I had no idea what he meant, but I felt a momentary tinge of apprehension.

He leant down and kissed me – an exciting kiss, like none I'd ever had before. With Ray it was just innocent pecks on the cheek or lips, but Clarry's was my first grown-up kiss. The next day was Saturday. I did think of going to see Ray to apologize, but he was at a Home Guard meeting, so I was in when Clarry knocked on our door.

'Hello, Margaret,' he said. 'I've come round to see if

you'd like to go for a walk with me. There's something I want to talk to you about.'

I was intrigued, so I agreed and we went off across the spare ground towards the country lanes beyond. It was a sunny day and at just fourteen I was rather in awe of Clarry. What did he want to talk to me about?

I soon discovered.

'Let's go and sit down on that wall,' he suggested. 'It's time somebody warned you about boys, and what they might want to do.'

'What do you mean?'

'Well, it's all right to be friends with boys, but you have to have limits.'

'What limits?'

'Well, you can let a boy kiss you, but you mustn't allow any touching of flesh.'

I wasn't sure I liked this sudden stern warning of his.

Clarry proceeded to give me the only grown-up talk I've ever had. He told me what was likely to happen with boys. He told me what I could allow, which wasn't much, and what I couldn't.

'There's a sort of line,' he said. 'And it's flesh.' He paused. 'You haven't to have flesh. No touching of flesh . . . and you certainly haven't to have anybody touch you under your skirt.' He carried on talking about this 'line'. I knew it wasn't a real line, of course, but I found it all quite shocking . . . and confusing.

The more he talked the more uncomfortable I felt at the thought of it all, and I was still trying to take in everything he had told me.

'I'm sorry if I've upset you, Margaret. But you needed to know.'

I nodded.

'It's very important, you see. There is this line, and you haven't to cross it until you are certain. It's only once in your life that you can cross this line, and then it's permanent. So there's no going back. It's forever. Do you understand?'

I nodded. In my mind I was thinking back to the nuns and their warnings to us about sin. I think flesh came into that somewhere. A Bible passage we once had to learn flashed into my head: *If you live by the deeds of the flesh, you will die.*

I never forgot what Clarry said to me that afternoon, but sometimes I did wonder if I'd have been better off without his advice.

One day at work, when Hilda and I were chatting during a break, she told me about her cousin who had recently joined up in the navy.

'The trouble is, Wilfred is feeling very low. He's at home on leave, staying with us for a couple of days, before he is posted overseas.'

'They're all coming and going, aren't they?' I said. 'As soon as I meet someone at Tony's and dance with him a couple of times, he's gone again. It must be very disruptive for them.'

'Yes. Wilfred is only young and he says that all the lads his age have sweethearts at home who write them letters, but he's the only one who doesn't have that. He says it doesn't have to be a sweetheart, just someone who is willing to write to him.'

'Like a pen pal, you mean?'

'Yes.' She paused, looking at me. 'I don't suppose you would write him a letter or two, would you? It would cheer him up tremendously if you could.' She smiled.

I knew she was hoping that I would agree and I did feel sorry for the poor boy, facing homesickness as well as the dangers and discomforts of war.

'All right,' I agreed.

'Oh, thank you, Margaret. You are such a good friend.'

'Well, I can't promise to write very often,' I warned her. 'You'd better tell him I'll write when I have time.' Then I thought how he would feel. 'I'll try to write once a week,' I added. 'I have other letters to write too, you see. There's Bobby, of course, but some of the other boys I've danced with also like me to write them letters when they're away.'

'I'm sure that will be fine, Margaret. He'll be grateful for anything, and I know this will cheer him up no end.'

'Did you say his name is Wilfred? What is he like?'

'I tell you what,' replied Hilda. 'He's coming to meet me to walk me home after work. If we leave together you'll see him.'

The afternoon rolled on, and I was so busy with a backlog of testing that I was surprised when Hilda came into my office.

'Are you ready?'

'Is it that time already? I'll just put these away and I'll be with you. Why don't you go and meet him and I'll join you in five minutes?'

By the time I left the building, Hilda was deep in conversation with a medium-height young man in uniform, with a rather earnest expression. I walked over to them and Hilda turned to give me a smile. 'This is Wilfred,' she said. 'I've just told him what we were talking about.'

'I'm pleased to meet you,' I said with a warm smile that made him seem a little more at ease as he gave me a tentative smile back.

That was it – less than two minutes. We said goodbye and went our separate ways home. The next day, Hilda gave me the address I should write to. 'And I've given Wilfred your address too,' she said.

So that was that. Over the next few weeks I wrote regular letters to this boy I hardly knew, and each time he wrote back. It did seem strange that we had only spent two minutes together, but he showed his gratitude in every letter, saying how much better he felt, just knowing that he would have regular letters from me, and thanking me every time.

'All the lads are teasing me now about my mystery sweetheart!' he wrote.

I was pleased that just by sending him the occasional letter I could cheer him up so much.

11

Red Alert!

1940

While Bobby was based in England, repairing damaged Mosquito fuselages, he continued to have occasional leave.

One time he met up with his old pal Maurice Haslam of the Inniskilling Dragoon Guards, or 'Skins' as he called them. He brought Maurice back to our house to join us for tea. Just as Bobby had been fed up because he wasn't allowed to fly the planes, Maurice had his own problems, but worse. He had been wounded at Dunkirk and was officially still recuperating from his injuries.

'I've got bits of shrapnel all over my body, but I'd better not tell you where!' he said with a grin. 'Here, feel my hands.' He held them out in front of me.

I felt gingerly across the back of one hand, till I came to a lumpy-looking area and found something hard and quite sharp embedded under his skin. I flinched. It made me feel quite weird.

'And try this one,' he said, attempting to encourage me.

I didn't really want to, but I didn't wish to upset him, so I couldn't refuse. I lightly touched where he was pointing, on the palm of his other hand. As soon as I felt the shrapnel, I recoiled again. It felt so wrong – a solid piece of metal lodged in his flesh. A part of me wanted to be sick, but I managed to control it and tried to smile with genuine sympathy.

'Does it hurt?' I asked him.

'Not so much now,' he replied. 'More of an ache. The wounds are healing well. But I still have a shock every morning, the first time I feel one of these pieces. It takes me right back to Dunkirk.'

'Was it terrible there?'

'I don't want to talk about it.'

'Couldn't they take the bits of shrapnel out?' I asked, curiosity getting the better of me, as usual.

'No, the medics said they were best left in for the time being. They did remove the largest pieces, in my back and one leg, but they told me it could cause more damage if they tried to dig out the smaller fragments, so they were best left alone. Some of them might give me trouble one day, but hopefully not.'

On another occasion, Bobby came back on leave with three of his pals. His main focus was to meet up with Nellie Forrester again at the dye works, and he knew I could get him in. The courtship had been continuing through letters and he was keen to see her on this trip, so he came in at lunchtime, as before, and they found a quiet place to chat and share their sandwiches. But things were not as he thought. Nellie had a sailor boyfriend as well, so he wasn't happy about that.

After he'd headed back to his base, Bobby wrote me a

letter to say that Nellie had turned him down and chosen her sailor boyfriend instead, because she thought he would be 'more settled' than Bobby. I could tell he was aggrieved about it. I worshipped my big brother Bobby, so I was almost as upset as he was.

Gordon Fudge was down in Blackburn at this time as well, visiting his grandmother, and came round to see us. It made me think back to those days when Gordon and Bobby were about the age I was now, and Gordon was always around at our house. For their holidays, Gordon and Bobby used to pack up the panniers on each side of the back wheels of Gordon's tandem, load up their cooking gear and cycle from Blackburn to Paisley in Scotland to stay with his sister. It was just under two hundred miles to ride each way, but they stopped and camped at points along the route, there and back, having a wonderful time. I used to wish they could take me with them, but, 'No room on the tandem,' as Bobby used to say, and I'm sure Mother would have forbidden it. After we'd chatted over a cup of tea, Gordon asked me if I would like to come with him back to Paisley to stay with his sister for a short holiday.

'On your tandem?' I asked him with a grin.

'Not this time, love. Let's travel in luxury!'

I had some leave owing from the dye works, so I agreed. It would be lovely to meet his family and to visit a new place. I'd never been further north than Blackpool. Gordon took me all the way on the train and I stared out of the window, fascinated to see how much the landscape changed along the way. The close-packed urban areas of

Lancashire gave way to lush green countryside, followed by the wild beauty of the Yorkshire Dales – its rolling hills, crags and streams. I kept asking Gordon where we were and he was very patient, trying to tell me, as best he could, what we were seeing out of the windows.

'What are those high hills?' I asked him.

'That's the Pennines,' he explained. 'They run down the middle of England.'

The train rumbled and clattered on northwards, clouds of steam shrouding our view every now and then. As we emerged from one such burst of steam, Gordon said, 'I think this is Otterburn, where the English fought the Scots about 5,550 years ago.'

'Who won?' I asked. 'The English?'

'No, the Scots,' he replied with a grin. 'They had fewer fighting men, but they still managed to win the battle.'

We sat in a companionable silence as we moved on through Settle and Appleby, after which Gordon told me about his and Bobby's favourite camping spot in the Lake District, which we were passing to our left.

'We used to put up the tent above a fast-running brook, get out our Primus stove and cook up a corned beef hash.' He paused. 'That makes me hungry. Shall we eat our sandwiches now?'

I got out the waxed-paper parcel and untied the string so that we could share the packed lunch Mother had made for us early that morning.

As we ate, Gordon told me about his family. 'My sister is deaf,' he told me. 'But she plays the piano beautifully.'

'How can she play the piano if she can't hear it?' I asked.

'She can hear it very faintly and she says she can feel the vibrations.'

He explained that she and her husband lived in a tenement building. I had never heard of such a thing, so I was looking forward to seeing it.

It was a long, rattling journey, stopping at Carlisle, crossing the border and on through the Galloway hills, grazed by the peculiar Belted Galloway cattle, past forests and heathlands to Glasgow station, where we got out of the train at last and caught a bus for the last leg of the journey.

At last we reached Paisley and arrived at the tenement building. I'd never seen anything like it before. It was one huge, long grey building, with four flats on each floor. On the ground floor there were alleyways, called ginnels, between each pair of flats. We went up to their flat on the third floor, and through their front door straight into the living room, which had a lovely view over the park. Gordon introduced me to his sister Isla and brother-in-law Robert, who were very kind and friendly and had a tea of scones and cake ready for us to eat. After our day-long travels and a pleasant evening, I was ready for bed. But what I didn't realize was that I was already in my bedroom! My bed was in an alcove in the living-room wall, with a curtain across it. There was no bathroom, toilet or kitchen in the flat, they were all out of the front door and down the corridor, shared with other tenants on this landing. So I would have to undress in the living room, where anyone could walk through to go for a wash or to use the toilet.

I was horrified at the thought and just couldn't do it. I could not get undressed in that situation knowing anyone could burst in. Maybe it was because I was so tired, and still only fourteen, but I'm afraid I caused something of a fuss. So, in the end, Gordon took me and my things round the corner, from 19 Cochrane Street to 23 Green Road, where his aunt lived, in a house more like ours. I was to stay here to sleep and felt a lot more comfortable.

The next morning, back in Cochrane Street, Isla and Robert went off to work and Gordon suggested we should go on a coach trip to Troon. We were dropped off right by the sea and decided to hire a boat. As we rowed around, enjoying ourselves, I suddenly caught sight of something away in the distance.

'Is that the top of a submarine?' I asked.

'Yes, it could be,' agreed Gordon. 'Let's row across and have a closer look.' So that's what we did. He took some photos with his box Brownie camera, but I wanted to go nearer.

'Closer, closer,' I said as we approached.

Finally we reached it and I particularly wanted to have a photograph taken of me and the submarine, so Gordon had his camera ready.

But just then, we realized we couldn't manoeuvre our boat at all. We were stuck, half on the top of the submarine! As we tried unsuccessfully to push ourselves off again, several heads popped out of the conning tower, shouting at us.

'Go away, get out of here!' yelled one.

'You're in dangerous waters,' added another.

'Don't you know there's a war on?' shouted the third.

Their voices were rising in anger and they continued to call things out at us.

Luckily they were on our side in the war, but they sounded furious as they produced a long pole and tried to push us off their deck. They kept yelling and shrieking and all the noise became really frightening, as they rocked our boat to dislodge it.

Eventually they succeeded in freeing us, but our boat rolled over and tossed us both into the sea. I was afraid because I couldn't swim far, but as I floundered about, Gordon took hold of me and helped me grab on to the upturned hull. Just then we spotted a larger boat on its way out from the shore to pick us up. As it approached, we realized this rescue boat had men in uniforms on it. They pulled us out of the water and righted our boat, tying it behind theirs. Soaking wet, we were taken back to the shore.

But that wasn't the end of the story. When we reached the beach, there were two policemen waiting for us. They caused a kerfuffle, grabbing hold of Gordon and pointing out a big sign that said 'Cameras not allowed.'

'But we didn't see that,' protested Gordon, still holding his dripping camera.

'It's quite hidden,' I added, helpfully . . . or otherwise.

The first thing the policemen did was to take Gordon's camera from him. We watched as they deliberately pulled all the film out of it. Then they took us to a hut-like building – more like a large shed, with some chairs in it – and asked us a lot of questions. Gordon answered most of them.

One of them turned to me and asked: 'Can we see your identity card?'

Well, I was so flustered, I searched my usual pocket but it wasn't there. 'I don't have it,' I said. 'I don't know why, but I suppose I must have forgotten it, or perhaps it fell into the sea.'

They were cross about that and they took all my details. I feared what would happen next. Would they arrest me, or both of us? Would we be able to get away?

I was worried about what could happen to Gordon as well. Being an officer in the Home Guard and an adult, he was responsible for me, so would he get into trouble because I couldn't show them my identity card? At that point, I don't think it had occurred to me that the real problem was much worse.

'I hope you both realize how serious this incident is,' scolded the senior police officer. 'You caused a red alert, rowing out to the submarine like that.'

'Sorry, Officer,' said Gordon, in a conciliatory voice. 'We didn't mean to cause any trouble.'

'I just wanted to see if it was a submarine,' I added.

The police officer gave us a strict telling-off and a lecture about the waters around Britain in wartime. I can't remember most of it. I was too worried to concentrate. But finally they let us go and took us back to the coach, which was waiting for us. By this time, we had dried out completely in the warmth of the day and were keen to get away.

So off we went after our day's adventure, with all the people on the coach singing to me: 'She's a Lassie from Lancashire'. That really cheered me up.

We talked about it all when we got back to Paisley and wondered whether they would summons us, but fortunately we never heard any more about it. And when I finally looked in my other pocket, there was my slightly water-damaged identity card. I'd had it all the time!

After a good night's sleep at Gordon's aunt's house again, I went back to the flat. Just as we were discussing what to do that day, the air-raid siren blared out and we all had to run downstairs.

Everybody in the building gathered in the ginnel, which was like a tunnel between the flats, open at each end. We had to wait, all huddled together, and this is where I met Cathy Renfrew, who also lived in the building and was almost my age.

'Do you think this is a real air raid?' I asked her tentatively.

'Och, I expect so,' she replied in a whisper. 'But maybe not here. Most of the raids have been dropping bombs on Glasgow, especially the shipyards on the Clyde.'

I was relieved to hear that. I could almost feel the tension as we all waited, without really knowing what for. It helped to have someone to talk to.

'Can you see the shipyards from here?' I asked.

'Aye,' nodded Cathy. 'When it's the night raids and the fires light up the sky.' She paused as some of the other residents, late arrivals, jostled to pack themselves in amongst us, under cover. 'What about you?'

'Our air-raid sirens only go off when the planes are flying low enough, but most of the warnings are for groups of German bombers or stray planes flying overhead,' I explained. 'On their way to Manchester and Liverpool. That's where the real raids are.'

Just as we were beginning to feel that this might be a false alarm, we heard the drone of a fighter plane approaching. It was the first enemy plane I'd heard at close quarters, but it was an unmistakable sound and coming closer still.

In the ginnel, it was hard at first to tell what direction it was coming from or its altitude, so we all hushed and listened as it grew louder and louder. Cathy and I managed to manoeuvre ourselves so that we could peek out of the street end of the ginnel, and that's when we saw the plane itself approaching at an angle, one wing higher than the other, so low that we could just make out the black-and-white cross under the wing. I wondered if Cathy could hear my heart beating fast. Suddenly the plane opened fire, its guns shooting *rat-a-tat-a-tat-a-tat*, non-stop, as it passed along the street. It seemed almost like a war film but it couldn't have been more real . . . or frightening. Cathy and I hugged each other close as the noise got louder.

We could see the hail of bullets hitting the grass in the park opposite, and the dust they threw up into the air. The German plane zoomed to the end of the street, where it rose and soared away, higher and higher, into the distance.

We heard later that this had been a 'rogue' event and that the plane had lost its bearings and crashed over the Braes, killing the pilot.

*

On our final day, a Sunday, we all set out to go to Mass at their nearby church. On the way we noticed that there was broken glass all over the place – across the roads, on the pavements, in the shopfronts. As we passed a lovely ice-cream parlour and the chip shop, we all had to tread very carefully. Wherever I put my feet, they were crunching on glass. All the shop windows had been smashed in.

'Excuse me,' I asked a passer-by. 'Do you know what happened here?'

'It was the Italians,' she said. 'The army came for them.'

'Why?' I asked, horrified.

'Because they are changing sides in the war,' explained the passer-by. 'The government has ruled that all Italians have to be rounded up and taken to internment camps. So that's what a group of our soldiers did last night, all around Paisley I should think, though there aren't many of them here.'

'Oh,' I gasped. 'Is that why the ice-cream parlour has been smashed up?'

'Yes. It's a shame, isn't it? They were lovely people.'

I nodded sadly and we hurried on, not wanting to be late for Mass. Fortunately, we made it just in time. 'Normally the church is packed,' whispered Gordon's sister, sitting next to me. 'But look at that bench over there.' She pointed across the aisle. 'That's where the Italian families from the ice-cream parlour and the chip shop sat, but now it's completely empty.' She paused. 'They were good people – always cheerful and friendly, especially with little children. How could anyone think they would do anything to harm us?'

As the Mass began, I couldn't help thinking back to the convent. I knew that Italian people were usually Roman Catholics – after all, Rome was in Italy. Were there any Italian girls at the convent? I thought there were, higher up the school. Would the same thing happen to them back in Blackburn?

I didn't understand the ins and outs of why they had been taken away, but I felt very sad about what had happened to them.

This was meant to have been a short holiday to get away from the war, but it had turned out to be quite the opposite, so I was unexpectedly glad to board the train back home again the following morning. I was certainly ready to go home by then.

By the end of summer 1940, the air raids were stepping up to three or four a month, as the Germans increased their attacks on Britain's strategic targets. We didn't have many of those in Blackburn, so the raids weren't as intense as in the bigger cities. However, it was still becoming a cause for concern, especially since, apart from the odd cellar or home-made back-yard bunker, there were no air-raid shelters in Blackburn.

We didn't have a cellar, so Mother had followed the government instructions and made up a sort of sleeping area under the stairs, which soon became crowded. Jeffrey and Alan would go in at the end, where the stairs came lowest overhead. Mother would put in her rocking chair at the other end, which was occupied by an old lady from the end of the street. As soon as the siren went off she'd arrive in her huge white nightdress under a thick black coat, carrying an enormous handbag. That had to be wedged in too. Rather than sheltering, Mother would be busy in the kitchen – usually making snacks and drinks for everyone. We'd sometimes be joined by a boy who was training to be a pilot. He used to leave his grandmother a few streets away and come over to see that we were all right. I never did work that one out. There certainly wasn't room for him under the stairs so he'd bed down on the couch until the all-clear sounded.

Usually, if I'd been at a dance, I couldn't be bothered to take shelter, so I'd just go up to bed. But I remember on one occasion, a bomb dropped nearby and it rattled the place so much that I fell out of bed, bleary-eyed, and opened the door to go down and join the others under the stairs. I thought I'd opened the door to the landing but I'd somehow walked into the fitted wardrobe instead, and its door shut behind me, leaving me completely in the dark. I didn't even realize what I'd done. I could feel a wall in front of me, so I thought it had fallen in and trapped me. I started scratching at it with my fingernails. Meanwhile, I could hear the muffled sounds of everybody panicking downstairs.

Then I heard Mother screaming from the bottom of the stairs: 'Margaret! Are you all right? Come down here at once!'

'I can't,' I shouted. 'I'm blocked in and I can't get out.' I wasn't sure whether she could hear me. I was still scratching at what I thought was the collapsed wall, but it wouldn't move.

'What are you doing, Margaret? For goodness sake come down.'

'Help me! I can't move.'

Just then, I realized what I'd done, turned round and found my way out of the wardrobe and stood at the top of the stairs. I must have been quite a sight, blinded by the light, embarrassed and no doubt looking rather sheepish.

This was the first of a series of bombs that fell in late August 1940 in the Blackburn area. A few dropped on Bennington Street, damaging several houses, but fortunately their occupants all escaped unharmed. Sadly, this was swiftly followed, just before midnight on 31 August, by a much more devastating raid.

Peggy, a friend from work, and I were walking home from the cinema when the air-raid siren went, wailing through the clear night air. We had nowhere to shelter, so just stepped up our pace homeward. Seconds after the siren stopped, we heard the distinctive sound of a single German plane's engine, then a whistling sound and an ear-shattering explosion a few streets away. Terrified, we started to run, trying to put as much distance between us and the area as possible. We found out later that evening that the bombing was a direct hit on two shops with residences in Ainsworth Street, in the centre of Blackburn. Two people were killed – the driver and conductor of a passing tram, which luckily was carrying no passengers as it was on its way back to the depot for the night. The explosion also injured eight others and caused a lot of structural damage to the nearby buildings.

From then on, I took the air raids a bit more seriously. A few days later a whole line of bombs fell in a field by the Livesey Branch Road, clearly intended for a large factory, but luckily they landed off course so no one was hurt. In October two more bombs fell between the power station and the gasworks, but again, very little harm was done.

In November, wanting a new challenge, I felt it was time for a change of job. I wanted to take the next step up in my career now I was the legal age, so started to scour the newspapers for opportunities. I soon found one at Philips, a big international company, with its headquarters in Holland and a factory, laboratories and offices in Blackburn. I was offered a bigger salary and had a proper contract. I had to sign the Official Secrets Act and wore a white coat, like a doctor or a scientist. The first job I had there was on the Photostat machine, making and checking copies of photographs of buildings. I never knew what for, but perhaps it was something to do with the war.

After a short while, I was moved to a research laboratory for testing the power, strength and duration of light bulbs of all shapes and sizes and some other related components. Here I had to learn to use a slide rule. I always loved learning. I liked the people at Philips and soon made several new friends.

Not long after I'd joined the company, while I was walking between rooms a rat suddenly appeared and scuttled across the floor in front of me. I screamed and leapt at the first figure coming along the corridor, who was a huge man, very tall and wide, called Mr Bruch. As I leapt, he caught me in his arms.

'What is it?' he asked, not unreasonably.

'A rat,' I replied. 'A huge rat just ran across in front of me.'

'Oh dear, we can't have that,' he said with a grin, still holding me safely. I didn't want him to let me down before I knew that rat had gone. So there he stood, with me in his arms, and I'd only seen him once before, at a meeting. What must he have thought of me?

Finally he set me down and assured me that the rat must certainly have gone into hiding by now. 'You will be quite safe,' he said, and I did feel a little reassured, but not altogether.

This Mr Bruch was Dutch – one of the top people from the company's office in Holland – and we had been told he would be joining us for the duration of the war. Just after he'd made that decision, the Dutch factory was bombed by the Allies to stop the invading Germans using it for the production of German bombs and ammunition, so he had a very lucky escape. Perhaps he was warned by the British and got out while he could.

I saw him a few times after that, usually when he was showing high-level visitors around, explaining to them what we were doing. He always smiled and wagged his finger at me, which was quite funny. I really enjoyed our little joke.

Ray had left school at fourteen, two years before, and now worked as a decorator in his Uncle Osbert's business.

Whenever Ray finished work early, he would come and meet me outside Philips to walk me home. We always had so much to talk about – often the funny or sad things that happened at work or at the Home Guard or to other friends round about.

He would go home for his tea, then often come back to my house to walk me to Tony's, to dance the evening away. We usually danced together, but sometimes we swapped partners. We could forget about the war and all our other troubles when we were at the dance hall.

One night, just before Christmas 1940, Ray and I were walking home from Tony's arm in arm, talking and laughing together as usual, when we noticed bright red and orange lights shining and leaping as they lit up the darkness of the night sky. It was nearly midnight and we couldn't think what it was.

'It looks like fire,' I said. 'A lot of fire. What else could it be?' We stood in silence for a few moments, taking it in.

'It must be a big fire,' said Ray quietly. 'And it looks a long way away, on the horizon.' He paused. 'I reckon that could be Manchester.'

'Yes, maybe,' I agreed. 'But what could be happening?'

It was so dramatic and, in a way, awe-inspiring, that we couldn't stop looking.

After watching the distant flames in companionable silence for ten minutes or so, we realized we couldn't stay there all night and finally went back to our own homes and went to bed. It was nearly the end of 1940, the first full year of the war, and the whole of Manchester looked to have been set alight by the bombings. As I turned off my lamp, the distant glow shone through my curtains, casting eerie lights and shadows on the opposite wall.

Sure enough, the next day I heard that we were right. It had been Manchester burning. It was something called a 'blitz' – the 'Christmas Blitz', as it came to be known, demolishing large swathes of the city and killing many people.

This was a daunting time for us all. What would the new year bring? Would we be next in line?

12

The Mystery Visitor

1941–1942

Despite the rationing, we managed to enjoy the usual Christmas lunch in 1940, thanks to Grandma and Grandad. They brought a large chicken, vegetables and eggs from neighbouring farms so we had everything we needed for a traditional lunch, and the whole family gathered together as usual for a good feast. Even Bobby was able to join us that year.

Every time Bobby came home on leave, I let him have my bedroom. A part of me was annoyed at the inconvenience but I always volunteered because he was the man and I thought the world of him. We had a settee in the sitting room that folded out into a bed, so I slept on that when he was home.

It was baby Alan's first Christmas, so there were ten of us plus the baby squashed together round my grandparents' big dining table: Granny, Grandad and Auntie Elsie of course, plus Uncle George and Auntie Evelyn with their spoilt son, Ronnie. Bobby, Mother, Jeffrey, Alan – in Mother's lap – and I made up the numbers.

Jeffrey and I arrived last, fresh from Mass, which was always a black mark against me, for being a Roman Catholic and, even worse, for making Jeffrey one as well, although that had been down to Father, who had him christened as a Catholic before he left.

After lunch, we all sat around and opened the presents from under the Christmas tree. The gifts were mostly knitted or sewn pieces of clothing from my mother to everyone, but there were also wooden animals or trains for the children and wooden boxes or ornaments for the adults, made and carved in Grandad's workshop by his workers throughout the year, whenever the building work was rained off. (He never wanted to lay the workers off because he knew they and their families needed their wages.)

In addition to the presents, Grandad always gave an envelope with money in it to each of his grandchildren . . . but not the same amounts! In his mind, the fairest way was to give the same amount to one side of the family as to the other. So if he was giving five pounds, the single child, Ronnie, seven years younger than me, would get the whole lot but Bobby, Jeffrey, Alan and I would end up with one pound five shillings each.

It was typical of the way Ronnie was treated. Although often naughty – a pest and a menace – he was never told off and had received all the help with his education that Grandad had denied me. I wasn't exactly jealous of Ronnie for this, or for the way everybody spoilt him. It wasn't his fault. But it did hurt me that those who could have helped me chose not to. Uncle George paid for Ronnie to attend all the best schools, while I, who passed the scholarship that would have funded all my years up to eighteen at the convent, couldn't even be given the uniform to stay on to the minimum school-leaving age. When Ronnie didn't reach the standard required to gain a scholarship, Grandad paid for a lot of extra tutoring to help him scrape through for a bursary, which covered only a small proportion of his school fees. Uncle George then paid the rest.

In early 1941 I had a pay rise at Philips. I was getting a bit bored with testing light bulbs all day but I did enjoy the slide-rule work, doing calculations, and of course the social side of work – chats with the girls and banter with the boys. There were a lot of girls working at Philips and they were as much in the dark as I was about how babies were made. It was the subject of many of our conversations during breaks at work. Or rather, it was the absence of any knowledge about it that we discussed. How could we find out? Who could we ask? Then Kathleen Dugdale came and sat with us one day. She had been training to become a nurse before she came to work at Philips, but for whatever reason she had given it up. We assumed she had learned about people's bodies, so we were all curious to find out what she knew.

'Where do babies come from?' I asked and we all waited, agog for her answer.

'Well,' she began, then a long pause.

'Did you learn about it in your training?' asked Vera, one of the girls.

'Ye-e-e-s,' she hesitated. 'I remember there was something about it.'

'What?'

'I think they told us how people make them,' said Kathleen.

'Do you remember how?'

'They gave us a book to read about it, but I wasn't well that day, so I didn't have it.'

'Well, what do you know?' We were all becoming a bit exasperated now.

'I saw a diagram,' she said and we all leaned forward again. She must have seen how desperate we were to find out something about this mystery. 'It showed a piece that is under a woman's bottom.' We waited impatiently for further explanation. 'I think that has something to do with it.'

'What else?' someone asked.

'They told us about people having piles.'

'Can anyone get piles?' I was confused. I knew there was something below, but I couldn't see how it could have anything to do with babies.

'Yes.' Kathleen looked a bit more confident now. Perhaps she was on firmer ground talking about this condition. 'Yes,' she said. 'And I think anyone can have babies too.'

'Is that all you know?'

'Yes,' she admitted, looking rather embarrassed. 'I didn't stay on long enough to find out any more.'

From what little Kathleen had said and described, I now had the idea that I must have piles, so I went to see the local doctor.

'Hello, Margaret. What have you come to see me about?'

'I have piles,' I blurted out.

He gave me a funny look. 'And where have you got these piles?' he asked.

I explained where I thought the problem was, under my bottom.

'Well, let's have a look, shall we?' He indicated for me to undress and lie down on his high bed so that he could examine me. But I wouldn't let him. I refused to undress in front of him.

'Right,' he said. 'Front or back bottom?'

'Front.'

'Then you haven't got piles,' he said, categorically. 'You're perfectly normal, so don't worry.'

When I left his surgery I still didn't really know what piles were or where they should be, and I certainly knew nothing more about where babies came from.

This was the same doctor that came to my aid the time that Alan, now a very active toddler, tripped over on the pavement and knocked his front teeth through his tongue. He shrieked and wailed. I didn't think of going to my mother for help, I just picked him up and carried him down the road, straight to the doctor's surgery, with blood pouring out of his mouth. The receptionist took one look and sent us straight through to the doctor. I watched as he treated Alan as best he could, with all his writhing and screaming. Then I heard the doctor say: 'I think it's you that needs me now, Margaret . . .' and I don't remember anything else. I had passed out from seeing all that blood.

When I came to, lying on the couch, the doctor was

back with Alan, who was now lying down with a nurse holding him as still as possible on the bed, looking very concerned. I sat up and craned my head to get a better look at my little brother and I saw that his face was white as chalk.

'What's wrong?' I asked.

Without turning, the doctor replied: 'He's suffering from shock and a fever, so I think we'd better take him to the hospital.' He paused. 'Is your mother at home?' he asked me.

'Yes, I think so.'

'Well, I will take Alan straight to the Infirmary and you can both meet me there.' And then, as an afterthought, carrying Alan to his car, he called after me: 'Don't worry. He will be all right.'

But I did worry, and I felt awful. It was all my fault as I was supposed to be looking after him. I ran home as fast as I could, my heart pounding. Mother turned pale when I told her. For once we took the bus, impatient to get there quicker. When we reached the ward where they'd taken Alan, I almost cried to see my livewire little brother lying very still on a hospital bed. Mother went straight to him and stroked his curly hair, soothing him with soft words.

'There, there, love. Ssh, ssh,' she murmured as he cried anew on seeing her. 'You haven't to worry. The doctors and nurses will soon have you well again and then you'll be able to come back home.'

Sure enough, he came home the next day and the doctor was right; Alan did get better in the end. It took a long time, or so it seemed to me, worrying constantly at the memory of his white face, presumably the result of shock. But it was actually only about two weeks before his tongue healed and he was back to his usual self.

This was all well before the NHS was founded. But I don't remember anybody not getting the help they needed. And somehow, everyone managed to pay for it. Most workers had basic health insurance taken from their wages, but only for themselves, not their families. Others could contribute to insurance through societies such as Working Men's Clubs. Those who were self-employed could pay into an insurance scheme, with the money collected weekly or monthly at their door. I think Mother must have done that, as I know she put money by when she could and I don't remember ever having to worry about doctors' bills.

In late 1941, the government issued supplies of a new kind – an air-raid shelter for the home called a Morrison shelter. It was a huge metal table-type contraption that looked like a cage. We had to crawl into it when the air-raid sirens sounded. It was a good idea as we didn't have an outdoor shelter, but it didn't look great, taking up most of the space in our front room. At least, with the area under the stairs as well, we now had enough safe space for all of us and our two extras to shelter.

As the war ground on through 1941 and into 1942 the number of air raids seemed to increase, but the planes were usually passing over us to go somewhere more important. They had their strategic targets and, fortunately for us, these were rarely in Blackburn. There was a fair bit of superficial damage from time to time, mainly the falling debris from damaged planes that clattered onto roofs, but there were no other fatalities in town from enemy bombs and no real destruction, so we were lucky.

Meanwhile, from spring 1942, Ray was only too aware that his eighteenth birthday was approaching the following March, and that he would have to go to war himself. He started to talk to the boys in blue, from the RAF and the navy, as well as those in khaki, wanting to know what they all did. Of course, they all tried to persuade him to join whatever branch they were in, but he kept an open mind. Knowing that he would be leaving in a matter of months we became inseparable, wanting to make the most of our friendship for as long as we could. We mostly avoided talking and even thinking much about the fact that time was passing. We just wanted to enjoy our precious time together.

One day in September 1942, I came home from work for lunch as I often did and let myself in.

'I'm home,' I called out to my mother. But as I walked through the sitting room and into the kitchen, there stood a stranger – a soldier, with his sleeves rolled up, washing his hands at our sink.

'Oh!' I said in surprise.

Mother was standing there with a quizzical expression, looking at me expectantly, hoping I'd enlighten her. Jeffrey was back from school for his lunch, so both of my younger brothers looked from me to the soldier and back to me. The soldier said nothing. He looked rather dour, or maybe sad, with a set expression and sealed lips. I didn't know what to say. We were all too polite to ask what he was doing in our house, so we went through to where the table was laid. As we all took our places and the soldier sat down on the vacant chair, still nobody said a word, and I was desperately trying to work out: who the heck can this be?

We had our lunch together, with ten-year-old Jeffrey telling us about his lessons that morning. Two-year-old Alan was sitting on a couple of cushions and kept falling off. Well, the first time he did it accidentally, but it made us laugh, so he slid off again . . . and again. It helped to break the ice with the stranger, who managed a momentary smile. As I helped Mother to clear away and got ready to go back to work, our anonymous visitor started to talk to me about somebody called Wolf.

'I'm sorry,' I said. 'But I don't know anyone called Wolf.'

'No, Wilf,' he corrected me. 'Wilfred.'

'Oh, do you mean Wilfred Taylor? I—'

'That's right,' he interrupted me. 'My brother. First of all, I had hoped to come here and congratulate you . . .' He paused, looking down and fidgeting with his hands.

'Really? I didn't know I'd done anything special. May I ask what for?' I really didn't know where this conversation was going.

'I wanted to congratulate you on your engagement.'

Now he'd really flummoxed me. 'Thank you,' I said, hesitantly.

'We were all so pleased when he told us in his last letter.'

Well, I was thinking, he didn't tell me! What could I say?

'Thank you, but . . .'

'All Wilf's friends are looking forward to meeting you.' He had started this sentence with an effort to look pleased, but he now looked as if he was about to cry.

I had no idea how to respond, so I suggested we go and sit down in the front room. I waited for him to compose himself sufficiently to go on.

'In his last letter, Wilf said he was coming home and he was going to get engaged . . . to you, Margaret. He even gave us your address.'

Now I realized how he came to be here, but I was still a bit puzzled.

He took a deep breath and looked me in the eyes for the first time. 'I don't know how to say this,' he began. Another deep breath. 'I'm afraid Wilfred was killed a few days ago. First he was wounded in action when he took part in a disastrous commando raid at Tobruk.' He paused, as much for himself as for me.

'Oh, I'm sorry to hear that,' I began. 'How badly?'

'Well, I'm not sure, but I know he had treatment and survived that. He was coming home on a British hospital ship, HMS *Coventry*, through the Eastern Mediterranean. They were just passing the coast of Egypt when they were dive-bombed by several German war planes. The letter we received today from a commanding officer says they had four direct hits and the ship sank, with the loss of sixty-three lives, including Wilfred's.' His brother paused to blow his nose, which gave me time to take it all in.

'How awful,' I said, genuinely upset. Even though I barely remembered meeting Wilf, I'd been getting to know him through our exchange of letters. He was only twenty and now his life had come to this horrible end. It really hit me again how cruel this war was and how close to home it could come.

'What a terrible shock for you all,' I added. 'I'm so sorry.'

'I'm sorry too, to bring you such bad news, when this should have been a happy occasion for you both, and for all of us.'

At that moment I just couldn't bring myself to tell him that I hardly knew Wilfred and we were just pen pals.

'I'm really sorry,' I said, looking at the clock on the mantelpiece. 'But I have to go back to work. I'm going to be late.'

'My father has a very serious illness,' he blurted out. 'And my mother is so upset she won't go out. They would both love to meet you. Could I please take you to meet them at the weekend?'

What could I say? I felt a fraud. Tragic as this was, it really didn't have anything to do with me. I couldn't pretend to have been Wilfred's fiancée . . . could I? In their eyes, we were engaged, so I suppose some people would say he was the first boy I was engaged to, but I couldn't see it that way, since I was never consulted. It was all so awkward and unfair.

I felt sorry for the brother, but there was something about him I wasn't too sure of. If I'd seen him in the street I probably would have kept my distance. I really didn't want to have to go and see Wilfred's parents and share their grief. It didn't seem right.

The brother looked at me with pleading eyes. 'Will you?'

'All right,' I agreed with a sigh. What choice did I have?

So on the Saturday morning, Wilfred's brother came round and took me to his parents' house in Montague Street, an area of Blackburn I didn't know. I still didn't feel comfortable going there under such false pretences. His father was lying in a bed in their living room. I think he had tuberculosis. His mother sat in an easy chair next to the bed. They seemed glad I had come, but the conversation felt very strained. I tried to say the right things, and I stayed for an hour or so, but couldn't wait to leave. I know that sounds awful, but I couldn't just make things up, so there wasn't much I could say.

Just six weeks later, in mid November 1942, I had another shock. Clarry was serving on HMS *Avenger*, an aircraft carrier, in the western Mediterranean. Most of the men had been on deck as they passed the Rock of Gibraltar, out towards the Atlantic, where they were unwittingly heading closer to a group of enemy submarines. All it took to sink the ship was one torpedo, with the terrible loss of 516 lives. The boy who used to whistle at me on my way home from the convent, the boy who gave me my first grown-up kiss, was killed. He was only twenty-two.

What an awful thing war is, when so many young men die.

13

Bittersweet

1943

It was a dramatic start to the new year, when a loud explosion resounded across our part of Blackburn. I was on my way home from the pictures with my friend Kathleen Cronshaw, who lived above her family's chip shop round the corner on Whalley Old Road. It was about nine o'clock and we were almost home when we heard the blast. We could see people in uniforms coming and going – the police, the fire service, an ambulance – and followed to have a closer look. They were all converging on what remained of a house across the road from Kathleen's family chip shop. I didn't know much about the family who lived there, just that the mother worked at the munitions factory, filling bombs and shells with gunpowder.

A policeman stopped us going any further, just as Kathleen recognized her father, blackened from the explosion that had broken their windows and caused havoc all around. The house had been reduced to a terrible mess of rubble and Mr Cronshaw was disappearing into the site of the debris.

'What happened?' Kathleen asked one of her neighbours. 'Did you see it?'

'I was at home when it went off . . . and I assumed it was an unannounced air raid,' he explained. 'But the policeman has just told me it was an explosion that happened from inside the house. No bombs were dropped.'

'How can that be?' Kathleen asked.

'Well, it could have been some kind of gas or other explosive.'

'Could it have been gunpowder?' she asked.

'Well . . . yes, it could be, if there was any around.'

'My younger brothers go over there to play sometimes,' explained Kathleen. 'And Derek, the eldest, told me that the boy who lives there – his mother works with gunpowder, just like Guy Fawkes.'

I waited a bit longer with Kathleen, until her father and some of the other men emerged from the building, covered in soot and dust, stumbling on the bricks and bits of wood on the ground, some of them bringing out the injured. Mr Cronshaw was carrying a child. The child didn't move, so he carefully laid him down and wiped some of the black stuff from the boy's face with his handkerchief. It was only then that he realized he had been carrying his own middle son.

'Frank, Frank,' he said frantically, sinking to his knees and gently trying to wake him. 'Come on, son.'

But it was no good. An ambulance man came over and took his pulse, then slowly shook his head and stood back.

Kathleen ran over to join her father, kneeling with him and gently stroking her brother's blackened arm, desperately hoping to find he had just been stunned. From where I was standing, only a few yards away, I could see quite a lot of blood on him. Kathleen was wailing by now, and the sound brought out her mother and her youngest brother, in his pyjamas. The family spent some minutes together with Frank, inconsolable in their grief. Watching this tragic scene I felt like an intruder, so I turned away from the gathered crowd. I walked sadly home and told Mother about what had happened, but I couldn't get that image of Kathleen's grief out of my mind for several days.

I didn't see her for some time after that, but when I did, she told me about Frank's funeral.

'It was awful, as we knew it would be, having to bury our dear boy. It was comforting to see his school friends, who came in a group . . .' She paused. 'Somehow they made it both easier and harder to bear, with their singing and their memories of him.' There were tears in her eyes as she told me about Frank, and in mine too, but I think it helped her to talk to me about it.

Ray had finally opted to serve in the navy, on the submarines if he could, though there was no guarantee he would be given his first choice. He enlisted, passed his medical and in late February he received his orders. Knowing what must be in the envelope, he brought it round so that we could open it together.

'Here it is,' he said, unfolding the letter. We read what it said with a great deal of apprehension. Up to now, Raymond had been quite excited at the thought of donning a handsome uniform and joining his friends to fight for our freedom. I suppose it was a mixture of patriotic fervour and bravado, tinged with a sense of duty and also perhaps a hint of apprehension – even fear. None of the boys wanted to be left out or, even worse, shamed for not joining up. And none of them wanted to go down the coal mines, which was always a threat. They weren't afraid of the mines, but they feared being regarded as cowards because they weren't in the armed services. Mining was an essential job, as everyone needed coal, so some men were ordered to do it, but nobody wanted it to be them. This letter would seal Ray's fate. It would be the final step towards his war service.

I know we both shared a great reluctance, to say the least, to be separated for the first time. We had been almost daily companions since my family had moved to Robinson Street, about seven years before. Friends and relations always joked that we were stuck together like glue. But now it really hit us that we would have to part.

'Well, they've confirmed that I'll serve on a submarine all right,' said Raymond.

'But they don't say which one,' I added.

'No, not yet. That's because they told me I'd have to go for training first.'

'Ah, so that's what this part is about,' I said, pointing at the longest paragraph.

'Yes. That's my orders. It says I have to get a train from Blackburn on the 8th March.'

'But that's the day after your eighteenth birthday,' I interrupted.

'Yes, I didn't realize it would be as soon as that.'

We sat in silence, just staring at the stark details.

Ray broke the tension: 'Orders is orders!' he grinned.

We spent as much time together as we could over the next few days, going down to the rec to sit on the end of the slide and reminisce about those days when we all gathered here and the times when I used to swing around above him on the ropes.

We went to the cinema one night and saw *Mrs Miniver* – what a wonderful, sad film that was, and of course it starred my favourites: Greer Garson and, especially, Walter Pidgeon – the man I would have chosen to be my father. Tears were streaming down my cheeks as we filed out that night. In fact, most of the other women and girls were weeping too. It was a great film, but maybe not the right one to see just before Raymond went to war.

We carried on dancing together most evenings. 'Next time we come to Tony's,' Ray said, on the eve of his eighteenth birthday, 'I will be in my naval uniform, and then, if I'm lucky, you might even think I look handsome.'

'You know I can't resist a good-looking boy in a uniform,' I agreed, squeezing his hand. 'Especially a blue uniform.' We both laughed at the thought.

On 7 March, Raymond celebrated his eighteenth birthday with a party at his house for his close family and me. Everybody was in a good mood, wanting to wish him well, not only because it was his birthday, but because by now everyone knew it was also his last day of 'freedom'.

It was a bittersweet evening for us both. I sat next to

Ray at the dinner table and later all his family smiled and spoke to me, as I stood proudly beside him.

After everyone else had gone, he walked me home, arm in arm, for the last time before he left. We talked non-stop all the way and continued on the doorstep.

'Come in and say goodbye to my mother,' I suggested.

'Good idea.'

'Ah, Raymond,' said Mother with a smile as she opened the door.

'Hello, Mrs Holden. I just came in to say goodbye. I'm leaving early tomorrow morning.' They shook hands.

'I'm very glad you came in. I wanted to have the chance to wish you all the best. I know Margaret will miss you.'

'And I will miss her too.' He nodded. 'Very much. But I will write letters – a lot of letters.'

'That will be lovely,' said Mother. 'Maybe Margaret will be able to read some of them to us, so that we can hear your news.'

'Yes, I'll tell you how my training goes and where I'll be going next.'

'Thank you, Raymond. Now you stay safe and come back to see us as soon as you possibly can.'

'I'll try my best,' he agreed.

We went back out to the front doorstep. Neither of us wanted the evening to end, but we knew it had to, so I gave him a big hug and a long, loving kiss and waved him off as he slowly walked up the road, turning to wave one last time at the corner before he disappeared.

He was my best friend, my confidant, my childhood playmate and . . . well, we had never talked of engagement or marriage, but we had a very special bond and there was an unspoken understanding between us. I'm sure we both assumed we would always be together.

Only the war could part us . . . but hopefully not for long.

Raymond and I wrote letters to each other almost every day. But there were others too. Every time a different boy walked me home from the dance halls, he would invariably ask me to write to him while he was away. I hadn't the heart to say no, so my address book soon filled up with the names and addresses of dance partners, some of whom I could barely remember. And that wasn't the only thing that filled up.

One morning, there was a knock on the door and it was our postman with yet another pile of letters from British forces overseas.

'I'm glad I caught you, Margaret,' he began, with a flustered look on his face. 'My mail bag is full every day with all these letters for you, all with different writing on. In fact, I have to use a bigger sack now and almost half of it is letters to you!'

Well, I knew that was an exaggeration, but I could see his point. Both Mother and I were trying to keep a straight face.

'You'll give me a hernia if this carries on!'

'I'm sorry,' I said.

I did try to keep up with replying to these boys. I knew from Bobby how important letters from home were to all the boys in the forces, most of them so far away. So I did my best to reply as quickly as I could, but sometimes I did get behind with the answers. Some of the boys were so impatient that they wrote to Mother, politely enquiring about my health, or more insistently requesting her to prompt me to write back more quickly. One of them even wrote to her to ask why I hadn't replied: 'Has Margaret broken her arm?' That made us laugh, but it worked. I wrote back to him straight away.

Usually the correspondence would begin by describing ordinary things, like the weather. But gradually the letters would become more daring. Quite often the boys would declare that they loved me.

I found this quite strange, since I had rarely spent more than a few hours with some of them, or a few evenings on the dance floor. I was just having fun in the moment, enjoying their company while it lasted – all very innocent. It meant much more to them, I think, than it did to me. So professions of love didn't seem appropriate.

I never did understand this business of the word 'love'. After all, you love your mother, you love the colour green, you love the cat and you love the weather . . . sometimes! It's a much misused word.

Occasionally a boy would come back from the war, or I'd see him the night after we'd danced, and he'd say: 'Do you still love me?' What could I say to that? I loved everybody and everything in a general way. But Ray was the only one I truly loved.

He wrote me letters about all the goings-on during his training, parts of which, especially the funny stories, I used to read out to Mother and the boys during lunchtimes or after work. I always went home for lunch in those days and after we'd eaten, Mother and I often played word or number games with Jeffrey and Alan. Lexicon was our favourite and it was great at teaching both the boys to spell, each at their own level. It was a card game and each card had one letter on it, so it was all about making words, a forerunner of Scrabble. Jeffrey was already quite good at spelling and he had a wide vocabulary, but he liked to use those skills to beat Mother and me. At the same time we all helped little Alan to see that letters made words and what some of the simple words looked like. Both the boys were very bright and keen to learn.

When Ray was first posted to his submarine, he wrote and told me they would be setting off for the Far East, where he would be based. We had hoped that he would have a short leave before he went, but apparently there wasn't time.

It all happened far too quickly and now he would only be able to write when he was on land, or in safe waters where post could be transferred between naval craft, which was quite sporadic. I did miss his letters on the days I had none, but once they started again, I would have several all at once – which was a joy. To start with, his letters were mostly light-hearted, telling me about the places he'd been, or giving nameless descriptions of them at least, trying to steer on the right side of the censor. He also described the inside of his submarine, the quirks of his fellow submariners, and the incidents and tales of his everyday life, all of which Mother and the boys loved to hear.

Increasingly he would write just to me, about his hopes
for the future, the plans we could make for when he came
home, or when the war was ended. Neither of us mentioned
marriage for some time, but it was obvious to both of us.
In one letter, Ray even described a length of delicate white
lace he had bought for me, and in another a beautiful
ring he had purchased for me to wear on our special day.
We exchanged ideas about the kind of house we would
like to live in and where it might be.

All of this sustained us over the months. Of course,
there was sadness too, on both sides. It was a cruel war,
especially in Asia. I worried about Raymond a lot, but
tried not to dwell on the risks and dangers he faced. I
preferred to fix my focus on keeping up his morale . . .
and to look forward to the day when he would finally
come back home.

If only he could have some leave, but apparently that
was not possible from where he was. All the other boys
were coming back every now and then for forty-eight
hours, or sometimes more, but never Ray. It was so unfair.
I longed to see him.

One of the sad things I wrote about to Raymond concerned
Bobby's old friend, Arthur Isherwood, who was killed in
action. Bobby had written to tell us about it. Arthur had
been a big part of our lives before the war accelerated. I
often remembered with fondness the lovely holiday I had
with Arthur, Bobby, Mother, her friend Alice and Jeffrey
in Blackpool. Those happy days seemed so long ago now.

We knew that Arthur had been trained to take photographs

on aerial reconnaissance missions. I hadn't really thought too much about it, assuming he would be flying behind the lines. But the most important part of his job was to fly over enemy territory, as low as his pilot dared and evading the German fighter planes, to photograph potential industrial targets, railways and roads. Bobby wrote that, on 9 June 1943, Arthur's plane was shot down in flames over Germany and he was killed – another dear friend gone to his Maker. A very sad loss.

That July, during Blackburn Wakes Week, I was with Peggy and some other girls at a dance in King George's Hall, when we decided to go across the road to the Jubilee Inn. We went to the bar and ordered 'Spitfires'. Well, no, I probably asked for my usual orange and lemon first, but when I saw that the Spitfire had a cherry on a stick, I decided I would have that instead . . . and that again. Suddenly I was seeing two cherries, and the ashtray looked like a box of matchsticks.

Peggy was playing the piano and we were listening.

'That sounds like camels coming across the desert,' I said. I do remember that.

The next thing I remember was being back in the toilet block at the dance hall, feeling as if I was dying.

Someone shouted at me, 'If your brother could see you now!' It was Nellie Forrester, Bobby's old crush.

Then I was staggering and stumbling along with Peggy holding me up and somehow getting me home, where Mother put me to bed. I was there for at least a week. The doctor called one day and checked me over.

'I think you've got some sort of flu, Margaret,' he said. Did I imagine that he winked ever so slightly at my mother?

'That's strange,' I said. 'I had the new flu injection at Philips last week.'

'What's that?' Mother asked in surprise.

'It's a trial,' I replied. 'I think it's the first time they've done it. They said it would stop me getting the flu, so how do I have it now?'

'Perhaps it's a different kind of flu,' suggested the doctor.

Luckily, I'd fully recovered in time for a family trip to Blackpool in August. We were in the Tower Ballroom at the 'tea dance', when a Polish officer came over to our table and clicked his heels together.

He turned to my mother. 'May I ask your daughter to dance?'

She was impressed by his good manners. 'Yes, you may,' she agreed with a smile.

He turned to me. 'May you dance with me?'

We went out together onto the dance floor. He was a good dancer and I was glad to have him as a partner. He spoke reasonably good English, so we were talking as we danced. He told me his name was Ivan and when I said my name was Margaret, he said 'Marishka', which sounded lovely.

Suddenly there was a commotion, as Alan pulled himself away from Mother and trotted onto the dance floor, straight towards me. He pulled at the Polish airman's trousers, then started smacking his legs. Well, by this time, everyone in the place was laughing, including the band who had seen it all and could hardly play another note, so the music petered out and everyone stopped dancing to look.

I was so embarrassed that I just picked up Alan and took him back to our table, to get us both out of trouble. It was at least two or three more minutes before everyone calmed down and the band struck up again.

I assumed that would be the last I would see of Ivan, but he came over to the table again and asked me if I would see him that evening.

'There will be party,' he said with a smile. 'You come with me? I bring you back after?' He looked from me to my mother and back again.

Then I looked at my mother. 'May I?'

'Yes, as long as you're back where we're staying by ten.'

So we all went back and I changed into a different dress, made by my mother. We were very lucky to have a place to stay, since so many of the boarding houses in Blackpool had been commandeered as billets for soldiers and airmen based nearby. But Auntie Evelyn's mother lived at 14 Gladstone Street and she was happy to have us for short stays.

Ivan came to call for me and we went to the party, which was held in a classy bar beneath Blackpool Tower. It wasn't at all what I expected. When we arrived, Ivan seemed to be the centre of attention. I found myself being introduced to various people, most of whose names I immediately forgot, with all the excitement going on. We were in the middle of a lot of backslapping – him, not me! Apparently, this so-called party was to celebrate Ivan being awarded the DFC (which I later found out meant the Distinguished Flying Cross, awarded for gallantry).

It was a wonderful atmosphere, but I was way out of my depth and could hardly follow what was going on – most of it in Polish. Everyone was so friendly and happy, but I was glad to get away and Ivan walked me back to where we were staying. He was the essence of politeness.

We went home the next day, so I never saw Ivan again. To this day, I have no idea whether he survived the war.

14

Making a Splash

1944

New Year 1944 burst in with a very welcome influx of glamorous American GIs to the town. Based nearby, they flocked into Blackburn and made a beeline for the dance halls most evenings, especially Tony's. They were so friendly and cheerful, which rubbed off on all of us. They loved to dance and they had money to spend. Above all, I could hardly believe how polite and courteous they were. I had watched a few wartime American films, but the GIs who came to Blackburn had very different stories and bore little if any resemblance to the actors or plots in those films.

My friends and I couldn't help flirting with our American visitors, most of whom were great dancers, good fun and very respectful of women. It was a promising start to the year and brightened up the monochrome aspects of Blackburn life in wartime.

There were more GIs than girls some nights, so we had our pick of them. Matt Karmelsky, however, was different from all the others. For a start, he didn't dance. He was a quiet man, an older American Tec. Sergeant, about twenty-eight to thirty years old, with a pale complexion, straight blond hair and blue eyes. He had his US Army pay but he was also paid a full salary by his former employer, GEC, because they wanted him back, so he had an awful lot of money.

I never went out with Matt. I never danced with him – nobody did, as he never asked. He used to watch the dancing with a benign smile as he spoke with his wonderful American drawl, telling his stories about the characters of his childhood in his home town. He was a great talker, but also a great listener. He had a way of making a girl feel she was the only person in the room. However, not surprisingly, there were always a lot of girls around him, including Peggy and Hilda. He was part of the crowd I was involved with. I knew he liked me, but then again, he liked a lot of other girls who were around him and they knew him a great deal better than I did. I realized he was generous, but I was surprised when, one evening, he came up to me and quietly slipped something into my hand, something wrapped in tissue paper, and gave me a smile, then a tilt of his head, suggesting he wanted me to open it. There was no box or anything showy; just the tissue paper. I gently unwrapped and opened it out. When I saw it for the first time, it took my breath away. It was the most beautiful thing I'd ever seen, let alone held in my hand.

It was a pretty golden watch, with what looked like diamonds around its face, but I knew they couldn't be real diamonds or real gold. It had a delicate black strap with a decorative loop. It was just perfect. I turned it over and saw, engraved on the back, the word 'Switzerland'.

'That's where I went to buy it for you,' he said. I was astonished. This was wartime and he was telling me that he'd flown over to Switzerland especially to buy a watch for me? He hardly knew me. It was like a fairy tale – even more so when he told me they were all real diamonds and the best-quality gold.

'How did you do this?' I whispered, overawed.

'Can you keep a secret?' he asked.

'Yes,' I replied. In fact, I was good at keeping secrets, so that was true.

'Well,' he continued. 'It's all very hush-hush. I work on something called radar, so I had to fly over to Switzerland for a meeting about it. That's the main reason I was there. But I had some time to spare, so I went round the jewellery shops to find a gift for you.'

'Why me?'

'Because I like you. You're different – special.'

'Thank you . . . thank you very much. It's a beautiful gift.'

We sat and chatted a while, then he walked me home, but that was all. He was very charming, very polite. It was just a walk with a friend.

'It's only me,' I called as I opened the door, in a happy mood and happier still to see Bobby, who had unexpectedly come home for a couple of days. He saw the gift, still in my hand, and questioned me about it. I didn't know what to say, except what actually happened. It was all very innocent. But Bobby took it the wrong way and

he said some awful things. As much as I loved him, I was
a little frightened of his cold, hard voice, accusing me of
things and making me feel cheap. Looking back on it now,
I realize that Bobby felt he was being protective of me.
He must have assumed that Matt's gift was a bribe to
lure me into the wrong kind of relationship. But he made
me feel it was my fault – that I had flirted with Matt and
led him on. Of course, that was far from the truth, so I
didn't understand why he was so cross with me. I had
done nothing wrong. After about half an hour of this, I
was in floods of tears.

'But you don't understand,' I wailed, one last time.

'Oh yes, I do understand,' he shouted, pointing his finger
at me in his rage. 'I understand only too well what men
like him want, and you're the kind of silly girl who falls
for it.' He paused for breath. 'But you can't keep that
monstrosity of a watch,' he told me. 'If you want a watch,
I'll buy you a watch.'

'But . . .'

'No buts. Tomorrow I insist that you give it straight
back to this man, and that's final.'

I looked again at Matt's beautiful gift when I was alone
that night. Not in my bedroom, of course, because Bobby
had that, but on the fold-out sofa downstairs. I turned
the watch over in my hand and watched the diamonds
sparkle in the light coming from the embers in the grate.
I sighed with sadness that things had turned out this way.

The next day, with great reluctance, I wrapped the
watch up again in the tissue paper, took it to the dance
hall with me and handed it back to Matt Karmelsky.

'I think it is a very beautiful gift,' I explained. 'But I'm afraid my family said I haven't to accept it.'

Matt gave me a disappointed look, then turned round and gave it to the girl next to him.

I had worked at Philips for a couple of years and I felt like a change – something that could lead to a proper career. So in spring 1944 I went to work for an accountant in Richmond Terrace. He was a big, hefty, middle-aged man with a ruddy complexion. He told me that he would pay me a wage and train me for free to become an accountant myself. That sounded good to me and it all started off all right. But gradually it became a little uncomfortable. It was a small office; just him and me working in the same room, and no other employees. It began with him asking me to come over to look at something, then I would feel his knee squeezing mine against the drawers of his big old-fashioned desk. I tried to avoid this as much as possible, but I didn't know what to do to stop him. Maybe he didn't realize. However, the training tailed off and I became more uncomfortable as his interest in me grew. I used to look up from my work to find he was staring at me.

At the end of each working day, my task was to lock the filing cabinets. The lock was right down at the bottom, so I had to kneel down and lean forward to put the key in the lock and turn it. He often watched me do this and I tried to ignore him. But one day, he stood so close behind me that as I got to my feet, awkwardly trying to lean away from him, I still couldn't avoid our bodies touching.

He took my chin in his hand and turned my face to his, trying to kiss me on the mouth, but I managed to jerk myself away and avoid it. So that was the end of that job.

In need of new employment quickly, I found out that the General Post Office was looking for a new telephonist, so I went to see the manager and I got the job. It might not have been a professional career, but it was a secure job. I was supposed to do six weeks' training, but they moved me on after three, perhaps because I was always making my fellow trainees laugh. I was put straight on the switchboard, so I had to learn the rest on the job. It was good fun: a new set of people and more contact with the public, which I enjoyed.

The 7th March was Ray's nineteenth birthday and I sent him a beautiful card with his letter, though I could not tell when or where he would be when he received it, possibly several days late. I thought a lot about him that day, as I did most days. The next day, the 8th, he had been gone for exactly a year. I was forlorn without him. Everybody else's sweethearts came home on leave, but not Ray. I longed for him to come back, even for just a short while. I just wanted him to hold me. It seemed most unfair to be separated for so long.

I knew I should not dwell on missing Ray, so instead I threw myself into my busy social life.

The next evening at Tony's, there was a tall, handsome boy with blond wavy hair. His name was Arnold Rouston, he told me, and he was in naval uniform – my favourite. We danced most of the evening and at the end he asked if he could walk me home. I liked his friendliness as well as his good looks, so I agreed.

'I've not seen you at Tony's before,' I said as we strolled along.

'No, I've not been before, but one of my friends suggested coming along to see what it was like. We don't live in Blackburn, you see.'

'Oh?'

'I live in Accrington . . . when I'm home, that is.'

'I suppose you're on leave? How long are you here?' I asked.

'It should be only forty-eight hours, but they're doing something to the railway track, so I can't go back till after the weekend.'

'Well, it's Thursday today, so that's another three evenings at the dance hall!'

'Yes,' he laughed. 'I suppose it is. What about the daytimes, though? Are you doing anything on Saturday and Sunday?'

'I am now,' I replied with a grin.

It was all light-hearted banter and friendship. Over that long weekend, Arnold Rouston and I became good pals. I was quite sorry when he had to go back, but there were plenty of other dance partners to choose from, so that was fine. I did stop and worry sometimes though about all these boys, going back to their terrible experiences in the war. I had already lost a number of friends. I couldn't even think about losing any more, yet I couldn't help fearing what news each passing day might bring.

*

The day after Arnold's leave ended, I took my mother to a private dance at Tony's, where I spotted another new face – a good-looking airman with wavy brown hair, a steady gaze and a confident manner. He came over and introduced himself to Mother and me.

'I'm Leslie Fielding. I'm a flight sergeant in the RAF – 576 Squadron.'

'I'm Margaret Holden.' I echoed his introduction. 'And I love dancing.'

'Well, that's good, because I was just going to ask you for a dance!'

As we danced we chatted.

'Are you home on leave?' I asked.

'Yes, just a short leave this time, but now I've met you, I think I might come again.'

I told him about my life, my family and my work. He told me about his work, his crew and some of his recent sorties in his Lancaster bomber – the regular ones he could talk about.

'I'm currently training on a new wireless system at Lindholme airbase near Doncaster,' he told me. 'But my home airfield is Elsham Wolds in Lincolnshire.'

I was eighteen and he was twenty-two. We danced a lot and we talked a lot more. In the break, Leslie came and sat down with us and Mother told him about Bobby being in the RAF and repairing Mosquitoes and I mentioned I had been the timekeeper at Bobby's model aircraft club.

The band struck up, so we walked out onto the dance floor again.

'What did you do before the war?' I asked.

'I worked in a tax office.'

'Well, that's a coincidence. I worked for a tax accountant in Blackburn.'

'We do have a lot in common,' he said with a smile.

We got on really well and by the end of the evening we felt like we'd known each other for ages.

'Let me walk you two ladies home,' he suggested, with a twinkle in his eyes, which seemed to impress my mother. Of course, once she had gone into the house, there was also the first, gentle kiss on the doorstep before he left.

The rest of the weekend we strolled along country lanes, arm in arm, and talked about our lives before the war, stopping every now and then for a kiss, and again when we ate our picnic, behind a hedge in one of the fields. I always loved kissing, but Leslie's kisses were special. There was something about him that really appealed to me and we quickly became closer than I had with any new dance partner since Ray had gone to war. But he had to go back to his temporary base at Lindholme, near Doncaster, so we exchanged addresses and kept in touch by letter. Our poor postman's bag must have been bulging more than ever.

When I opened the door a few days later, I was amazed to see Les back quite so soon.

'How did you manage to get more leave?' I asked.

'Why? Don't you want me?' he grinned.

'It's not that. I'm really glad to see you. But nobody else I know in the forces gets two lots of leave so close together.'

'Are you going to Tony's?' he asked. He knew it was a rhetorical question. 'Why don't we go down there together and I'll tell you all about it.

'Every time we fly off on a raid over Europe,' he explained, 'I come back and have nothing to do until the next raid, so I thought I'd come over and see you again.' We kissed outside the dance hall. 'I can only stay a few hours, but you're worth it.'

That made me feel good, and I liked his cheeky grin. 'Is it a few hours of my stimulating company? Or is it the dancing?'

'Yes,' he said with a lopsided smile. 'Something like that.'

'Which?' I put him on the spot.

'Both.' We laughed.

Now that we had arrived in the well-lit dance hall I could see his pallor and the lines of fatigue on his face.

'You look tired,' I said, with concern.

'Yes, I'm whacked. We've been on a raid over Germany today and I came straight here to see you.'

'Well, thank you,' I said with a smile. 'But you must try to get enough sleep.'

'Maybe I can just lie down on this settee for a bit of shut-eye, and then I'll be the life and soul of the party.'

For the rest of the evening, Les slept as if he hadn't been to bed for months. Perhaps he hadn't, with so many sorties. I woke him when it was time to leave and he walked me home, before going back to his airbase at Elsham Wolds.

Over the next few weeks, after most raids, Les used to

turn up at Tony's and slump down on a settee to sleep, still in his white roll-neck flying jersey, until it was time for him to walk me home. It was always lovely to see him, but he spent a lot more time catching up on lost sleep than we had awake together.

I wondered how long this could continue. Surely he would be missed at his base? But it wasn't long before the pattern changed.

'When an aircraft is shot down or any of the crew members are injured, the rest of the crew are "laid down" until the pilot forms a new crew,' he explained to me one evening, as he walked me home, arm in arm. 'Well, that has just happened to us. Our gunner was hit by a stray German bullet, so now, until we have a new gunner, we're all at a loose end. We spend pretty well all our time sitting at our base, watching and waiting as other crews take off and seeing who returns.' He paused. 'Well, that wasn't what we signed up for, doing nothing for days on end, so one of my pals, an officer, hatched a plan for me. He got hold of a batch of leave passes and signed them all for me to go home when I wasn't needed and just come back every other Tuesday for a briefing and to draw my pay.'

This went on for several weeks, so it was the perfect opportunity for us to spend time together, growing closer every day. However, one Tuesday he didn't return and I later found out from one of his letters that the RAF had discovered the ruse with the leave passes, so they arrested Les and confined him to his quarters at Elsham Wolds, awaiting trial.

I was very worried about him and wrote to him every

day. I couldn't wait to find out the date of the trial, or
the court martial, and what the outcome would be. I found
I really missed him, which surprised me. I couldn't believe
he would be convicted of anything. Yet I knew it must be
a possibility.

One evening, I heard from another RAF sergeant who
knew him that Les had been tried and acquitted. More
than that, he had been awarded an extra fourteen days'
leave as a reward for 'the outstanding performance of his
duties'. This 'punishment' was hilarious, and amazing. I
was thrilled with the outcome and wondered when next
he would be able to come over to see me.

Halfway through that evening, when I was dancing
with one of my GI friends, the music abruptly changed
to Ray McKinley's 'My Guy's Come Back'. We all looked
at the band and followed their gaze to the door, just as
Les walked in, with a big grin on his face. Everyone
surrounded him, patting him on the back and making a
fuss of him. Only ten or fifteen seconds later, though it
seemed a lot longer, the crowd parted so that he could
come over and give me a long kiss, to the enthusiastic
applause of all our audience.

It was great news and we made the most of it. During
those two weeks of extra leave, we walked arm in arm
and talked, about our families and friends, news of the
war, our pasts and our futures.

'If I survive this awful war, I'd like to go back to
accountancy and settle down here in Blackburn,' he said
with a smile. 'What about you?'

'Well, I'm younger than you, so I haven't really thought

about the future. But I'd like to get a better job, with my own office again, and I suppose I might like to settle down too one day, with the right man.'

'And do you think that man could be me?'

'Well,' I laughed, 'you never know. It might be!' I didn't want him to think it wasn't . . . but although I was beginning to realize that Leslie meant a lot to me, I hadn't told him about Ray, who was so far away, but still in my thoughts. I couldn't think about the future yet. I wasn't sure how I felt. I needed time to think it all through . . . and I hadn't seen Ray for so long.

Les and I both loved the cinema and musicals. His favourite song was 'You'll Never Know How Much I Love You'. Even now I can't hear it without thinking back to those times.

We talked about everything, but only rarely would he talk about his fears, though sometimes it just came out.

'My worst fear is being burned,' he told me, with a pained expression. 'I've been on raids where I've seen planes being shot out of the sky, their whole fuselages alight, and knowing there were men inside. I could almost hear them screaming.' His face contorted and I was afraid he was going to say more, but he stopped, as if suddenly aware that he'd said more than enough.

'How awful.' I really felt for him and all those brave airmen.

'Yes, this is an awful war, but I've come to see you for a break from all that.' He tried to make light of it, protecting me from any more horror stories.

We packed in a lot of fun and a good deal of serious

courting as well, though, while I felt a lot for him, I tried to keep it as light-hearted as possible most of the time.

There was one funny incident that stood out, though Les didn't notice. It happened one night, when we were coming down the stairs at the Rialto and I suddenly spotted Glen Douglas, an Australian pilot I'd been out with. His aunt lived near me in Little Harwood. I hadn't seen him for a while and I was glad he was all right, but I realized this could be awkward if he saw me. What would Les think?

But I needn't have worried, as when Les caught sight of Glen, he called out his name to attract his attention. Well, I might as well not have been there. They were the ones who were embracing. It turned out that they were old pals from their RAF training and so glad to see each other that they made a big noise and show of it. Everyone in the place must have noticed. When Les 'introduced' us and Glen saw my face, he just winked and we went our separate ways. I never saw him again.

Our two weeks were nearly up and we talked quite a lot about our feelings for each other, in a restrained way, neither of us being certain what lay ahead. But before he went back to Elsham Wolds, Les started a serious conversation.

'You're a very special girl, Margaret. I've fallen in love with you, and I think you may feel the same about me.'

I opened my mouth to respond, though I'm not certain what I was going to say, but he stopped me.

'Let me have my say first, because it's important that we are both honest with each other. These are dangerous days for aircrewmen like me, so any kind of commitment is unreliable. Two of my close friends on the base were killed in separate raids last week. So I know at first hand how risky it is to make any kind of plan for the future.'

'Yes, I know,' I said, with genuine sadness, for him even more than for me. 'You are special to me too,' I said. 'We've been together longer than I have with any of my previous boyfriends, apart from my childhood sweetheart. But we had been friends for years as children, so that was different.'

'Where is he now?'

'On a submarine in the Far East. I haven't seen him since he enlisted.'

'I hope perhaps I will meet him one day,' said Les. I suppose it was his kindest way of saying he hoped they both survived.

How could I know how I felt? I was so confused that I just had to separate them in my thoughts. Right now I had to focus on Les. I didn't know when Ray would be coming home.

Les's expression became more sombre. 'There is so much I want to say . . .'

'There is still a war on,' I interrupted. 'It's not the time for making promises. Let's just carry on as we are for now. We're happy, aren't we?'

'Yes, of course.' He smiled, reluctantly. 'That's decided, then.'

Finally, it was the last night before Les had to return to his base and his crew.

'You know my favourite song?' he asked as he walked me home.

'Yes, it's our song now.'

'It's how I feel about you . . . and about our situation.'

'I know. I feel the same.'

'But do you?' He cupped his hands gently round my face and looked into my eyes for a few silent seconds, as I returned his gaze.

'Yes,' I confirmed. 'We've had a wonderful time, haven't we? And I hope we'll have many more, but it isn't the right time to make plans.'

'But we do have an agreement, don't we?' he asked. 'If we . . .'

I put my finger to his lips. 'You don't have to say it. We do have an agreement and I look forward to what the future may bring.'

I think we both knew the odds were against us with every new raid he flew on, but neither of us put it into cold, hard words that night.

'We have some major missions coming up,' he told me. 'A big project, any day now, so I may not be able to see you for a while.'

'You will still be able to come over sometimes, won't you?' I asked.

'If I can.' He gave me a wistful smile. 'So you'd better behave yourself while I'm away!'

We kissed, a long kiss, and I waved him off as he left. I watched him stride down the road and stop again at the corner for another heartfelt wave.

That night in bed, I did think about what I would have said if he had asked me outright to marry him. It was difficult to know. Les and I had grown very close, and I did love being with him. Perhaps I was in love with him. But the war was a dangerous place to live. One of our friends, who was part of our group, was tall, thin, doll-faced Isobel. She had a very pale complexion, with the most gorgeous dark hair. One day she didn't turn up and for the next two weeks we wondered what had happened to her. When she did reappear, even thinner and paler than before, she told us that, following a whirlwind courtship with a dashing pilot, she had married her man. They had a wonderful weekend's honeymoon, after which he returned to the war. Four days after their wedding he was gone – killed in action. It was awful! My gosh . . . She looked like death on a stick.

Inevitably, I thought of Les and was glad we had agreed not to make any promises, yet. In peacetime it might have been different, but then I would have had Ray as my companion and would probably never have met Les.

I didn't know it then, but all the aircrews, and all the other services, were preparing for a huge Allied operation that could change the course of the war.

Sunday, 27 May 1944 was my eighteenth birthday. Instead of a party, I had arranged to have a short holiday with Jenny Bolton, who was a farmer's daughter and a good friend from Tony's. She was always up for a lark. I got up early, joining Jenny on her milk round, which was great fun. We chatted as we went along, and all the customers were so friendly, coming out to greet us with their jugs, some of them paying with eggs or vegetables instead of money. When we returned to the farm, Jenny's mother had baked us some potatoes, which we ate with lashings of home-made butter. This was a delicious treat, at a time when butter in the shops was strictly rationed.

My mother had made me a special outfit for my birthday. She had managed to get hold of some gabardine material, so she made me a raincoat, with the back like a battledress top and a band drawing in the waist over quite a full skirt, and with a hat and holdall bag to match. Under this I wore a tight-fitting black woollen dress she had recently made me.

We collected our tickets and set off on the train to Leamington Spa. It was quite a long journey, so when we arrived we checked in at our boarding house and had a brief walk around the town with its elegant buildings, before having something to eat at a riverside cafe.

After our late lunch we strolled along the bank of the river Avon and met two pilots, Maurice and Ted, who joined us and chatted until we reached a little jetty where a man was renting out rowing boats.

'Let's hire a boat and row downstream,' said Maurice.

We all agreed, they paid and helped us into the boat. It was a warm afternoon, so Jenny and I were just in our dresses. We sat on the wooden seat at one end as the boys rowed us around and bantered with us, showing off the skills they didn't seem to have.

'Let's row over to that sunny glade,' suggested Ted.

'Good idea,' agreed Maurice. 'How do you steer this thing?'

They managed to row us in the general direction, but before we reached it, disaster struck. Ted stood up, for a better view of the glade I suppose, just as another boat bumped into us from behind. Our boat wobbled, then overturned and we all fell in! Fortunately, I managed to hang on to my handbag, with both our train tickets and our money in it, or it would have sunk into the murky depths never to be seen again. It was a weedy stretch of the river so Jenny and I got our legs a bit tangled up as we flailed about and tried to swim towards the nearest bank. I wasn't a strong swimmer, so I was anxious that I wouldn't make it without help. Meanwhile, the boys had swum back towards the jetty on the other side.

As we neared our bank, we saw that this was where the fire station was situated. Three burly firemen ran out and leapt into the water, wading out to rescue us. By this time, Jenny and I were shivering from the cold water, and perhaps from shock as well.

As we stood on the bank, we must have been a comical sight, both of us squelching in our sodden clothes, with weeds hanging from our arms and our hair bedraggled.

The firemen led us into their fire station. 'What you need,' said one of them, 'is a good cup of hot, sweet tea and a chance to warm up.'

That sounded good to me. The friendly firemen led us through to a cosy room at the back of the station, made us some sweet tea, then gave us a blanket each and a heater to dry our clothes on.

There was even a lock on the inside of the door, so we were able to take off our sopping wet clothes and put them on a rack in front of the heater. After drying ourselves with towels we draped the firemen's blankets round us to drink our tea. We sat and laughed about our escapade and the pilots. Which one did we each like best? Where had they gone? Would we ever see them again?

Finally, our dresses were dry. I helped Jenny into hers, then she helped me slip mine over my head . . . but that's when my troubles began. The short back zip was undone, so it went over my head all right, but it was a struggle getting my arms into it. That was as far as it went. When I tried to pull it down, it wouldn't go. I couldn't get it over my bust.

'Here, let me help you,' said Jenny, and we both pulled and tugged, in fits of giggles, to no avail.

'My mother made it out of a woollen material,' I said. 'It must have shrunk.' It seemed the more we pulled, the worse it got.

'You are not going to get this dress on,' said Jenny. 'You'll have to go back to the boarding house with a fireman's blanket round you.'

The thought of me in nothing but my underwear and a fireman's blanket sent us off into more fits of giggles. Finally, the firemen asked where we were staying and one of them drove us back there in a fire engine.

'I'll go in first,' said Jenny. 'Just to make sure the coast is clear. Then you can run in when I wave at you.'

'I don't think I'd better run. The blanket might fly up or slip off.'

The lovely fireman, grinning all the way, parked right outside and everything went to plan. The coast was clear, with nobody in the street or in the hallway of the house.

I was so relieved to get back into our room at last and put on the other dress I had brought with me. Phew.

We thought that would be the end of the story, but somehow the pilots found out where we were staying, maybe from the fireman, and they turned up a couple of hours later to take us out dancing. It was their last night of leave and we had a great evening with them. The next day Jenny and I strolled around Leamington again, then we went into a bar and ordered a drink each, to celebrate my birthday. The barman served Jenny all right, but he wouldn't serve me at first.

'You don't look old enough,' he said.

'Well, I am. I was eighteen years old yesterday.'

'If you want me to believe that, you'll have to show me your identity card.'

So I did. 'There, see? I'm now eighteen years old.'

'Sorry, madam,' he said with a rueful smile. 'And happy birthday for yesterday.'

We took our drinks to a table and sipped them while we decided what to do next. We got through the drinks quicker than we'd expected, so we decided to order another – perhaps a cocktail this time. After that, my mind went blank. I don't remember anything, until I woke up in my narrow bed in our room in the boarding house.

Was I dreaming it? I rubbed my eyes, but yes, that's where I was. Jenny was with me and so was the landlady and a middle-aged man wearing a spotted bow tie.

'Thank goodness you've woken up at last,' said Jenny, looking anxious. 'This is the doctor and he's come to see what made you collapse in the bar.'

'What?' I asked in a weak voice that didn't sound at all like me.

'Ssh, don't fret,' said the landlady, a kindly soul.

Now it was the doctor's turn. 'Your friend Jenny tells me you had a couple of drinks to celebrate your eighteenth birthday. Do you remember that?'

'Yes, I remember the first one, but I don't remember whether I drank the second one, or anything after that.' I turned to Jenny. 'How did I get back here?'

'I was so worried about you. I didn't know quite what to do, but the barman called the landlord and he brought us both back here in his car.'

'That was kind.' I tried to smile, to stop her worrying so much. But when I tried to sit up, it was too much of a struggle and I had to lie flat again. The room was spinning.

'You'll need to stay in bed for the rest of the day,' said the doctor. 'And maybe longer.'

'What's the matter with me?' I asked.

'I think it's some kind of flu,' replied the doctor. Did I imagine his slight wink towards the landlady?

Now where had I heard these words before? Some kind of flu . . . Was it a coincidence? I couldn't quite remember.

'Your friend tells me that you both fell in the river yesterday, then went dancing all the evening,' continued the doctor. 'So that might have something to do with it too.'

'Maybe you swallowed some water?' suggested the landlady.

'I wouldn't be surprised,' agreed Jenny.

Well, whatever it was, I had collapsed and been unconscious for several minutes, so the doctor would not let me take the train home until I was well enough. Jenny couldn't stay with me. She had to return the next day as planned, as she had her duties on the farm to get back to.

'Can this young lady stay an extra day or two?' the doctor asked the landlady.

'Yes, I won't charge you for an extra day in the circumstances,' she assured me.

'Thank you,' I replied. 'That's very kind.'

As soon as Jenny got back to Blackburn the next morning, she went straight round to my mother's to explain what had happened. Mother got her friend Alice to have Jeffrey and Alan, so that she could get the train to Leamington Spa to look after me and accompany me back home again. What a palaver it all was, but it certainly turned out to be a memorable eighteenth birthday trip!

15

Let Me Go!

June–December 1944

One day they were at Tony's and the next day they were gone. What had happened? Where did they go? For months now, the GIs had lit up the dance hall, and one evening, without any warning, the place was almost empty. The Americans had been the life and soul of the dance floor, for me anyway. They livened up every party. But now, my friends and I found ourselves competing for the few men in uniform who were left. A few days later, some of those had also disappeared.

The previous weekend, I had overheard Uncle George telling Grandad that there was something going on, some sort of 'campaign to turn around the war'. But then they started whispering and I didn't hear the rest.

The build-up and preparation for something big was unmistakable, but I had no idea what. Even Les, when he had said goodbye that night a week or so ago, had only hinted at some big project coming up, but said nothing more.

*

One evening at the beginning of June 1944, I was walking home with one of the few boys remaining, when the low sound of several planes grew louder and louder.

'There's no air-raid warning,' he said. 'So they must be our planes.'

'They're getting much louder now, like a grinding, unstoppable flood,' I panicked. 'It sounds like they're heading straight for us.'

'Not for us,' he said. 'Beyond us.'

We looked up as the sky grew black with planes.

'There must be hundreds of them,' I gasped in wonderment. 'Where have they come from? Where are they going?'

'Perhaps there are planes flying across other parts of Britain too, going south like these.' He sounded as awestruck as I was.

As we stood there, watching them passing endlessly overhead, my thoughts turned to Les. Maybe he too would be flying his plane southwards. I said a fervent prayer for him and for all of them. It was a night to remember.

It was only days later that I discovered why: 6 June was D-Day – the beginning of our huge campaign to take back Normandy on the way to repelling the Germans from France. It wasn't just RAF and US bombers going south; there were Canadians, Australians and other Allies too. The navy sent troop ships, landing craft, floating bridges and all kinds of seagoing vessels, packed full of men, mostly army, ready with their packs and rifles to land on the beaches of northern France and run for their lives, dodging artillery fire as they headed inland if they could.

I learned all this with interest from the newspaper

hoardings and the radio news bulletins that Mother listened to avidly every night, while she knitted jumpers for the boys. As I sat with her on these evenings, I heard the newsreaders heaping praise on the huge and efficient organization of the Normandy landings, the largest seaborne invasion in history. They told how it involved all three armed services, with backup from US Coast Guards to rescue soldiers wounded or stranded on the beaches or in the water. They also said that the RAF had been bombing the beaches and inland in preparation for D-Day and I wondered whether Les or any of Bobby's friends were involved.

Now he was getting older, twelve-year-old Jeffrey was taking much more interest in the military operations and he was eager to talk about it to Bobby, the next time he came home.

A few days later, I heard on the grapevine, with great sadness, that most of our GI friends had been killed on the D-Day beaches. What lovely men they were. I felt sure I would never forget them.

One evening I was having a quiet night in, catching up on all the letters I had to write to boys in the services, and doing a bit of Fair Isle knitting, which Mother had recently taught me. I was just getting the hang of it when there was a loud, insistent knock on our front door.

'I'll get it,' said Mother. I immediately recognized Peggy's voice, faster and higher than usual.

'Hello, Mrs Holden.' She sounded out of breath. 'Is Margaret in?'

'Yes, she's in the sitting room.'

Peggy burst through. 'Oh Margaret, you'll have to come. It's awful, truly awful . . . and he's asking for you. You'd better come . . . quick.'

Peggy wasn't usually like this, so I knew it must be something serious, but she hadn't given any clues.

'What is it, Peggy? I'll put my cardigan on and come with you. Do I need anything else?'

'No, he's waiting for you . . .' She was so breathless that I thought she must have run all the way here. 'And I had to talk to you first.'

This was becoming more and more mysterious. Even my mother seemed curious and gave me a look as I went out.

'We'll have to hurry, Margaret,' said Peggy as I closed the front door behind us. 'He's been looking for you, so I said I'd come and find you for him.'

I stopped. 'Who is looking for me?'

'Come on, don't keep him there too long. He's waiting for you outside Tony's. I'll tell you as we go.'

'Right, but first tell me who is waiting for me.'

'Arnold Rouston,' she finally managed.

'Ah, that's the good-looking sailor that I made friends with last winter. He's a good dancer too, and . . .'

'Stop, Margaret.' She was strangely insistent. 'You can't think about all that now.'

'Why not?'

'Oh dear. I have to warn you – his face has been badly burned, and his hands, and other parts . . .'

I stopped in disbelief. 'Oh no! How dreadful. He's one of the most handsome boys I know.'

'Was,' she said. 'But you'll have to brace yourself now. Try not to look too shocked when you see him. You must look him in the eyes and try not to appear too upset.'

'Yes, of course. You're right, Peggy.' I paused to think. 'Is it bad? Very bad?'

'Yes, although he's still having treatment, so it will get a bit better over time. But he won't be as you remember him.'

'Well, he has a great personality,' I said, determined to look on the positive side. 'That's what I like most about him.'

Peggy walked part of the way back with me and left me at the corner so that I could go alone to meet Arnold. There he stood, outside Tony's, still wearing his uniform and lit only by the moonlight. He had his back to me. I was determined not to act any differently, so I called his name as I came close and he turned round.

'Hello, Arnold. Peggy came and told me you were back and looking for me, so here I am,' I said, in as bright a voice as I could. He pulled back slightly, as if to protect me from too close a look. His face was a terrible shock, but I didn't turn away. Instead, I tucked my arm in his. 'Let's go inside and have a dance.'

'Are you sure?' he asked. 'I look even worse with the lights on,' he added, with a smile in his voice.

'Not to me,' I reassured him. 'It's you I'm here for, not your face or your hands. Oh, come on, Arnold, let's dance!'

We went inside and spent the rest of the evening on the dance floor. He had always been a nifty dancer and he still was. He might have lost some of his confidence, but he still had his sense of humour, so we had a good evening, catching up with each other as we danced the night away. Other people may have given him looks, or talked behind his back, but I didn't notice.

In the band's break, we went to sit down and Arnold told me about his accident. The fire was caused by one of the giant boilers on his ship and he'd been rescued and taken for treatment, but not before he'd sustained these terrible burns.

'It was just after I saw you in January,' he said. 'I've been in and out of the military hospital ever since. It's not so painful now, and they say they can do some more work on my face to make it look better. I think I may have to go down south for that. I'll never be handsome again, but better than this would be a good start.' He gave me a one-sided smile.

'You'll always be handsome on the inside,' I said. 'What about your hands?'

'I think they're going to do some more work on them too,' he explained. 'Don't worry. They look worse than they feel. And I have some lovely nurses looking after me, so I can't complain!'

I waved Arnold off at the station on 24 July 1944 and went to work with a heavy heart. He needed his friends right now, but I was glad he was going back to the nurses he was so fond of.

Later that day, Leslie Fielding turned up unannounced at Tony's, as he had so often done earlier in the year. We hadn't seen each other since before D-Day, though we had exchanged a lot of letters, so I knew he had lived through it. What a huge relief that was.

The only problem on this evening at Tony's was that when Les arrived, I was dancing and laughing with one of the Americans who had come back from D-Day and I didn't see him come in. In the old days, he would just have lain down to have a sleep. But this evening was different.

When the music stopped, I turned around and there he was, standing watching me from the edge of the dance floor, with a scowl on his face. I went straight over to give him a hug, and he did return it briefly.

'Come on,' he said in a gruff voice, which I'd never heard before. 'Let's get your jacket and I'll walk you home.' Normally I would have said it was too early, or maybe made a quip to cheer him up, but he seemed preoccupied, so I just nodded and collected my jacket. We stepped out into the warm evening air, I tucked my arm into his and we walked along, talking about nothing very much. I was making most of the conversation, as he was unusually quiet.

I felt as if I'd upset him somehow, but couldn't think how unless he was upset to find me dancing and laughing with my American dance partner. Did Les feel jealous? No, I didn't think so – it wasn't like him. Or maybe he thought I should have seen him come in. I assumed it was something I'd done or said and it made me feel guilty. I certainly never wanted to upset him.

He had his head down as we walked and seemed very unhappy. Had he stopped loving me? Was he preparing to 'dump' me? I was really worried and stopped talking, as he didn't seem in the mood for everyday conversation. We turned into Robinson Street and stopped outside my house, as we always did. But Leslie was still distant and it unnerved me.

We kissed outside my door but it seemed different when he pulled away. He stood back and took both my hands in his.

'I can't tell you anything,' he began, 'but I'm sure this is the last time I will see you.' His eyes looked loving for a moment, then steely cold. Something was very wrong and I was trying not to tremble.

'Is it because of the American I was dancing with?' I asked him.

'You can think that if you like,' he replied.

I felt so hurt I couldn't speak.

'This is our last goodbye,' he said with a solemn expression, still holding my hands in his. He kissed me strongly, then abruptly pulled away, turned and strode off down the road. I was bewildered as I watched him walk heavily down Robinson Street. I waited to wave him off at the corner, as usual, but he didn't turn round. He just quickened his pace round the corner and out of sight. Selfishly, I felt let down and very hurt.

As I went to bed that night, I thought it all through and couldn't work it out. Was it really the last time? Why? Les was not a petty sort of man. He'd never complained before when I danced with all the boys while he was resting on Tony's couch. Why now? Perhaps he'd just gone off me.

*

Three days later, when I'd just got back from work, there was an urgent-sounding knock at our door. It was Jackie Fielding, Leslie's brother, with a letter in his hand. As soon as I saw the official envelope I had a horrible premonition. My heart was racing, as Jackie read out the letter to us, announcing the death of Flight Sergeant Leslie Fielding on 29 July 1944. He had been on a major raid to bomb Stuttgart when his Lancaster plane was shot down over Northern France, exploding in the air before any of the crew had a chance to escape, other than the pilot, who was the only survivor and was taken prisoner.

I turned cold. Mother had come in and heard most of what Jackie read out.

'I'm so sorry, Margaret,' he said. 'But Les told us that if anything happened to him, we were to come round and tell you straight away.'

'Thanks, Jackie,' I said, numb with shock. 'I appreciate that.'

After he left, I confided in Mother how I felt about Les. I told her about his last visit, suddenly realizing that it was just the evening before that final night's raid, only hours before he was killed. At that moment, I had a great urge to be on my own and ran up the stairs to my bedroom, closed the door and lay on my bed.

How could I have been so heartless? It was as if he knew he was going to be killed. He clearly knew that he would be on a massive mission, involving thousands of Allied planes bombing all German cities repeatedly over five nights. Les had been killed on the fifth and last night. Could he have known he would be killed? A premonition, perhaps? Is that why he was so quiet and distant with me? Or was he deliberately trying to make me cross with him, perhaps to cushion the inevitable outcome? I wouldn't put it past him. He was always so caring and protective of me. Maybe he thought his aloofness would make it less painful for me to hear he'd been killed. He'd once told me the average life expectancy of aircrew in bombers at that time was four raids. I knew he had done over one hundred.

I had so many thoughts going round and round in my head that evening. My emotions too were all over the place – shock and grief, of course, but also a great sadness that our final goodbye had been so unsatisfactory and upsetting for us both. Why was I so thoughtless as to leave him feeling insecure, and maybe even unloved, the very day above all others when he needed to feel confident and positive? I was ashamed of myself. He must have felt so miserable walking home alone that night and then travelling back to the airfield. He must have felt even more miserable on that flight. And it was all my fault. I wasn't quite sure how it had happened, but I had to take at least some of the blame.

If only he had survived that raid and come back. I was certain that all would have been forgiven and forgotten. We would have been back to normal and happy again . . . but it wasn't to be. Only he knew the ending and he did his best to prepare me for it.

Thus my close companion for several intense weeks – the man who wanted to marry me one day, and yes, the man I was in love with – Flight Sergeant Leslie Fielding, had been killed on a clear summer's night, 29 July 1944.

I gulped and the tears came. He was only twenty-two, a great friend and companion who could have had a fine future. I wasn't quite as sure as he was that we would have married after the war, but he was very special to me and I would never forget him.

Losing Leslie like that made me feel restless. I couldn't settle at anything. All these boys were going off to fight for our benefit, but what was I doing to help the war effort?

It came to me one day. I should give up my cosy job at the Post Office and go and do 'war work'. Quite what kind of war work I could do, I didn't know, but I asked around and found out what there was in the Blackburn area.

I worked out my notice at the Post Office, had a good send-off, and the following day I turned up to clock in – or was it clock on? – for the first time in my life, at the fuse factory.

I'd never seen anything like it. I had to wear a green overall and a green hat thing pulled over my head to keep my hair away from the machinery. It clearly wasn't designed to hold my curly hair, which kept bursting out. We made lorry-doll fuse light strips, whatever they were. I never saw the finished product as I only worked on one part. It was nearly all women in the factory, but there were a few men. The manager, Mr Greenwood, went to the same church as me and knew my father and his side of the family. He also knew I had been a pupil at the convent, which was rather unusual in his factory.

Mr Greenwood would go around the factory floor every day, talking to all the staff. I worked on the capstan lathe machine. I stood on a box, with a wheel to my right that I had to spin, which sent a rod through the machine, then it was washed and cooled by some white, soapy liquid. In my first break, one of the girls told me that I hadn't to do it too well, or they would be out of a job, so I tried to keep that in mind. It wasn't difficult, because I really struggled to make the machine work properly and was always catching my fingers on the rough bits, so it wasn't long before I had pretty well all of them bandaged up! I had a great time there chatting to the other girls, but I was hopeless with all the mechanical bits and pieces. I'm just not cut out for that sort of thing. But I did persevere, and finally got the knack of it.

One night at Tony's, in autumn 1944, my friend Kathleen Brown introduced me to her latest boyfriend, Joe, the most handsome boy in the room. He spent most of the evening with her and walked her home. A few days later, however, Kathleen and Joe had split up and he came and asked me to dance. Well, I thought that was great. Joe had it all. He was in the Coldstream Guards, a talented athlete, the life and soul of any party, a good singer . . . and he seemed able to do anything one could want. He was so good-looking, with his blond hair and bright-blue eyes, that he had all the girls gravitating around him. Tony Billington's wife used to call him a 'Greek god'. She would say, 'Where's the Greek god tonight?' But from that evening on, he seemed to have eyes only for me. I was very flattered.

All my friends, especially Peggy and Irene, would have loved Joe to dance with them, but he always asked me. When he started to take me out on dates or to any of the dance halls, Peggy and my other friends admitted they were all envious of me. His dancing was very good. He did everything better than most and he could be great fun, but there turned out to be a darker side to him too.

I could soon tell Joe was getting serious. He was about Bobby's age, so five years older than me, and I thought it was probably the war that made him think it was time for him to settle down. But what about me? I was only eighteen, and, crucially, I didn't love Joe. I don't know what it was. I liked him. I liked the idea. Let's be honest, he was an Adonis, wanted by everyone, and I liked the idea of 'he's mine!' But I didn't want a serious relationship and Joe did, though I didn't realize it until he pretended to ask me to marry him – at least, I thought he was pretending.

We were standing on my doorstep at the end of an evening.

'Did you know that Tony's wife calls you "the Greek god"?' I asked him.

'Does she?' he said with a grin, then got down on one knee, still laughing. 'In that case, will you marry me and be my Greek goddess?' he asked with what I took to be mock seriousness.

I was embarrassed in case anyone came along or my mother came out, and I was sure he was joking, so I said, 'Oh, all right. Now get up off our step and say goodnight.'

'Let's go to Manchester tomorrow and buy you a ring,'

he suggested with a grin. 'And we could have a nice lunch there to celebrate, then go and see a film.'

'All right,' I agreed – anything to get him away home!

But as I went in, it sounded like a good day out, so I was glad. It just didn't occur to me that he really meant any of it. I thought that if we bought a ring, it would be a penny ring from Woolworths, just for fun.

So that's what we did, except it was a jeweller's, which surprised me. I chose the cheapest pretty ring they had and, with what I took to be mock ceremony, he put it on my finger. I always liked jewellery, so that's how I saw it really, as enjoying ourselves rather than as a serious commitment. In my mind it was nothing more than carrying on the joke with, at most, a temporary 'engagement' until Ray returned.

We had a lovely lunch and found a cinema that was showing *Meet me in St Louis*. Being Manchester, it cost us five shillings each, so it was an expensive day, but it was fun.

'Let's go in and tell your mother,' he said, when we got back home that evening.

'Tell her what?' I asked, laughing.

'About our engagement, of course.'

'Oh, all right. If we must.' I was obviously very naive, as I still thought this a continuation of the charade. But it turned quite serious when we got inside.

'Hello, Mrs Holden,' he began. 'I've asked Margaret to marry me and she has said yes. Will you give us your blessing?'

Mother looked at me with a surprised expression. I

gave a slight shrug, hoping to suggest I wasn't necessarily in agreement.

She turned back to Joe.

'Well, Joe, Margaret can get engaged as often as she likes, but she hasn't to marry till she's twenty-one.'

Looking back, I can see I should have made clear that this was all a misunderstanding, but at the time I failed to take the initiative . . . and then it was too late.

Once it was in his mind that we were engaged, Joe changed. He became very possessive and jealous. He seemed to want to control me, but I wasn't having any of that. I already had a possessive brother, which I could cope with because I knew he had always been like that, out of love for me. But I couldn't take it from Joe.

When he saw me talking with my old crowd the next evening at Tony's, including a couple of boys home on leave, Joe erupted: 'You've got to stop talking to other boys.'

'But they're just old friends,' I explained.

'I will not have you talking with any other boys. I don't care who they are. You're mine now and you do as I say. You only talk to me.'

I wasn't going to let anybody stop me from talking with my friends, so I decided I had to try and break off this engagement. However, knowing him better now, I was afraid he might be angry if I just told him that I wanted to call it off and gave back his ring. So I came up with an idea that I thought would put him off me.

We still used to meet at Tony's a lot, so instead of walking in on my own, or just with my girlfriends, I thought I could occasionally arrange to meet up with other boys, big, strong ones, who were good friends and who understood my predicament, so that they could walk me in. With luck, Joe might realize I wasn't serious about him, or anyone else.

So one evening I asked Bert Cave, a Lancaster pilot who had been a prisoner of war, to come with me. He had recently arrived back from Germany following an exchange of prisoners. Bert was good fun and I enjoyed his company. I walked to Tony's with him and I was laughing with him as we walked in. I looked across at Joe, whose expression changed to a black look . . . and not just at me. At that moment I feared for Bert and maybe even for myself, as Joe raced across the room, took my arm and pulled me aside, before picking a fight with Bert.

'Quick, hurry,' I said to Bert, 'you've got to get away.' But he only took a few steps outside, then hesitated and turned, worried about me. Joe flashed across the road, socked him a punch and knocked Bert right over the wall. I realized I couldn't try that again.

The relationship was all very on–off, as far as I could make it. I hadn't meant to get engaged to Joe and hadn't recognized his mercurial nature, nor his jealousy and possessiveness. In his good moments, I liked him and enjoyed his company, especially amongst a crowd of friends. I liked seeing strangers turn their heads at his chiselled good looks and his confidence. I liked all the girls being impressed that I was going out with him, engaged or not. But I didn't love him and couldn't help flirting with other boys from time to time – it was just part of my nature. I should have realized, though, after what happened to Bert, how it would make Joe's anger boil up to the surface.

One night, at a special dance, his frustrations came to a head. I remember I was wearing a long pale-blue evening dress at the time, and was dancing and flirting with an American GI, while Joe was with my crowd of friends, entertaining them with one of his stories. Joe saw me and stepped onto the dance floor towards us. My partner saw him coming and rushed off to the gents, followed hotfoot by Joe, who cornered him there and started a fight with him. The band played as loudly as they could, but they couldn't drown the shouts. I knew it was all about me, and I felt bad about it, but I couldn't do anything. Feeling trapped, I slipped away and set off for home. It was a moonlit night and I was walking as quickly as I could, but my evening dress and shoes slowed me down. I hadn't got far when I heard a man's running footsteps behind me. Joe caught up with me, took hold of my arm and pushed me roughly into a doorway.

'No, Joe. Let me go!' I shrieked. 'You're hurting me.'

He had his hands round my neck and tightened his grip. I froze, but I knew I had to get away, somehow. I remember the terrible fear as I tried to struggle, but he wouldn't let me go.

'If I didn't love you so much,' he said, 'I would kill you.'

He held me like that for what seemed like several minutes, his steely eyes staring into mine, piercing right through me. I wanted to shout for help, but I could barely breathe and I felt like I was going to faint. I suppose he must have realized . . . and loosened his grip. I saw my chance and, with a supreme effort, I pulled myself loose, but slipped on the doorstep. Realizing I was trying to escape, he put his foot firmly on the hem of my dress. I struggled as he pinned me to the door again and expressed his fury. 'Did you hear me?'

I nodded.

'You are engaged to me now, so I don't want you to go out with any other boy, or even dance with them. You should not even speak to any other boy, unless you are with me. We are engaged, so you belong to me now; remember that!' He paused again for my answer.

'Yes,' I said, trying to stall him, as I looked for an opportunity to escape. Finally, he let go of my neck and I slipped right down to the ground. To help me up, he took my hand, more gently this time, but I summoned enough strength and pulled free of his grip at last. I ran and ran, all the way home. I think he may have been following me, to make sure I was all right, but I didn't dare stop till I got through our front door, to the safety of our fireside, where my mother was sewing in her rocking chair.

She must have realized something was wrong. I was out of breath, dishevelled, and I noticed her gaze went straight to the large footprint on the bottom of my pale-blue dress, then back up at my face with a silent question mark.

'It's all right,' I said. 'It was just Joe, having a tantrum.'

I don't know why I tried to make light of the danger I had been in. Perhaps because it already seemed unreal. We never spoke about it again, but I knew for certain now that I had to break up with Joe.

I stayed away from Tony's the next day, but the day after I met Joe there and told him that, instead of dancing, I wanted to get a drink of lemonade and sit down at a table. I had thought about what I wanted to say, so I plucked up my courage and began by taking off my ring.

'Joe, I'm really sorry,' I started. 'I didn't know you were serious when you asked me to marry you. Because you were joking around, I thought it was just a stunt, a bit of fun.' I could see his face reddening and his mouth open to speak. 'Please just let me finish,' I said. 'I never meant for all this to happen and I certainly didn't want to upset you. But in the circumstances, I am asking you to accept that our engagement is off.' I placed the ring on the table and slid it across towards him. 'It's a beautiful ring, but I'm sorry I didn't realize you meant it to be an engagement ring.'

He looked as if he was going to explode at me. I was a bit scared, but determined not to show it.

'I'm really sorry, Joe,' I repeated.

He opened his mouth, but said nothing . . . Then he dropped his shoulders and gave in. He just nodded. He must have realized that shouting in a place like this would do no good.

'Keep the ring,' he suddenly said, shoving it back towards me. Then he got up, pushed past the table and walked away.

I felt as if a huge weight had been lifted from my shoulders.

At the end of his leave, Joe went back to the war and I went back to the dance hall, feeling free again.

In late 1944, Kathleen Cronshaw and I decided to go on a short trip to Blackpool. On the first evening, we were dancing in the Tower Ballroom when we met George Slack, who was a singer with the RAF Entertainment Troupe. He sang brilliantly, but he was also a good dancer, so we got on well and started to write to each other.

A few weeks later he wrote that his troupe were bringing their show to the Grand Theatre in Blackburn as part of an evening performance. With this advance notice, I was able to buy tickets for the front row downstairs, for Kathleen, me, Mother and her friend Alice Westwell. I had recently found out that Alice's brother Sydney was serving on HMS *Maidstone*, the mother ship for Raymond's submarine. I could hardly believe this coincidence as I knew him well, and it definitely brought me closer to Ray. It's a small world, isn't it?

On the night of the show, we dressed up and went to settle in our seats, ready for it to start. Alex Munro, a well-known popular Scottish comedian, was the host of the show, introducing each act. It was what was called a variety show, so it included comedians, magicians and all sorts of other performers.

Finally it was George's moment, as he came onto the stage and started straight into a medley of Italian songs. He had a beautiful, lilting voice. For his final number he came to the front of the stage, dropped on one knee right in front of me and sang an Italian love-song, looking straight at me. Then he produced a single red rose and leant across to pass it to me.

'For you, Margaret.'

Embarrassed in front of this large audience, which included many people I knew, I stood up, reached across and took it.

Alex Munro strode onto the stage and said, for all to hear: 'Come on, Margaret. Put him out of his misery and say "yes".'

This was all good-natured fun, but it was never serious. I described it all to Ray in my letter that evening. Throughout his time away – nearly two years now without seeing him – we had kept up our correspondence almost daily, and our affection for each other had grown into a pure and abiding love. We both treasured plans for the future – the rest of our lives together. Why had he still not been allowed any leave? And when would we finally meet again? I yearned for him to come home and hold me close.

16

The Worst Tragedy

1945

Christmas 1944 was more upbeat than the earlier wartime Christmases. Since D-Day, things had been progressing well for the Allies, who were driving back the enemy. We really felt this might be our last wartime Christmas.

But in the meantime we had to maintain our patience and frugality for just a little while longer, or so we thought. Rations had been gradually reduced throughout the war and were now at their lowest levels. As a family, we continued to receive fresh food grown by Grandma and Grandad Harrison or procured by them from nearby farms: all surplus to rations, of course, but it was a very different story for most people in Blackburn. Even if they had a ration coupon for butter (two ounces per person per week), or eggs (one egg per young or elderly person per week), there was no guarantee they would be available at their designated shop. Every individual was entitled to a maximum of one shilling and two pennies' worth of meat – the equivalent of two chops – per week, which was much lower than when rationing started in 1940, and there was often little choice of meat. I don't know how we would have managed without the dozen eggs from Grandad's hens or the pound of butter and the slab of cheese made at their friends' farm. Businesses too were suffering more than at any previous time during the war, especially from the rationing of paper and petrol.

On the morning of New Year's Day 1945, I had an unexpected visit at home from Arnold Rouston. This was a very welcome surprise and I could see considerable improvements to the scars on his face and hands. They were still badly disfigured and always would be, but it was wonderful to see what the medics had done to help him.

'I've had some more operations at a specialist burns unit in East Grinstead, where everyone is in the forces, and we made a jolly crowd while we were there, all bandaged up and cracking jokes nineteen to the dozen.'

'Your scars certainly look less angry than last time I saw you,' I said. 'It's quite a miracle really, how much better and more comfortable your face looks. Does it feel better for you?'

'Yes, and they say they can still do a bit more here and there.'

'I do admire your positive attitude, Arnold.'

'Thank you. But I reckon it's the only way.'

'How long are you here for?' I asked, thinking we might go out somewhere.

'For a couple of days, mainly with the family,' he replied. 'But we could maybe go dancing at Tony's one night if you like?'

'Yes please, that would be great – just like old times.'

'Well, not quite!'

'Oh, I'm sorry . . .'

'It's fine. Don't worry. I was only teasing.' He took a deep breath and told me the real reason for his visit. 'I'm not on my own this time. I've brought someone special with me to meet my family. In fact, she's with them now. And you've been such a good friend to me, Margaret, over the past few months, that I'd like to introduce her to you as well. Can I bring her round at four-ish this afternoon?'

Ooh, that sounds exciting, I thought. Could it be? Well, I'd soon find out. 'Yes please, that will be a perfect time to come. If she's special to you, I'd love to meet her. What a lovely start to the new year.'

'Yes, very special. She nursed me with great care and dedication for several months in the hospital, after I was first wounded . . . and now she's agreed to marry me!'

'That's wonderful,' I exclaimed, giving him an impromptu hug.

'Yes, isn't it? I'm the luckiest man alive.'

As I waited to greet them with scones and tea that afternoon, I was still feeling delighted at Arnold's wonderful news. This nurse had obviously grown to know and love him for what he was, a remarkable individual, without any comparisons to his good looks before. What a wonderful person the woman must be.

And indeed she was. They arrived arm in arm.

'This is Eunice, my fiancée,' Arnold said as they came in. She was a pretty girl – petite like me, with auburn hair.

'I'm so glad to meet you, Eunice. Come on through to the front room.'

'It's lovely to meet you too,' she said, giving Arnold's arm a squeeze before they sat down close to each other on the sofa.

'Show Margaret your engagement ring,' he suggested, and grinned as she held out her hand.

'Arnold chose it before he asked me to marry him,' she explained. 'And he couldn't have chosen better.' She gave him a conspiratorial smile. 'Did you tell Margaret how we met?'

'Yes, but I didn't tell her how I proposed.'

'Oh yes,' she giggled. 'Well. He did it the old-fashioned way, in a tea room, down on one knee,' she told me.

'And some of the other customers started clapping,' said Arnold with a grin.

'Only he lost his balance and toppled over.'

'Yes, and I dropped the ring,' he added. 'It rolled across the floor, under the tables, and before long we had nearly everyone on the floor searching for it!'

'Did you find it all right?'

'Yes, we did,' replied Arnold. 'And a good job too, or we might not be engaged now!' They exchanged loving glances.

Eunice was a lovely girl and I was so pleased for Arnold. They evidently adored each other, but I couldn't help feeling pangs of deep sadness. The way they were with each other reminded me of the special closeness Ray and I had shared in those last months before he left for the war. It wasn't that I was jealous – not at all. I was delighted for Arnold in his new happiness, but if only Ray could come home. I longed for that time . . . for his handsome smile and his loving kisses.

I'd had time now to think about things and I knew that my love for Leslie had been different from what I felt about Ray. Yes, I loved them both, but whilst Leslie was the serious wartime romance, which was very real for a time, Ray was the one I always knew would be there for me in the long term, the one who would love me unconditionally, and I him . . . even if we had to wait till the end of the war. But it was a long time. If only he could be allowed some leave . . .

The following day, I had a long, loving letter from Ray, from somewhere under the Indian Ocean. That was all he could tell me about his location, of course. He wrote about the fantastic Christmas lunch they had been given on his submarine. By the sound of it, they were eating a lot better than we were in Britain, with our meagre rations! Later in the day, he wrote, the whole crew put on a talent show for themselves and each other. Ray was good at so many things that I wondered what he had chosen to do for it. I sat down straight away to write back and ask him. I could also tell him about Arnold and the lovely news about his engagement.

Ray had written this letter on the evening of Christmas Day and he said that they were going on special exercises, so he would keep writing me letters, as always, but I was not to worry if I didn't hear from him for a couple of weeks or so, as they would be out of contact for at least

that long. This seemed to be nothing unusual for submariners, so I looked forward to an avalanche of letters
all at once, whenever they finally arrived.

'But what about his leave?' I wanted to scream across
the oceans at his commanding officer. I knew Ray had
put in several written requests for leave over the nearly
two years that he'd been away, but he said that he wasn't
the only one who had been refused, so there wasn't much
we could do. It seemed that the best we could hope for
would be an early end to the war.

The days passed slowly, with no news from Ray; then,
in the last week of January, I heard the letter box bang
and found two letters on the mat. I picked them up,
puzzled to recognize my own handwriting and Raymond's
address. Then I saw the words stamped across them in
black: *Missing, presumed dead.*

'What?' I gasped, and turned cold. I must have cried
out, because Mother hurried through to the hall to see
what had happened. By now I was shaking, so I handed
her the letters.

'What does that mean?' I asked her, in a confusion of
fear and disbelief. 'Surely they can't presume someone is
dead? If they don't know he's dead, he could easily still
be alive . . . couldn't he?' I was clutching at straws, because
I needed to. 'Surely there's a good chance that some junior
clerk has stamped this on a lot of envelopes, without
checking if they are all correct?' I could hear my voice
rising to a near-hysterical pitch. 'It must be wrong . . .
mustn't it?'

'Well . . .' Mother paused, as she led me to sit down

and sat with me, wondering how to respond. 'I very much hope it's wrong,' she said. 'But I'm afraid you must try to steel yourself . . .' Uncharacteristically, she put her arm round me. That meant a lot, but it couldn't change the words.

That awful phrase, 'missing, presumed dead', might as well have been a knife to my heart. I couldn't think of anything else.

'I wonder whether Alice could find out,' she suggested. 'I'll be seeing her tomorrow. If you remember, Alice's brother is on the supply ship for Raymond's submarine, HMS *Porpoise*.'

'Yes, maybe she can ask?'

'But he might not be able to tell us anything, if it was a secret mission, or something like that.'

I was desperate to know now, but of course it might take time. 'Do you think Ray's parents would know anything?' I asked.

'They may do, if the War Office has contacted them direct.'

I tossed and turned in my bed nearly all night, the dreaded phrase continually running through my mind, along with all the possible ways I desperately hoped it could be wrong. Maybe tomorrow I would get a letter from him, to show he was alive . . . but I didn't. I went to work as I always did, but I was in a state all day and probably got everything wrong. I walked back home in a daze. Not knowing was surely even worse than knowing, except that there was a small chink of hope.

Poor Ray, far from home and desperate to get back to see me again, while I had been able to carry on dancing with all the boys in uniform. This thought made me feel terribly guilty. But in the months since Les's tragic death, I had focused my thoughts and future hopes back on Ray, who had never wavered in his love for me, nor I in mine for him. We both wrote of our longing for the war to end, bringing nearer the time when we could be together again at last. Now that dream was turning into a nightmare.

I let myself in, calling out, 'It's only me.' I could hear voices in the front room, but I didn't feel like talking to visitors. As I took off my coat, Mother came out into the hall.

'Ray's father is here,' she said.

My heart leapt with hope. 'Have they found him? Is he alive?'

My mother looked stunned, then gave a very slight shake of her head . . . and my hopes plummeted.

'Come and join him. I'll go and make us all some tea.'

I walked into the front room, just as Raymond's father stood up. We took one look at each other and hugged. Neither of us spoke at first. It was a great comfort for me, and I think for him too, that we could share that moment without the need for words.

Ever since Ray and I first played together, we had often been to each other's houses and came to know each other's parents well. Mr Nash felt more like family to me than some of my blood relations.

'Is it true?' I asked him as we both sat down. 'Can he be dead?'

'Yes, Margaret. I'm afraid it is true,' he said in a gentle voice.

The shock was like a physical punch to the stomach. I could barely breathe.

'That's why I wanted to come round straight away to tell you what we know.'

'Thank you,' I whispered.

'Your mother tells me you had a couple of letters returned with that terrible message stamped on them?'

'Yes. I thought it must be wrong,' I said.

'So did we.'

'I was so shocked when I saw it – I couldn't believe it. I still can't,' I added. 'I suppose that's because I don't want to.'

'You've put that very well,' he said. 'We feel just the same. Raymond's mother would have liked to come with me to see you, but she is so distraught that she cannot leave the house at the moment. I'm sure you of all people can understand that, Margaret.'

'Yes,' I nodded, with tears in my eyes. 'It must be terrible for her.'

He put his hand in his jacket's inside pocket and took out a buff-coloured envelope. 'We received the telegram from the War Office yesterday afternoon, but we were all so upset that I couldn't even come round to let you know, and anyway, we didn't know anything about what had happened.' He paused to open the envelope. 'This is the official letter we received today from the War Office. It doesn't say much.' He unfolded it to show me, but the print seemed to swim in front of my eyes.

'Could you please just tell me what it says?' I asked him.

'Yes. It seems that HMS *Porpoise* travelled on the surface to this position and submerged for Raymond and the rest of the crew to lay mines in the sea. It doesn't say where, but I think it was probably somewhere off Malaya. When they had finished, they surfaced again and a lone Japanese fighter pilot saw the submarine. His crew loosed a bomb. That was all it took – one plane with one bomb. It was a direct hit and badly damaged the submarine, which sank below the surface, leaking oil. Then two more attacks followed and dispatched the ailing submarine, which sank with all hands. It now lies on the bottom of the ocean.'

He looked up to see if I was all right. 'The only nugget of comfort I take from this,' he said, 'is that if there was an explosion, Raymond and all the crew could not have had time to realize what was happening. They almost certainly would have died immediately.'

I wasn't sure whether Mr Nash was just saying that to give me some consolation, but I could see that it might have been true. I desperately wanted it to be true.

'This letter also says,' continued Mr Nash, 'that Raymond's personal possessions, which he left on the support ship, will be gathered together, listed and sent back to us.' He paused. 'I will let you know, Margaret, when they arrive. I've talked about this with my wife, and we would both like you to choose something of his to keep.'

'Thank you,' I said. 'That is very kind, but . . .'

'We insist,' he interrupted. 'It's what Raymond would have wanted.'

I nodded, the tears trickling silently down my face.

As I closed the front door after him, I knew I had to accept the facts. John Raymond Nash, aged twenty, had been killed in action. It was a shock of immeasurable proportion. I went up to my bedroom to be alone for a while. I was devastated by this terrible news and needed time to myself to think.

Throughout the two years since Ray had gone to war, we had corresponded as often as his submarine's locations would allow, growing ever closer, sharing an understanding that we would be back together again for good one day. I'd known Ray since he was in short pants. He was my first love, my best friend and my sweetheart – the child I played with, the boy I danced with and the young man I had assumed I would marry one day.

When Les died, I told Ray all about it, pouring out some of my sadness and sense of guilt in my letters to him, all of which Ray nobly understood. He really was a very special person. He knew me so well. We were always together and expected to stay that way. Our families and friends knew we were inseparable . . . or had been, until the day after his eighteenth birthday, when Ray went to war. And now I would never see him again.

A few days later, Mr Nash came round again and I took him through to the front room.

'A box of Raymond's possessions has arrived from the

War Office,' he told me. 'And there is a package with a label on it for you. We haven't opened it. I was going to bring it with me, but my wife would especially like to give it to you herself.'

'Thank you.'

'She still refuses to go out. She is too upset and the doctor has said she should stay at home and rest.' He paused, with a worried frown. 'I'm afraid she doesn't want to see anybody . . . except for you. She particularly asked me to invite you to visit her at our house, when you are free.' He paused. 'It would mean so much to her to see you and share her memories of him with you.'

'Yes, I will come,' I promised. 'Perhaps after work tomorrow – about half past five?'

'Yes. Thank you, Margaret. That will be perfect. We'll see you then.'

The path from our house to Raymond's was so familiar to me and as I walked it once more, down Robinson Street and round the corner, it was impossible to believe my childhood sweetheart would never again be there to greet me. I knocked on the door and it was opened almost immediately. Mr Nash welcomed me into their sitting room, where his wife was sitting in an easy chair by the fire. 'Hello, Mrs Nash,' I said with a sympathetic half-smile as she wiped away her tears and held her arms out. I gave her a long hug. Finally, as she loosened her grip, I sat down on the chair beside her.

She turned to pick up a long brown-paper package in her trembling hands and showed it reverently to me. 'There,' she said with a weak smile. 'Look,' she added, pointing at a label. I saw my name, Margaret Holden, written very carefully in Raymond's best handwriting. My heart lurched. I would have recognized his handwriting anywhere.

I hesitated to take it.

'Please,' urged his father. 'He left it especially for you.'

This time I let his mother pass it to me and I held it in my hands, knowing that he had held it too. I gently traced his writing with my fingertip, gulping the air, my tears trickling down my cheeks. 'If you don't mind, Mrs Nash, I'll open it later.'

'Yes, quite right,' she said kindly. 'Best to open it on your own.'

'Thank you for being so understanding.'

I could tell from their expressions they were disappointed I didn't want to open it whilst there with them. But I didn't think I could cope with that. I stayed and had a cup of tea with them, however, and we reminisced about the days when Ray and I played, carefree, around the neighbourhood, coming back into one or other of our houses at regular intervals for refuelling with snacks and drinks.

Finally, it was time to go, so I said my goodbyes and promised to visit them both again soon.

I went straight home, where I took the package upstairs to my bedroom and shut the door. I placed it gently on the bed and sat next to it, just looking at it. I don't know how long it was before I touched it again. It was long and soft on the outside, with something small and hard in the middle. As I traced my name again, I imagined him writing this himself, in his quarters on the submarine. I touched the wrapping where he must have touched it himself, when he was doing up the string. A shiver went through my body. This was torture.

Finally I decided to open the parcel. I suddenly had an idea of what might be inside it, something that he had written about in one of his letters, to form part of our future plans.

I took a little while to unknot the string, as I didn't want to tear the paper, especially where he had so lovingly written my name. I set aside the string and unfolded the brown paper, inside which I found another layer of tissue paper. I carefully opened that out to reveal the most beautiful white lace I had ever seen. Unlike some of the English lace I'd touched, this was feather-soft and delicate, intricately patterned in what I guessed was an oriental style.

The tears fell once again as I gently opened out the lace, one fold at a time, to reveal a small, separately wrapped package between the layers. This was the hard item I had felt earlier . . . and now I knew what it was.

Raymond wrote in a letter that he had bought a length of white lace for my wedding dress and I sobbed as I held it against me. What a beautiful dress my mother could have made out of it . . . but it was not to be. Exquisite as it was, I could never wear it now.

I hesitated for a moment when it came to the small package, but I knew it held the rings that Raymond had also written about buying for me, for our special day. Part of me thought I'd rather not see them, but my curiosity got the better of me and I undid the box to reveal two gold rings. One plain, and the other a solitaire diamond, beautifully cut and sparkling, set on a matching band of gold. I tried them on. They were a perfect fit. How did he manage that? I wore them for only a few sad seconds, then put them away again and wrapped the package up to look as it was before.

It upset me too much to have this in my room, so I asked Mother to look after it for me. When I came back from work the following day, I collected that precious package and took it back to Raymond's parents.

'I'm really sorry,' I said as I handed it back to Mrs Nash. 'But I did undo it all to see what it was. It was a length of beautiful white lace that he told me in one of his letters he had bought for my wedding dress. And inside that were two rings – engagement and wedding rings.' The tears were running down my cheeks again. 'It was lovely to see it all, but I'll never feel able to wear them, so I'd rather you look after it for me, or use the material for something else.'

They both looked sadly at me. 'But why, Margaret?' asked Raymond's mother.

'Because it would upset me too much to keep it in my house,' I explained. 'I hope you understand.'

'I see – yes, of course we understand,' she assured me.

'Yes, I can see how much these things must have upset you, but Raymond left them for you, so we shall be their keepers, until you want to take them back again,' said his father. 'You'll always be welcome here,' he added. 'We always thought of you as our future daughter-in-law, and I see no need to change that.'

'And I agree,' echoed Mrs Nash.

I was relieved that they had taken it so well and grateful for their encouragement to come and see them whenever I wanted.

Walking home, however, I felt lost and guilty. I had lived for the day, having fun, while he was imprisoned in a large metal box under the sea, far from everyone and everything he loved. And now that metal box had become his tomb.

Although Raymond's body would never be recovered, his parents still wanted to have a proper funeral for him. I too felt bereft. So when I received a note from them, asking me to attend his funeral, I knew I had to be there. In those days, it was not permitted for a Roman Catholic to attend a service in any other Christian church, so I went to see the priest at my church and explained the situation. It was wartime, and he understood. He approached the bishop and I was given special dispensation to attend the C. of E. church for Raymond's funeral.

Raymond's funeral service was conducted at St Stephen's Church in Little Harwood, by our friend George Heaton's father. I was close to tears throughout the service, but especially when the vicar mentioned my name with Raymond's, as always being inseparable, until the war parted us. That went straight to my heart. It was very hard, but also very special. He was always with me as we grew up, and I have thought of him every day, ever since. This hasn't stopped me living my life, enjoying my days, but I have never forgotten my first love.

Although Raymond Nash had no grave, other than the submarine in which he lived and died, his name is remembered, engraved on the Royal Naval Memorial on Plymouth Hoe.

17

The Palais Glide

1945

It was January 1945. The snow fell and lay thick on the ground, bringing the buses and trams to a halt. But the most urgent requirement for us was our outside lavatory. It was the only lavatory we had for up to five people, when Bobby was home on leave.

One Friday night the snow was particularly heavy, with a strong wind. When I got up the next morning and opened the back door, leading into the yard, the snow had drifted so high that it was over the door. This was not funny when the lavatory was at the far end of the yard, next to the coal bunker.

Thank goodness for a good fire, despite the scarcity of coal. It also heated the water in our back boiler. Mother and I first had to dig out a path to get to the lavatory, which we had to make sure didn't become slippery. We then had to heat up extra bucketfuls of water on the fire to carry out to the lavatory to melt the ice in it, before anyone could use it.

Jeffrey came down and helped us dig, while Alan, who

was still only five and full of mischief, decided the best way to help would be to make snowballs and pelt his brother with them. Meanwhile, Mother swept the path as clean and dry as she could while I brought through the containers of steaming water, trying my best not to slip nor to slop any of it out to scald any of us.

Once we had the lavatory in working order, temporarily at least, we could then get on with our day. It wasn't too bad if the snow fell on a weekend, but I do remember one snowy week when there was no bus running to my war-work factory in Lower Darwen. I had to muffle myself up in the warmest clothes I had, pull on my thickest socks, my stoutest shoes and hat, then set off to trudge all the way – about four miles – through the snow to work. My legs, bare above my socks, smarted from the biting cold. Some days, the snow was so thick that I didn't arrive till nearly lunchtime. I did maybe an hour or two of work, and then had to set off back home to Blackburn again. On one frightening day everything was so white, like a fantasy land, that I got lost, walking in circles until I finally found a landmark to steer me back in the right direction.

My mother sometimes listened to the radio and kept me up to date with whatever was going on – mostly news of the war. I didn't take too much notice, now that Ray would never come back. I had lost the two most important loves of my life, so now I put my energies into enjoying the dances and my friends – anything to brighten my days, and other people's too.

*

In the spring, Joe came home on leave. He came round to our house, hoping to pick up where he thought we had left off. I had written the occasional letter to him while he was away, just because I wrote to all the boys to cheer them up . . . and perhaps also, in a strange way, because I felt guilty that I couldn't return his love. But my letters to Joe were all about Blackburn gossip and people he knew and nothing about anything personal or about the future, which I certainly didn't intend to spend with him.

He still refused to accept that we were not engaged and insisted on my wearing his ring. He got so cross if I didn't that he frightened me. He would grasp my left wrist and tighten his grip till I winced. I feared he might lose control, so it was safer to go along with it. But I never wore it when he wasn't there. I agreed to go dancing with him one night, afraid of him flying into a rage if I didn't, but when I talked to any of my friends, especially Bert, or the other boys, he made his jealous anger clear.

'When I take you dancing, as my fiancée, I expect you to have eyes only for me,' he said as he walked me home. I hadn't wanted him to walk me home, but he gave me no choice.

I took a sly look at his face. Even when cross, he was undeniably handsome – he could have been a film star walking down the street. But I could not shake off the memory of the night when he tried to strangle me. I chose to say nothing, to avoid another such scene, but once he had gone I breathed a huge sigh of relief and just carried on as usual.

*

On Monday, 7 May 1945, everyone seemed to be smiling. At first I didn't know why, but I met an air force boy, Peter, at the dance that night and he told me.

'Now that Hitler is dead, most of the chaps at my base think the war will be ending very soon. We are having a sweepstake on what day we think it will be.'

'Do you have a ticket?' I asked.

'Yes, I went for Friday this week.'

'As soon as that?' I was astonished. But then I hadn't listened to any news bulletins lately, so I didn't even know that Hitler was dead. Mother must have forgotten to tell me.

'It's quite a big thing,' he explained as he walked me home. 'Even some of the officers have joined in the sweepstake!'

As we reached my house and were stood on the doorstep saying goodbye, the front door burst open and Mother came out with a triumphant look.

'The war in Europe is over!' she exclaimed. 'Well, it will be in a few minutes, just after midnight. It was announced on the wireless this evening. I can't believe it! We're free! No more blackouts.'

I don't think I'd ever seen my mother look so delighted about anything.

'Yes, it's great. But what . . . How do you know?' I asked, catching her enthusiasm.

'It was a short announcement,' she explained. 'The Germans signed the surrender today! Winston Churchill will give a speech tomorrow, followed by King George.' She paused for me to take it in. 'Isn't that wonderful?

We're going to have a national holiday tomorrow to celebrate. VE Day, for victory in Europe. So you'll have a day off from work.'

'Let's not wait till tomorrow,' I suggested to Peter. 'We have to celebrate right now!' I knew Mother had to stay in as Jeffrey and Alan were asleep, but I was too thrilled and now much too wide awake to go to bed, so Peter and I turned around and walked, full of joy, back into town.

'Close, but no cigar,' he said with a grin.

'What do you mean?'

'I was out by two days,' he said. 'On the sweepstake, I mean. But I don't care – this is the best evening I've had in years. Let's go and live it up!'

As we walked past the empty spaces where the iron railings had been, some of them now replaced by other makeshift barriers, people were coming out of their houses, laughing and joking with each other, pulling down their wooden fences to pile up on a big celebration bonfire. The mood was joyous as complete strangers talked with each other and worked together in their preparations for the big day. Some of them put up bunting that had been stored away since the war began. Others blew up balloons.

We were jubilant as we walked along, meeting Bert, Kathleen, Peggy and most of my other friends, who joined us along the way so that by the time we reached the Market Square in the centre of Blackburn we were already a large party. We were all standing there, thinking what we could do to mark this special occasion, when the clock struck midnight. Suddenly all the street lights came on, for the first time since 1939. It was magnificent.

'Let's light a bonfire,' I shouted out, clambering onto a market table. 'Who's got some matches?'

'What can we light a fire with?' yelled a voice from the back of the square.

Bert got up and joined me. 'Let's gather all the stalls and tables together and fire up the market to celebrate!'

'Yes, that's all we've got.' I was always inclined to be mischievous when I could, but now I was really charged up with euphoria and keen to do something extraordinary. In all the excitement, we didn't even think about the damage we would cause.

Everyone dragged the tables and stalls together and some matches were found, so I struck one and tried to light the stall nearest to me. Everyone else soon joined in. But try as we might, we couldn't get them to stay alight.

By this time, a band had arrived and set up their instruments, and jolly music filled the square. As we gathered round they started to play familiar, morale-boosting songs from both the world wars for us to join in with. Songs like 'Bluebirds over the White Cliffs of Dover' and 'Pack up your Troubles' were the most popular. It was marvellous to hear everyone sing so happily. By now we had gathered a huge crowd. The whole square was packed with hundreds of people – mostly young like us.

While the band took a rest, I suddenly had another idea. 'Everyone get into long lines,' I shouted, climbing on top of one of the stalls to be heard over the crowd.

Somebody found me a megaphone and I shouted it out again, even louder. 'Let's do the old "Palais Glide"!' I suggested, and looked over at the band to see if they were ready. They were all smiling and nodding as they sorted out their sheet music. Bert, Peter and some of the other boys, still in their uniforms, organized the lines, so that we would all have enough space if we went the same way.

The band started to play and everyone laughed and cheered as they joined in, draping arms round each other and doing the steps . . . or any steps, as long as they managed to keep upright and in line, which most did.

I have no idea what time I got home, but there wasn't much sleep for anyone that night!

The next day, I went back into the centre of town again, where I had arranged to meet with all my friends. Kathleen and Peggy were there, along with Hilda, Bert, Peter and Jenny from the farm. I even met up with Philomena, my old friend from the convent. It was wonderful to catch up with her after so long.

Almost every building I saw was festooned with flags, bunting or some sort of colourful decorations – even Christmas-tree baubles. The whole of Blackburn had erupted in a frenzy of joyous celebrations. The day was packed with impromptu, bring-your-own street parties across the town. Bands were playing, there were games for the children, a bonfire in the Market Square and a happy fairground atmosphere.

It was a great community celebration of the freedom

we had gained. We were drunk on relief and hope. It was a day never to be forgotten.

Now at last we could burn the blackout curtains, tear up the ration books, get back our iron railings, switch on the lights and live! Well, not entirely, as it turned out. The blackout material could go, but the ration books had to stay, temporarily we thought, but in fact they were still needed for another nine years for some shortage items. Our beautiful railings wouldn't be back for some time either, if ever, but it was a joy to be able to switch on our lights whenever we wanted and especially good to see the warm glow in other people's windows again as I walked home from the Market Square.

One of the GI boys I used to dance with quite a lot at this time was called Hank, and we started to go out together for a while as friends. Of course, we knew that he would have to go back home to the USA soon with his pals, just as our boys would soon start coming home. But we made the best we could of that time between, when he didn't have too many duties and the light evenings beckoned us to explore the English countryside that he liked so much.

My family was not strong on shortening names, except for Bobby's. However, Hank used to call me Margie, and I quite liked it when he said it, with his American drawl. So it was always Margie . . . but not in front of my mother.

I had never visited an American base, so I was looking forward to going with Hank to a special dance they were holding at Bamber Bridge near Preston, before the GIs started to leave, either for the Far East, where the war still raged, or for home. My friend Peggy and I received our special invitations and were taken there, about twelve miles, in a huge army truck, which was quite a novelty for us. Hank and Peggy's partner Omar were waiting to greet us on our arrival.

The dance was a lot of fun and a great success. We each had some time to kiss and say goodbye – me with Hank and Peggy with Omar – and we were all very happy as we went to board the truck taking us back home, which was parked next to another large truck going somewhere else. I don't know how it happened. We were obviously not concentrating and, as Peggy boarded first, I suddenly realized that she was on the wrong truck. I was gesturing to her, trying to explain and reaching to grasp her arm and pull her down, while Omar was standing beside me, encouraging her to get out and change trucks. Suddenly Hank grabbed me and dragged me away from the vehicle. A van flashed past us, missing me by inches, and smashed into Omar, pinning him to the truck.

Being a medic, Hank quickly turned to a bystander and rasped, 'Take her away . . . and quickly. Take her back inside – anywhere away from here!' As I was ushered away by another GI, Hank took his jacket off and turned back towards the scene of the accident. 'I'm a medic! I'll stay with him.'

It was so fast that I didn't see much of what happened to Omar, which was just as well. I knew that he'd been hurt and Hank would be busy treating him, but it wasn't till later, as an officer drove us home, that I found out how awful it had been. Peggy was in a terrible state as she had seen it all. She sat with me in the back seat shaking with shock and inconsolable. I put my arm round her, trying to soothe her.

Omar was taken to hospital where he survived, unconscious, for two days before he died of his internal injuries. Peggy was distraught. He must have meant a lot to her, but I think she felt guilty as well, because he was trying to help her down from the truck when he was hit.

The Americans were preparing to leave, while our boys were beginning to come back and being demobbed. Every day I wished Ray could have been among them. It was hard to be cheerful, but I knew I must be.

They came to the dances in their civvies with big smiles on their faces, visibly relieved to be home at last. But within days their good moods had faded as many of them failed to find work and couldn't settle back into their old lives as easily as they had expected. Everybody they left behind had moved on, whilst all these boys wanted to do was to get married, settle down and have families.

Some of the boys I'd played with as a child, and grown up with, came back to the neighbourhood, and when they met my mother in the street, they were all asking her: 'Has Margaret made her mind up yet?' What they were keen to know, of course, was whether I'd decided who I wanted to marry, or if I wanted to marry and therefore whether I was still eligible.

To which Mother would give her usual answer:

'Margaret can get engaged as often as she likes, but she hasn't to get married till she's twenty-one.'

Well, that was telling them. They didn't want to wait that long so they looked for potential marriage partners elsewhere, which suited me.

Many of us shared a depressed, let-down feeling after the euphoria of VE Day, only a few weeks before. Things hadn't improved as quickly as we expected. There were still long queues outside shops and shortages of all sorts. Unemployment of ex-servicemen was high and there was not much prospect of work for most of them. It would take some time for the factories and businesses to adjust their plans and return to their pre-war production. Many returning men also suffered from physical wounds, and they had witnessed terrible traumas on the front line but were unable or unwilling to talk about their inner turmoil. A lot of young couples had sudden short courtships, marrying quickly in the months following VE Day, and there were then not enough houses and flats to go around, which was another source of discord.

During the war, women had taken on many of the men's jobs – finding exhilarating and fulfilling work, with new social networks which they were reluctant to forego. They too were affected by the expectation that they would give up their work to provide employment for their menfolk and go back to what some thought of as the drudgery and boredom of their former lives, always taking second place.

As someone who had been independent from an early age, I agreed with them. I had always enjoyed working so I wouldn't have wanted to stop either. I decided to leave my 'war work', however, now that we were no longer at war in Europe, so I approached the Post Office and they offered me my old job back from the following Monday. That meant I would now be working nearer home again, and I was doing work that suited me better – I never was any good at machines and physical work. First, though, I decided to have a break. A couple of days in Scotland was just what I needed, so I arranged to take the train up to Paisley on Thursday to stay with Gordon and his new wife Betty.

'Hank came to see me this afternoon,' said my mother while we were having tea on the Wednesday.

'Really? What did he want?' It was a surprise to me and I couldn't think why he would have come.

'The usual,' she replied, with a smile.

'What do you mean?'

'He wants to marry you and take you back with him to America.'

'Oh . . . I had no idea!'

'Well, I did wonder. I know you're friends, but I wasn't expecting that, were you?'

'No, he hasn't asked me. I knew he would have to go back sometime soon, but we haven't even talked about the future.' I was genuinely astonished. 'What did you say?'

'The usual, that you can get engaged as many times as you like, but you haven't to marry till you're twenty-one.'

I smiled. 'Yes, that's fine.'

'Would you want to go and live in America?'

'I don't think so. I wouldn't even want to marry him. He's a good man and I enjoy his company, but he's a friend. There isn't that spark. It would never work.'

'He said to tell you he'll see you at Tony's tonight.'

'Thanks for warning me,' I smiled. 'But I wasn't thinking of going dancing tonight.' I needed to iron some things and pack my bag, so that I could leave for Paisley straight from work tomorrow. It was my last day at the factory, so they were letting me go at lunchtime. 'I'll see Hank when I get back and sort it all out with him,' I added.

It was lovely to get away on the train, winding through all the different patches of countryside. Gordon and Betty were at the station to meet me and we had a good chat over supper that evening at their house. 'Tomorrow night, if it's all right with you, we've all been invited to a ball.'

'Oh yes. It will be lovely to dance somewhere new and meet different people.'

Sure enough, we went to the ball on the Friday evening and I met a good-looking English captain, in uniform. We danced most of the evening and arranged to meet the next day, Saturday. His name was Alastair and he had a car, so we drove over to Glasgow for the day. He had it all planned out. He took me to a lovely restaurant where we had lunch and, unusually for me, some wine. Then we went to the cinema and afterwards we strolled up Sauchiehall Street.

Unexpectedly, we bumped into another officer who was an old friend of Alistair's and he joined us, so now we were a threesome. While we were deciding what to do next, I came up with an idea.

'I know what we can do. I've heard such a lot about dancing at the Barrowland Ballroom. Why don't we go there?'

I noticed that they gave each other strange looks.

'Why not?' said my escort.

So off we went. I was quite excited to see this place that I'd heard people rave about at Tony's. But when we got there, the vast size of the dance hall, the crowded floor and the famous band playing stopped me in the doorway. For the first time ever at a dance hall, I felt frightened. Here I was in an unfamiliar city, with two men I hardly knew. What if they preferred to dance with other girls and left me on my own, or if someone else came up and asked me to dance? Would we be able to find each other again if we were parted in the crowd?

I wished I hadn't had all that wine at lunchtime. I was sure I was going to be sick. But where was the cloakroom? Now the captain wanted to dance, so we took to the floor, but I knew I wasn't much company; I felt awful and I just wanted to get back to Paisley. I couldn't say so straight away, so we stayed for a short while and then I asked to go. I could see my captain was disappointed that I seemed to have changed so much from the brave, vivacious girl I was in the morning, to the timid, uncertain mouse I had become in that place.

He drove me back to Gordon's house in Paisley and we parted as friends. I was so relieved the following day to be on the train home, to security and an evening with

Hank, dancing at good old Tony's on the Monday evening.

I did go dancing on Monday, but couldn't find Hank anywhere. I asked around and one of our friends told me he had gone.

'He had no choice,' she said. 'He so much wanted to see you before he left, but we found out you were away in Scotland, so he had to leave without saying goodbye.'

'Where did he go?' I asked, knowing it could either be to another posting or back to the States.

'He went home. Back to his mom's cooking, he said. But he asked me to tell you he would miss you and would write soon.'

Indeed, Hank did write me a letter. He was very sad to have missed me, he wrote. But would I consider getting engaged, and going out to visit him when I could get the time off work?

He was a lovely guy, and would make someone a funny, kind and loyal husband, but not me, and especially not in America. It wasn't going to happen.

In August 1945 the surrender of Japan was officially announced, giving us another public holiday and a new excuse for celebrations, with all the bunting back up for the street parties and merrymaking across Blackburn. This lifted the mood for a few days. The war was over across the whole world now and our prisoners of war from the Far East might at last be able to come home. But once again, many families would be disappointed and dispirited. Most of their POW boys were so close to death that it would take up to two years before they were allowed back, since they needed so much medical treatment following their long starvation and the accompanying diseases.

In the autumn, Bobby came home for a rare two weeks' leave, as possessive as ever, wanting to escort me wherever I went. By coincidence, only a day or two later Joe was also back for forty-eight hours and he came straight round to see me, once again insisting we were still engaged. Sitting with him at our kitchen table, I tried to tell him, yet again, that it was over.

'Joe, it's really good to see you again, but it would be so much better and easier for me if you could accept that we are just friends – good friends. I tried to make it clear when I told you I didn't want to be engaged any more. Will you please accept that our engagement is over? It was finished when I tried to give you back your ring.'

'I never agreed to that.' He raised his voice and his whole face turned to anger. 'You cannot be serious about this, Margaret. I will not hear of it. We are engaged to be married because we are made for each other . . . and that's that!' He slammed his hand palm-down on the table.

I gulped, then looked steadily at him as I tried to keep my voice calm. 'I've always liked you, Joe, and I'm glad of your friendship . . .' I took a deep breath. 'But I'm afraid I don't love you.'

He pushed the table roughly and stood up, towering over me. 'I don't believe you, Margaret. I'm not standing for any more of this. Come on.' He grasped my wrist tightly and pulled me up. 'You're coming with me to the cinema this afternoon.' And that was it.

He just wouldn't listen to what he didn't want to hear, and I was too fearful of his temper to push him any further this time, so for his two days of leave I had no choice but to go along with what he wanted to believe. But I was determined to change his mind about going to the cinema and at least I got my way over that.

I told Joe I had arranged to meet some of my friends that evening down at the George and Dragon, where our newly formed choir were having a practice, and I wanted to wash my hair first.

'My older brother Bobby is on leave too, so I've already agreed to let him walk me down town tonight, and I'll meet you there.'

Joe reluctantly agreed to this change of plan. 'Well, all right,' he said, letting go of my wrist. 'But you're my fiancée, so you will sit with me.'

Bobby chatted all the way as we strolled down to the pub together that evening.

'There will be quite a few people there that you know,' I said.

'What about your fiancé?' he asked.

'Joe? He's not my fiancé,' I explained. 'The engagement was over ages ago, when I told him and gave him back his ring. But Joe wouldn't accept it.'

Not having met Joe yet, he shrugged, but looked quietly pleased. I expect he wanted to keep on protecting me himself, at least until I met someone who would protect me as well as he did, which he no doubt thought would never happen.

By the time we arrived, the choir had finished singing and were settling themselves down with a drink to chat. Joe was there and made a big thing of standing and greeting me with a kiss, though I turned my head to make sure it was only a peck on the cheek.

'Joe, this is my brother Bobby, home on leave for a fortnight.'

'Lucky man,' said Joe as they shook hands. 'I've only got a couple of days, so I want to make the most of it.'

Joe had saved me a seat next to him, which he signalled to me, but before I could sit down, Bobby took my place. Good old Bobby! For a moment I thought Joe was going to make a scene about me sitting there instead, but Bobby got straight in, talking to him, and it was as if all Joe's momentary resentment just dissipated.

I left the two of them to talk together and went over to chat with the girls. Later, when I looked back at them, Bobby and Joe were still deep in conversation together, as if they were good pals. How strange, I thought, since they didn't have that much in common . . . other than me. Were my ears getting red?

We all met up again the following night, including Bobby and Joe who once again were getting on like a house on fire, standing by the bar and exchanging banter most of the evening. I was getting worried now that they might gang up on me. Thank goodness Joe would be leaving the next day and they probably wouldn't be at home at the same time again for quite a while, since Bobby was staying on in the RAF at his base in Africa.

From then on, for the rest of his leave, Bobby seemed

to turn up almost everywhere I went, whether at the George and Dragon or at Tony's. Had he made a pact with Joe? Or was I imagining it? Perhaps he was just being his usual protective self . . . but I had the distinct feeling that Bobby's ulterior motive was to make sure I didn't pick up with any of the other boys.

Little did he know!

18

The Bush Hat

1946

It was 22 March 1946, the day of the Annual Northrop Ball at King George's Hall, Blackburn, which was always a big occasion for my mother and her extended family. I was expected to be there, of course, whether I wanted to go or not. This year was a not. I tried everything to get out of going.

'Why do I have to go?' I asked over breakfast that morning. 'It's a stuffy dance for the old folks.'

'So are you saying I'm an "old folk"?'

'No, of course not. But what's wrong with wanting to be with my friends?'

'Nothing, but you're with your friends every night of the year, except this one.' Mother paused. 'I'd like you to be there. I've made you a beautiful new dress, so you'll be the star of the ball, and all the family will be proud of you. I will be proud of you. I know everyone would be very disappointed if you were missing.'

'But it's Friday. All my friends will be at Tony's. I'll have the pick of dance partners there. Friday's the best night at Tony's and I don't want to miss the fun. I could wear my new dress there instead.'

'No. I made it for the Northrop Ball. I'm sure there will be young men there too. You'll enjoy it once you're there.'

My mother could be very determined and this was one of those occasions. So, with great reluctance, I gave in.

That evening, when I got in from work, I laid out on the bed the dress Mother had made me, along with my new bra, stockings and dancing shoes. I admired the dress – Mother really had excelled herself. It was a beautiful black ballgown, with short sleeves, a sweetheart neckline and a v-shape from each side of my waist coming to a point at the back, made to one of my designs. Nobody would know that parts of it were made from our redundant blackout curtains. It was so elegant and close-fitting that when I put it on and did up the zip, it reminded me of what an old boyfriend had once said to me: 'Oh Margaret, you look like you've been poured into that frock!'

This was one dance where I wasn't really bothered what I looked like, so instead of taking time to put my hair up as usual, I left it curly and loose on my shoulders. I was sure there would not be anybody there to impress. But I did put on some lipstick and a bit of mascara, just to please my mother.

I went downstairs for her to put the finishing touch to my dress, as she always did. She had a way of putting a pin in that meant nobody could find it and undo the dress except her. 'There,' she said as she stood back. 'That will keep it all in place.'

I think I must have been a bit dim about that pin, as it was quite some time later that it finally occurred to me she had an ulterior motive for this!

It was time to leave and Grandad Harrison – whose business had the contract for building works at the Northrop Loom Company – had sent a car for us, so off we went in style. When we arrived at King George's Hall, the foyer was brightly lit, like a public square. We went through to the hall itself and there were all my relations on my mother's side, sitting in a long row along the far wall. I smiled nicely at all the old aunts and uncles but my heart sank. This was going to be a terrible evening, sitting there like birds on a telegraph wire hour after hour, with all the fuddy-duddies gossiping amongst themselves. The hall was dimly lit and the band hadn't started yet, so I was bored already, and there would be three or four hours of this.

I recognized a lot of the people coming and going, fetching their drinks. Mother waved at them now and then, but mostly she was chatting with her friend Alice.

My attention switched to the musicians setting up. It was Oscar Rabin's band, who had an excellent reputation, so at least I would be able to listen to their music to while away the time.

The main doors to the foyer were still open, with more people coming in . . . and that's when I saw, silhouetted against the bright light behind him, a tall, uniformed soldier, wearing a bush hat. As he walked away from the door, I could make out his face enough to see his fair good looks. I was fascinated by his bush hat. I had only ever seen those in wartime films.

'Ooh,' I said to my mother. 'I wonder if he's Australian.' The band started up, the noise drowning her reply.

I looked around and by now there were some other men still in uniform. I saw a naval officer, an airman and a couple of soldiers, but my eyes were on the man in the bush hat as he took it to check in at the cloakroom counter, then returned to the hall. After a quick look round the room, he made a beeline for me. As he walked towards me, I noticed his thick blond wavy hair, his sky-blue eyes and his rugged, sunburnt skin. But the features that stood out most were his big smile and the twinkle in his eyes. I must have smiled back as he approached and asked me to dance.

As soon as we stepped onto the dance floor, my heart sank. I wasn't the best dancer ever, but I was very good, thanks to the convent, and I realized this clodhopper had probably never danced in his life. He hadn't a clue. After we'd introduced ourselves and he told me his name was Jim, we shared a bit of small talk and he told me he had a month's leave before he had to go back to India. I knew I liked him, but I couldn't go on with this embarrassing charade, with him struggling over every step and everyone looking at us. I'd never live it down if any of my friends came in now.

Then, to make it worse, because of the sweetheart neckline of my dress, he'd somehow, unintentionally got part of my new bra strap in his hand and it started to unravel.

'What's this?' he asked.

I was mortified.

'Oh, Mother!' She always had pins, so when she saw

what had happened she came over and did something to sort it out.

'Phew! Let's sit down and have a drink,' I suggested firmly, already pulling him away from the dance floor.

He ordered a beer and I had my usual orange and lemonade that cost the princely sum of fourpence.

'Well, you're very cheap!' said Jim and we both laughed.

I didn't want to have to sit down with the family again, so I suggested we go and sit up in the balcony instead.

We went up the stairs and there was nobody there, so we had our pick of the seats, choosing two overlooking the dance floor, but far enough up that the music wasn't too loud, and we chatted away. If I went to a dance I expected to dance all night – this was the first time, the one and only time, that I'd sat down for the whole evening! But the hours flew by as we talked and talked, just getting to know each other.

'I went to St Mary's College,' he told me.

'Really? That's where my brother Jeffrey is now.'

'Where did you go to school?' asked Jim.

'The Convent of Notre Dame.'

'Well, how strange. We're both Catholics, then? And my sister is at the same convent. She'll be leaving this year.'

'So she must be a couple of years younger than me?'

'How old are you?'

'Nineteen. I'll be twenty in May. What about you?'

'Just a year older than you. I'll be twenty-one in July.'

Jim was very easy to talk to and, with three brothers, I was used to talking with boys. We chatted mostly about our families, our early childhoods and our first memories.

'So if your grandfather was the landlord at the Tanners'

Arms, and my father used to take me with him when he went for a drink in their beer-garden, and I think we children had free lemonades, do you think we might have met, playing in the garden?'

'Yes!' I was quite excited at the thought. 'I played with all the children who came and, being almost the same age, we probably did play together in those days. Isn't that amazing?'

'Yes, quite a coincidence, but a shame we don't remember each other.'

'We must have been very young.'

The longer we chatted, the more coincidences we discovered. It was as if we were meant to meet. Maybe we were.

'I won our section of the Border Regiment's lottery in India to come here tonight,' Jim told me. 'We put all our names in a hat and mine was picked out, so I won my passage home for a whole month's leave! Now I feel as if I was meant to meet you on my very first evening.'

Before we knew it, the taxi arrived to take us home. My mother had to come up to find me.

'Sorry to end your evening,' she said. 'But we have to go now. Our taxi is waiting.'

Not for the first time in my life, I felt a bit like Cinderella, having to rush away before the clock struck twelve.

'Can't we stay a bit longer?' I asked her.

'No, we can't keep him waiting, or Grandad might make us pay!'

'Hello, Mrs Holden,' said Jim. 'I'm James Ford of the

Border Regiment.' Then he took me by surprise. 'We're only just getting to know each other,' he explained. 'And we have so much more to talk about. I'd like to walk your daughter home, if that's all right with you. I promise I'll look after her.'

Mother hesitated for only a couple of seconds. 'All right,' she said, then turned to me. 'Mind you come in by midnight.' Now I really was like Cinderella.

Jim got that too. 'I'll make sure she doesn't turn into a pumpkin!' We all smiled at that and off she went to the waiting taxi, while we went down to collect my coat and his bush hat, which he put on as we left the building.

We must have talked for at least four hours already that evening, and we carried on talking all the long walk home. When we arrived back at my house, we went up the path. There were two steps in front of our front door, so he stood at the bottom and I was on the first step. He was six foot two inches, you see, and I was only five foot three. I always loved the six-footers.

Neither of us wanted the evening to end, although it was very late. I was probably being a bit coy, not wanting to seem too keen, and we must have annoyed the man who lived next door. He pulled open his upstairs window and shouted down.

'For goodness sake, Margaret, let him kiss you and then we can all get some sleep!'

It was difficult with the bush hat in the way, but he managed to kiss me. Just then Mother, having heard the neighbour's voice, opened the door.

'Will you bring him in?' she said. It was more of an order than a question.

So we followed her in. Mother sat back down in her rocking chair in front of the fire and picked up her crocheting to finish off, while Jim sat in my chair, to the side, and I perched on the stool in front of him. While we talked quietly he started to play with my hair. I didn't like anyone fiddling with my hair, so I pulled my head away a bit to give him the hint. After a few minutes, Mother put her crocheting down and rested her head back, eyes down, but still gently rocking.

We sat silently, watching the glowing embers, and when it looked like Mother had fallen asleep, Jim leant over to me.

'Does she never go to bed?' he asked me in a whisper.

'Not until you've gone, Jim,' she said, without opening her eyes.

As I lay in bed that night, still wide awake, I relived the evening. If I'd gone to Tony's, as I wanted, I probably wouldn't have met Jim, so I was very glad Mother had persuaded me to go with her and the family instead.

I'd known Jim for less than a day, so far. It seemed so strange that we'd only met a few hours before and yet already I felt very much at ease with him. There was definitely a spark between us.

I knew Jim felt it too when the next day, a Saturday, he was back at our house unexpectedly, just after breakfast, eager for us to go out for a walk.

'I don't want to waste one minute of my leave,' he explained.

The sun shone and I looked forward to a lovely day out with him. If it went as well as I thought, we would have a whole month to enjoy after that.

I made some sandwiches to take with us and we set off together for a tour of our childhood haunts, starting with the sandy patch we called 'Little Blackpool' on the bank of the river Ribble, where I had played with otters as a toddler. We didn't see any otters that day, so we walked on, hand in hand, along the river bank, past the ferryman who took paying passengers across the river to Hurst Green and Stonyhurst College, where my Holden grandparents were buried.

'We never took the ferry,' said Jim. 'I used to swim across the river, with my friends.'

'With your clothes on?' I laughed.

'No, we used to take them off and wind them round our heads, with our snake-clip belts fastened round to keep them there.'

'Did they ever fall off?'

'Only once,' said Jim with a grin. 'Luckily they floated, but I had to go home in wet clothes that day.'

We walked on to Sale Wheel Woods, with its wild spring flowers, then sat on a log to eat our sandwiches and watched the birds rooting around for comfy twigs which they took up into the trees to make their nests.

There was so much to talk about and so much to see on that first day, so we walked on and talked about the eccentricities of our families. I told Jim about my two sets of grandparents being at loggerheads with each other and putting up a sheet to hide their houses from each other.

I told him about my father, all the trips to the coast at weekends and the time he fell over a cow coming back one Sunday night.

Jim told me stories of his family too, but none quite as eccentric as mine. I learned that his father was Irish and served in the Connaught Rangers. He had been wounded in the Great War, shot in the eye.

'He was on the way home on a hospital ship when it was sunk,' said Jim. 'He survived and was taken onto another hospital ship which was also sunk. He was rescued again. It was a case of third time lucky for him and he finally got back to England, where he was classified as disabled, so he's been unable to work for most of his life.'

'Oh dear. But thank goodness he survived.'

'Yes, but I nearly didn't.'

'What do you mean?'

'You see this scar?' asked Jim, pointing to a red-and-white mark on his neck.

'Yes. What happened?'

'When I was about eleven, I was knocked down by a car. I don't remember it, but they told me about it afterwards. In fact, I didn't know anything as I was lying unconscious in hospital for a week before I woke up.'

'Your parents must have been very worried.'

'Yes, it was touch and go, the doctor told them. But I survived it all right. In fact, it probably knocked some sense into me!' He grinned.

'What about your family? Do you have any brothers and sisters?'

'Yes, three brothers and one sister. Jack is a chief petty officer in the navy, with a medal for gallantry. He's four years older than me. Then there's Louis in the air force, three years older than me. I'm in the middle, with David two years younger and Margaret, the youngest, still at school.'

He then told me about some of the antics he and his brothers got up to as children. In fact, there were so many stories to tell that we spent most of Sunday, after church, carrying on with our reminiscences. We took a tram to Wilpshire and walked the country lanes near where my Harrison grandparents still lived.

It was on this route that we bumped into a character from my childhood at the Tanners' Arms. I saw him walking towards us and thought I recognized him, but I wasn't certain till he came close. There was something about his face that looked familiar . . . and then I noticed it: the skiver bag that he always kept with him at the Tanners' Arms, and obviously still had – the bag that contained the big, gold sovereign coins that I loved playing with. He gave me a puzzled look, then uncertain recognition dawned.

'Margaret?' he said.

'Yes, that's right. How lovely to see you after all these years . . . and you still have your skiver bag.' I smiled with fondness for those days, and for the man. 'David Furness, isn't it?'

'Spot on, love,' he said. 'What a memory you have. You must have only been about three or four when you used to climb onto that high stool at the Tanners' Arms.'

'Yes, I remember. And you said that the head on the coins was better-looking than yours! But I didn't agree.'

We laughed.

'This is my friend Jim,' I said, introducing them to each other.

'I'm delighted to meet you, Jim. Anyone who has this girl for a friend is a lucky man. I always felt she would be a catch for someone special when she grew up.'

'Hey, enough of that,' I said with a grin. 'I only met Jim yesterday.'

'Well, you look like you already make a happy couple,' he said.

'Yes, I think we are,' agreed Jim, squeezing my hand.

'I'm so glad to have bumped into you, Margaret, after all this time,' said David. 'Hopefully it won't be so long before we meet again.'

We said our farewells and each walked on our separate ways, happier for having had that brief encounter with our past. Jim too was pleased to have met him and amused by what he said about us.

That evening, Jim joined us for tea at our house and met my younger brothers. Luckily, Bobby was still in the RAF, away overseas, but I dreaded what he would have said if he saw me walking out with Jim, instead of his new pal Joe, who was now serving in Germany. I could see trouble brewing. I knew I should warn Jim about this potentially tricky situation, but not tonight. Not yet. First I just wanted to enjoy some relaxed happiness – a happiness I didn't expect to find so soon after losing so much to the war.

19

Tickling Trout

1946

I had just finished my breakfast on Monday morning when
there was a knock at the door. I opened it and there stood
Jim on the doorstep, with a big grin and a bunch of
flowers.

'Good morning, Margaret. I've come to escort you to
work!'

Well, that was a happy surprise. I picked up my bag
and off we went, chatting while we walked.

'I'm going to ask for the rest of the week off,' I said.
'Then we can go for more days out.'

'Good idea. Will they let you?'

'Oh, I think they will. They're very good, and anyway
they owe me some holiday.'

We walked as slowly as we dared and I got there with
only a minute to spare.

'Just time for a kiss?' asked Jim with a cheeky grin.

I stood on tiptoes – it was definitely a 'kiss and run'
situation.

'I'll come for you after work,' he called after me as I

ran in through the door, holding my hat on and ready to apologize. A couple of the post girls had seen and shared a giggle.

True to his word, when I came out at the end of the day, Jim was there, standing to the side of the building, not wanting to show me up, but I'm sure it was noticed. I didn't mind. I felt quite spoilt, having a handsome man to walk me home.

'Did you get the time off?' he asked as we crossed the road.

'Yes, that was fine, so we've got the whole week to do what we like.'

'That's great.'

'What have you been doing today?'

'Well, I spent most of my day looking forward to coming to meet you.' He smiled. 'But I also helped my parents with a few things and did some errands of my own, like going into the bank and the dentist.'

'I thought the army had its own doctors and dentists?'

'Yes, it does, when we're living on an army base, but there aren't any dentists in the jungles of Burma.'

'You didn't tell me last night that you'd served in Burma.'

'You didn't ask,' he said with a smile. 'I wanted to hear all about you first.'

'It must have been awful, fighting out there.'

'Yes, for quite a while. It was tough, and the terrain made it harder, not to mention the poisonous wildlife and the tropical climate – like an inferno at times, carrying our packs and beating our way through with machetes.'

'That sounds terrible.'

'It's all part of the job.' He shrugged modestly. 'At least I just avoided the worst thing.'

'What was that?'

'Well, after two years in the Burmese jungle, we had orders to prepare to invade Japan. A lot of our troops were rerouted from Europe to join us for this massive invasion to try and end the war in Asia.'

'I thought the bombs on Hiroshima and Nagasaki did that?'

'Yes, they did. And that was what saved us. If those atom bombs hadn't been dropped on Japan, or if the Emperor had refused to surrender, our invasion would have gone ahead. If that had happened, millions would have died . . . and I might not have survived to meet you at the Northrop Ball!'

We carried on talking, happy to know that we had the whole week to continue learning about each other.

'Come and have some tea at our house,' I suggested. 'Then let's go and see what's on at the cinema.'

That first week together went by in a happy haze of sharing memories, walking and talking: strolling by the river, round the park or visiting the places we knew as children. Jim spoke quite a bit more about his time in Burma, which I knew from what other soldiers had told me was one of the most feared postings in the army, and any man who came through that was one to admire. Jim said very little about any of the worst things that happened, or the terrible things he saw. I suppose he didn't want to upset me – like my brother Bobby, always protecting me from anything bad.

We grew closer every day, though there was a part of me that wanted to keep it all light – nothing too serious. I had lost too many special people during the war, and if Jim was going away to fight or put himself in any more danger, I feared finding myself in that position again.

One day we took a walk through our childhoods, going to see all our old schools and sharing stories of our schooldays. As we went from one school to another we found out that we both knew quite a few of each other's school friends – yet more coincidences.

At the end of each afternoon, we walked back home up Robinson Street, past the playground where Ray and I had played as children, past Howarth's Pens, where hundreds of chickens roamed before the war, in large wood and wire-mesh pens. The hens went when war was declared, the wire went soon after to the ammunition factories and the wooden frameworks were ripped up to fuel the VE Day bonfires. So now it was bare ground, but we still called it Howarth's Pens.

The surface of our road hadn't been kept up during the war. It remained a black and rather sooty-surfaced asphalt, with random potholes and wagon tracks. Now that the weather was warming up, most of the children were playing outside after school, skipping and playing hopscotch, or its variation, 'airplane hopscotch', just like my friends and I used to play in the St Alban's Junior School playground.

Even after the war, there still wasn't much traffic along Robinson Street, but tradesmen came on their rounds, some of whom we hadn't seen since the early days of the war, before rationing took over. We had a twice-daily milk cart. The first visit was early morning and the other late afternoon. The milk was in 'kits' or churns and we had to bring our own jugs for the milkman to pour the milk into. The children had great fun with the horse-drawn coal wagon, petting the coalman's beautiful shire horse and running after him with buckets, some for loose coals and others for manure to nourish their parents' tomatoes.

We had missed our rag-and-bone man during the war, poor chap, with the metal all taken for the war effort and the 'rags' or old clothes going to the WVS (Women's Voluntary Service), where the volunteers would unpick the seams and unravel knitted garments to make new ones – a helpful way to stretch the clothing coupons in our ration books, except that Mother was an expert at that in our house. I don't remember any of our neighbours giving our rag-and-bone man bones, but still he called out 'Rag and bone' in a gruff, sing-song voice as he rounded the corner into our street. 'Any old metal. Bring out yer rags.' We were pleased to see him back again. I suppose it was a sign that all was well with the world once more. He smiled as we passed him. 'Hello, love. Tell yer mother I'm back,' he said.

'Yes, I will.' I returned his smile. 'I expect she heard you.'

On our second weekend I managed to persuade Jim to come to a dance – the first time since the Northrop Ball.

'You know I don't like dancing,' complained Jim. 'And, as I remember, you didn't like my style.'

'What style?'

'Whatever it was, you certainly pulled me off the dance floor quickly enough!'

'Yes, before anyone I know saw us.'

'So why do you want us to go tonight?'

'I haven't been to Tony's all week! Besides, I want you to meet some of my friends. But you don't have to dance. You could always talk to them while I'm dancing – I'm sure you'll like them.'

'All right, then. I'm not going to get any peace if I don't!'

With reluctance, Jim came into Tony's with me and I introduced him to all the gang. He talked a bit to Kathleen, Peggy and Jenny, plus Bert and the other boys, while I danced with various partners, until finally he'd had enough.

'Come on, Margaret. Let's go back to your mother's.'

So I agreed and we walked back home again. 'How did you like my friends?' I asked him.

'They were all right,' he said, but the messages were obvious – he didn't like me dancing with other boys and he didn't like having to make polite conversation with my friends, of whom he didn't seem particularly enamoured. Perhaps it was just how he felt that evening. But I noticed that, as he relaxed a bit, he was very charming with the girls and I was dying to find out what they thought of him. I'd have to wait to ask them, though I was sure they appreciated his tall good looks.

He soon livened up when it was just the two of us again, walking home. Mother invited him in, as always. I think she was already growing rather fond of him. So was I, but rather more than just fond, despite his moodiness tonight. On the Sunday, Jim's parents had invited me to come and meet them for tea, so we walked over there, taking some flowers that I'd bought with Jim on the Saturday. Although his house wasn't very far as the crow flies, it was a long walk to Mary Street in Eanam, with there being only one way of going under the railway line. We set out in good time and, as always, talked non-stop all the way.

Finally we arrived at a neat-looking terraced house, smaller than ours and without a garden, but inside it was immaculate. All the furniture was polished to a high shine. Jim's parents were welcoming and friendly, so it was lovely to meet them. His mother cooked a delicious tea, despite the continuation of rations, and we all had a good chat about the latest post-war news and our childhoods.

'What do you think, Ma?' Jim said as we all sat down together after tea. 'Wasn't I right?'

His mother turned to me and smiled warmly. 'Yes, you were right. But I'm not going to embarrass Margaret while she is here by praising her.'

'Why do you think none of your brothers or your sister were at home?' I asked after we left.

'Just as well,' said Jim. 'You'll get to know them soon enough.'

I sensed a slight note of tension in his voice, but thought it better to say nothing.

On the long walk back to my house, I asked Jim whether he knew Joe Walker.

'Vaguely, but I don't think I've ever spoken to him.'

'I was sort of engaged to him for a short while last year. I thought he was pretending to propose, but he was being serious. Not only that, he was terribly jealous if I even looked at another man, let alone danced with any of the boys at Tony's, especially the Americans. I didn't like that and I didn't like the way he tried to control me,' I explained. I decided not to mention his near-strangulation attempt. 'I had to break the engagement.'

'Good,' said Jim with a sigh of relief, although I think he was already confident in my growing relationship with him.

'The only trouble is, Joe wouldn't accept it. He still calls me his fiancée, tries to get back with me and won't acknowledge that it's over.'

'Well, it takes two to be engaged, so if you don't want to be, there can't be an engagement to Joe any more,' Jim said with certainty. I just wasn't sure Joe would see it that way.

Every working day, Jim turned up at breakfast time, walked me to work, then often went back to my mother's for a bit. Mother liked Jim and seemed happy to have him around, whether I was there or not. He might go back to his parents' house for the afternoon, then he walked all the way back to pick me up at the end of my working day. We rarely went to Tony's in the evenings as Jim didn't enjoy it, but there would be plenty of time for me to make up for that when his leave was over.

Time was running out, however. It was a Saturday morning, the third and last weekend of his leave, and we strolled through the park, enjoying the spring bulbs, the newly mown lawns and the blossom on some of the trees.

We sat down together on a nearby bench to relax.

'It's such a lovely time of the year in England,' said Jim. 'I shall miss it when I go back to the sweltering heat, this time in India.' He paused, turning to face me. 'And that won't be the only thing I will miss.'

'I should hope not!' I replied. 'If you mean me.'

'Will you miss me too?'

I pretended to think about it . . . but not for too long. 'Yes,' I agreed. 'I will miss you and all our walks and chats. It's going to seem very strange without you, and yet we've only known each other for three weeks.'

'I know. I feel as if I've known you for months or years – not just weeks. But we still have six days to fill before I have to leave.'

'Will you write to me when you are away?' I asked, thinking back to all those letters I used to receive from boys abroad during the war, and the struggle I had to find time to reply to them. The special ones, particularly Ray, I always answered first. They were the ones I looked out for when the postman came, but now there were no more letters from Ray or Les, Clarry or even Wilfred. I told Jim all about these boys and how much I felt for them, but I'm sure he also knew now that he was special to me too. I found it strange, in a way, that we had become a couple in such a short time, but it felt right.

'You bet I'll write to you – every day. What else will I have to do?' He grinned. 'You'd better make sure you write back and tell me everything you've been doing.'

'Everything?' I teased.

'Well, you know what I mean.'

Jim was due to leave from the station on Friday morning, so we made the best we could of the few remaining days, until midweek, when I suddenly developed a rash. As soon as she saw it, Mother dabbed gentian violet on the spots, leaving mauve blotches all over my face. I looked such a sight that I didn't dare go to work that day. I'd have frightened away the customers' children!

So I sent Jeffrey before school to tell a girl round the corner who worked at the Post Office to let them know that I couldn't come to work today.

As soon as he left, there was a familiar knock on the door and Mother opened it, to let Jim into the vestibule.

'Where's Margaret?' he asked. 'Isn't she ready yet?'

'Don't let him in,' I cried.

'She's got a rash on her face,' explained Mother.

'You can't see me like this,' I called out to him. 'I'm covered in gentian violet.'

'What?' I don't suppose he had a clue what I meant. 'Please let me in to see you. I want to talk to you.'

'Well, I'm not going out anywhere,' I said as he came through the door to our sitting room. I held up a cushion to hide part of my face.

'Nobody will see you if we just go for a walk.'

'Why can't you talk to me here?'

'Because I'd like to have a serious talk with you and . . .' He looked around. Jeffrey had just come back to collect his school bag. Alan was trying to chop up an apple on the tablecloth with a blunt knife and Mother was clearing the breakfast things.

'It's time you left for school, Jeffrey,' she told him. 'Alan, put that knife down and help me clear up. We have to get you to school too or you'll be late.'

Jim and I sat together yet apart on the sofa, watching all this with some amusement and, in Jim's case, frustration.

'Come on, Margaret. It's a lovely day. Let's go out for a walk.'

'But somebody might see me.'

'Who are you afraid of seeing you?'

'Anyone from the Post Office.'

'But how can they see you if they're at work?'

'Oh . . . all right, then, but maybe later, when my face isn't such a bright colour.'

Of course, we could have had the talk that Jim wanted at home, but he was unusually determined that nobody should interrupt us, even my mother who would return shortly. So I went and washed my face to try and remove some of the vivid colouring, then cut us some sandwiches and off we went.

'Let's go to Corporation Park first,' he suggested.

'We went there the other day, why don't we go somewhere in the country instead?'

'Well, we've got all day – we can do both.'

As we walked through Little Harwood, I remember feeling guilty not to be at work. After all, it was only a rash . . . but it was on my face, except that it seemed better now.

'I feel a fraud,' I confessed. 'I hope nobody sees me.'

'Never mind. If anyone should recognize you, they will probably just assume you're having a day off.'

'Y-e-s, maybe.' I wasn't too certain about that.

As we approached the grand Victorian entrance to the park, Jim slowed me down to a stop. 'Have you heard the song "Macushla"?' he asked.

'Yes. I've heard it on the radio, when Mother listens to songs in the evenings.'

'It's one of my favourites.' He paused. 'Because of what the word "Macushla" means.'

'Oh yes? Is it a real word, then?'

'Yes, it's an Irish word. In Gaelic, "Macushla" means "my pulse" or "pulse of my heart". Isn't that wonderfully romantic?'

'Yes, it is rather.'

'Sometimes people in Ireland use "Macushla" instead of "Darling", so that's what I'm going to call you.'

We walked through the gateway and along the paths round the park, then came to the seat we'd sat on last time. Jim seemed a bit tense and I was just about to ask him if he was all right, when he put his hand in his pocket and brought something out, then opened it to show me. I could see it looked like gold, but it was quite unusual.

'What is it?' I asked.

'It's called a rosary ring,' said Jim. 'Try it on.'

So I slipped it onto the ring finger of my right hand, held it away and admired it. 'It looks very pretty,' I said. 'I've never seen one of these before. Why is it called a rosary ring?'

'Because . . . can you see these ten little knobs on it? They're the rosary.'

'Oh, that's clever.'

'It used to belong to my grandmother when she was young.'

'Oh. Shouldn't your sister have it?'

'No, she has another of our grandmother's rings.'

'Well, I really like it, thank you.'

So there we were, sat on a bench in Corporation Park, when Jim shuffled himself forward and got down on one knee. He took my hand and said, 'Will you agree to become engaged to me?'

Out of the corner of my eye, I noticed there were some people walking down the path towards us. 'Will you ask me again, so that these people can see?'

Jim looked a bit surprised, then smiled, kissed the back of my hand and asked me again, a little louder this time, 'Will you agree to get engaged to me?'

'Yes,' I replied in a clear voice.

The elderly couple smiled at us as they walked past.

'Good luck,' said the woman.

'Be happy,' added the man.

'We will,' responded Jim. 'Won't we, Margaret?'

'Yes,' I said again. 'I really think we will.'

Jim gave me a big hug, lifting me off my feet and twirling me round.

'Why did you make me do it again?' he asked with a quizzical expression.

'I just wanted other people to see.' I paused. 'I'm a terrible show-off, aren't I?'

'Yes, even with your gentian violets.'

'Oh, I had forgotten about that!' We had a giggle together.

'So we're engaged?' asked Jim, as if wanting to make sure he hadn't dreamt it.

'Yes, we're engaged,' I confirmed. 'Isn't it great?' It wasn't a surprise, but it was exciting, though I didn't take it too seriously at the time after the fracas with Joe, although this was entirely different. Everybody wanted to get married after the war, but my friendship and easy familiarity with Jim had grown into love, rather as it had with Ray, though this time it had been over a much shorter time and still needed developing.

'I'll save up and buy you a proper engagement ring as soon as I can,' he said. 'But I'll just put the rosary ring on your left hand for now.' It fitted perfectly.

'Let's go and tell someone,' I suggested. 'We could go and tell my mother. I think I know what she will say.'

'What's that?' He looked a bit worried.

'I'll let you find out. But don't worry, it's nothing bad,' I laughed.

When we got back to the house and told her, she seemed genuinely pleased. Then she turned to Jim: 'I'll tell you what I've told all the others. Margaret can get engaged as many times as she likes, but she hasn't to marry till she's twenty-one.'

He turned to me. 'Have there been a lot of others, then?'

'Not many,' I said. 'I've already told you about them,

but I was younger then and most of them were lost in the war.'

'But will you give us your blessing to marry after that, Mrs Holden?'

'Yes,' she said with a nod of her head. 'I can see that Margaret thinks a lot of you, Jim, and so do I. But I'm afraid you may have a different response from other people.'

'Do you mean Joe?' he asked.

'Yes, I'm sure Joe won't be happy. But also, more importantly, I'm thinking of Bobby. You know how protective he's always been of you, Margaret. And he still thinks of you as his little sister – far too young to make your own decisions. He wants to make them for you. I think he may have something to say about it, but you'll have to tell him yourself, not me.'

I knew Bobby's next leave wasn't till after Jim had gone, so I would have time to work out the best way to tell him. And at least Jim wouldn't be there to complicate things.

The next stop was Jim's parents and they were delighted for us, though I found out later that his brothers were not so happy. I didn't know why. Perhaps because they hardly knew me, and it had all happened so quickly.

We spent our last two days visiting other relatives and meeting up with friends to announce our engagement. Everyone seemed happy for us. Of course, it would be more than a year before we could marry, as I would only be twenty the next month, and Jim could be away in India for up to two years before his next leave. My emotions were all over the place as these idyllic four weeks came to an end.

As I lay in bed that last night before Jim's departure, I was in quite a state – a mixture of happiness, sadness and anxiety. Our four weeks together had been a blur of happiness and I knew that Jim was the one I loved. But now he was going off, far away, and leaving me for goodness knows how long without him.

I dreaded having to tell Bobby. I was frightened of angering or upsetting him. I knew he had my best interests at heart, but he didn't always have a clear view of what my best interests might be. I desperately wanted his blessing. I hoped for the best, but feared the worst.

In the end, whatever Bobby said, it was Jim that mattered most now. If only I could be sure he would not be killed.

I slept fitfully that night.

20

A Long Goodbye

1946

The dreaded day dawned – Friday, 19 April 1946. I met Jim at the station, as planned. He was back in his uniform, complete with the bush hat that had first attracted my attention just four weeks before. He dropped his kitbag and gave me a long embrace, twirling me off my feet and right round.

'Didn't your parents want to come and see you off?' I asked, once he'd put me down.

'Yes, but I told them I wanted it just to be you and me and I think they understood. I said all my family goodbyes at home.'

We went straight to the platform, sat on a bench and waited for the train, holding hands and chatting non-stop, trying to be cheerful for each other's sake, but feeling the opposite inside.

Far too soon, the train pulled into the station, then screeched and clattered to a halt in front of us. One last kiss and Jim climbed aboard. He sat by the window next to where I stood, and as the guard blew his whistle and waved his green flag, the train slowly clanked and trundled into action. As it began to move out along the track, he waved as furiously as I did, through the clouds of steam, until well after he and the train were out of sight. How long till we could be together again?

I don't remember doing as much work that day as I should have done. I couldn't stop thinking about Jim, watching the clock for the time he would change trains and then when he was due to arrive at Southampton. I wondered what his quarters would be like and how long it would be before he embarked on the troop ship, bound for India.

By the end of Friday afternoon, I felt drained. On my walk home, I weighed up the alternatives – stay in and mooch about Jim not being around any more, or go out on the town. So I went dancing at Tony's, caught up with my old friends and told them about Jim's proposal. They all seemed very pleased for me, but perhaps also a bit uncertain.

'Do you think it's serious this time, Margaret?' one of the boys grinned. 'Or do we still have a chance?'

The music, the fun and of course the dancing lifted my spirits and a funny lad I used to play with in the rec walked me home, telling me jokes all the way back to my house.

The weekend stretched out ahead of me, but I went back to my Fair Isle knitting, playing Lexicon with Jeffrey and Alan, plus of course dancing in the evenings.

On Tuesday I received my first letter from Jim. He was still in Southampton, awaiting his ship. It was a very long letter – several pages, so he must have been bored . . . or besotted with me! Perhaps both, judging by what he wrote.

I took it unopened up to my bedroom and shut the door before I looked at the envelope with his neat writing and the Southampton postmark, then slit the envelope and took out the letter, written on several pages of thin white paper. I began to read it:

Transit Camp,
Southampton.
Sunday morning, 10 a.m.

My own darling Macushla,
I have just had my breakfast after coming back from Church. The atmosphere in the Church just suited my mood, peaceful and quiet. I was waiting in the Church for quite a while before Mass started and as I was waiting, you were in my heart and talking to me, just as if you were sitting beside me, telling me of the day we will be joined together in Holy Matrimony, and of the joy and happiness we will be experiencing on that day.
Macushla, I love you with all my heart and soul, and the day of our reunion cannot come too fast. That Heavenly day when time stands still and everything is hushed . . . We shall be oblivious to everything else, time and people.

Jim had written each page in the same vein as the first – very loving and longing. I felt that too as I read it, right the way through to his last paragraph.

*The clock on the civic building outside has just
struck four. Every four hours the clock chimes out
a few bars from a hymn. I know the tune, but I
can't name it. With every chime that sounds, I am
coming nearer to you, Macushla. I may be sailing
vast oceans or in foreign lands, but I am always
with you in Blackburn, as you will always be by
my side. We shall be waiting patiently and saving
and planning for the happy and joyous day we are
together again.*

*I will close to catch the early post of the day, so
until this evening, au revoir, my darling Macushla.
I am yours, body and soul.*

Your loving Jim x x x x x x x x x x x x x x x

*I shall love you and keep on loving you till my
breath fails me, and my heart stops beating. From
my heart to your heart, Macushla.*

*'I'll walk beside you through the world today'
[written entirely in kisses]*

Letters from Jim arrived daily, sometimes two or three
a day. I used to take some of them to work with me to
read extracts out to the other girls. I also read out the
more descriptive parts of them to Mother, as she liked to
hear about the things he had to do while he waited for
his ship to come. I wrote to him too, almost as often as
he wrote to me.

As Jim was still in Southampton the following weekend,
I took the train down to see him. This was how I knew

he was different from all the others. I really wanted to spend more time with him, while we still could. I left early on Saturday morning and bought a return ticket to arrive back home again on Sunday evening. The night in between I was booked in to stay at the Girls' Friendly Society in Southampton.

I got up very early, boarded the Blackburn 'milk train' to London and settled down for a long journey. At first I seemed to be the only person in my carriage, but a few stops later a young RAF lad got on. We said hello to each other and, being me, I started chatting, asking him about himself and where he was based. His name was David.

'Why are you going to Southampton?' I asked. 'Are you on leave?'

'Yes.' He nodded. 'I'm going home to stay the weekend with my parents.' He paused. 'What about you?'

'I'm going to Southampton for the weekend too,' I said. 'To visit my fiancé.'

We carried on chatting and looking out of the windows at the passing countryside. It helped pass the time, but we were glad when we arrived at Euston station in London. Then we had to find our way to Waterloo station. I was relieved I didn't have to navigate London on my own. It seemed such a huge, busy, noisy city and we had to walk, of course, carrying our overnight bags, as neither of us could afford buses on top of the train fares. It was quite a long walk, but on the way I was amazed to find we were crossing London Bridge, the one in the rhyme, but it wasn't falling down at all.

By the time we had reached Waterloo, found the

platform and boarded the train, I was tired out. Before
long, with the movement of the train, I felt more and
more sleepy. David seemed to notice it.

'You look tired,' he said.

'Yes, it's been a very long journey, all the way from
Blackburn.'

'Why don't you just lie down across the seat and have
a sleep. I'll keep guard.'

I was a bit unsure at first . . . would I be putting myself
in danger? But he was such a nice, innocent-looking young
man that I had the feeling I could trust him . . . and I did
need a nap.

'Thank you,' I said with a smile, as I lay down along
the bench seat and put my coat over me as a cover. The
rhythmic sounds of the train lulled me straight to sleep
and I only woke up as it slowed to a stop.

'That was well timed,' David said with a grin. 'I hope
you enjoy your weekend.'

'You too,' I said as we parted ways.

He turned, put his kitbag over his shoulder and strode
off towards his home.

It was wonderful to see Jim in the station forecourt, waiting
for me with a huge smile. He ran towards me and, being
a whole foot taller than me, swept me off my feet.

'I can't tell you how wonderful it feels to have you in
my arms again,' he said. We walked on a few paces, arm
in arm. 'Are you hungry?'

'A bit,' I admitted. 'But I've got two rounds of sandwiches
with me. Shall we find somewhere to sit and share them?'

After we'd eaten and I'd told Jim how I'd fallen asleep on the train he suggested going to the pictures. 'It's nice and dark in there,' he said with a twinkle in his eyes. 'And we could sit on the back row.'

'Yes, let's,' I agreed. So we did. I can't remember what the film was – I don't think we watched much of it. But I do remember the lovely time we had in the interval, when the organ played and the whole place was in an uproar, singing 'Deep in the Heart of Texas'.

At the end, we all poured out of the cinema into the street. By now it was about teatime and Jim carried my bag for me. 'What time do you have to be at the Girls' Friendly Society hostel?' he asked.

'Well, they close the doors at ten and apparently they don't let anyone in after that, no matter what. So I guess I should be there by around quarter to ten.'

'Right, that gives us a few hours,' said Jim. 'Let me show you the sights of Southampton,' he said with a grin.

'What sights are those?'

'You're right. You're the only sight I wanted to see,' he said, giving me another kiss, right there in the street. Luckily there was nobody around to see us. I was afraid he might be court-martialled for kissing a girl in the street while he was in uniform.

'Let's just go and walk around the port and the town,' I suggested, so that's what we did.

We hadn't got far when, heading along the pavement in the opposite direction, I saw a familiar face.

'Who's that smiling at you?' asked Jim, sounding suspicious.

'It's all right,' I said. 'It's David, the RAF boy I told you about – the one who guarded me while I slept on the train. And that must be his father with him.'

We stopped and did the introductions and then the father invited us back to their house.

'Do come back and have a cup of tea with us.'

I glanced at Jim, whose face told a story.

'Well,' I began. 'I'm afraid we . . .'

'I insist,' interrupted the father. 'Just for a cup of tea and some of my wife's cake. You needn't stay long.'

'Well . . .' Jim hesitated.

'That's decided, then. Come along with us. It's only five minutes' walk away.'

So we walked along with David and his father to a sweet little house in a quiet street, where we were invited to sit down in their comfortable living room, while his cheery wife brought tea and cake on a tray.

I've never known anyone to talk as much as David's father. He talked and talked. A fresh tray of teas appeared after the first hour, with biscuits this time and delicious home-made crumpets.

Jim was asked about his war service in Burma, which astonished them and took us well into the evening. Darkness fell and the blackout curtains were drawn tight across the windows, even though the war was over, and still David's father was talking and talking. I looked at my watch as obviously as I could, but he didn't take the hint. A few minutes later Jim too looked at his watch but there was still no break in the conversation to allow us to stand up. Neither of us wanted to be rude to these lovely people, but Jim was worried about losing the opportunity to have time alone with me, and I was becoming increasingly anxious about getting to the GFS hostel before they locked up at ten.

In the end, we just had to insist on leaving so that both of us could get back in time to where we were meant to be. After hurried goodbyes, we finally left their house at 9.30 in the evening. As soon as they closed their front door, we ran through the streets of Southampton. Luckily, Jim had already been to find out where the GFS hostel was and we just made it, arriving with only two minutes to spare.

On the Sunday morning, as early as allowed, Jim came to meet me and this time we really did walk around the port and the town, talking all the time we had – only a few hours before I had to catch my train back. I desperately didn't want to go. The relationship was becoming more and more special to me with every moment I spent with Jim. We shared our thoughts and feelings as we planned for the day we could marry and the future that would lie ahead. I was rather pensive on the journey back to London and then onwards to Blackburn. I was pretty certain of my feelings for him, the spark we had for each other, the loving letters he wrote every day. When would I see Jim again?

By the end of the next week, surprisingly, Jim's ship still hadn't arrived, so I travelled down to Southampton again. This time the Girls' Friendly Society was full, so I had to

stay at the YWCA. That was a novelty! It was clean and
had what I needed, but was a little less genteel. The
previous weekend we had walked around the city, but this
time we took a packed lunch with us and kept going till
we came to the countryside, where we found a stretch of
open woodland. We picked our way between the tall trees
and found a little clearing where perhaps only animals
gathered. Here we sat on a fallen tree trunk and ate our
lunch – sandwiches first, then a small cake each. I bit into
my piece, but the sponge was so dense that I couldn't eat
it all.

The forest was green and peaceful, save for the natural
orchestra of lively birdsong. Jim laid down his army coat
and we lay side by side, holding hands and looking up
through the branches to the blue sky, enjoying the spring
warmth. The weekend was too brief and the parting was
painful, but it had to be. We knew this might be the
beginning of many months apart, with half the world
between us.

Jim continued writing his letters after that brief but
glorious weekend. Towards the end of the next week, I
received three letters on the same day, all written on the
Wednesday and recalling the carefree time we had spent
together. The first was written in the early hours, when
Jim couldn't sleep.

Transit Camp,
Southampton.
Wednesday morning, 2 a.m.

Dearest Macushla,

We have parted for a while, but compared with the happy lifetime we are going to spend together it is but a few seconds. We were made for each other . . .

In this letter, Jim told more of his love for me and his dreams for our future. He urged me to keep in touch with his mother and visit her whenever I could.

I am going on the BOAT tomorrow, Margaret, for my long ocean journey and long train rides. Through Monsoons, sweat and glaring sunshine, you will always be with me. Just one thought of you and I can take everything else in my stride.

I have just been paid and this afternoon we have an FFI (do you know what that is?). We cannot leave Camp as Guards have been placed at the gates.

I am thinking of you all the time. Our love for each other is like a fierce fire which will never be quenched.

I don't suppose I will get any mail from you until I get off the Boat, but I know you will be thinking of me and writing as often as you can . . .

The second letter I received that day was written at 11 a.m., just a few hours after the first, and included four lines of a popular song: 'Happy Days, Happy Hours, Happy Years', which expressed his love for me.

The third letter was also written on the same date.

Wednesday, 8.30 p.m.

My dearest Macushla,

It is getting dark here and I have just left the NAAFI Canteen, where a soldier was playing the piano. He played 'our' tune and it was just as if my stomach was coming up through my mouth, dragging my heart with it.

I told you in my previous letter that we could not leave Camp because of the Guards, but I sneaked out.

I went to the bench where we had been sitting on Saturday and stayed there for half an hour. I would have given my right arm to have had you there by my side. Then I wandered off to where we had been in the woods on Sunday. The foot-marks were still there and the grass was still flat where my overcoat had been. Then, can you remember giving me part of a cake which you couldn't eat? We put it into a paper bag in the bushes. I found it – the piece of cake you had bitten was in the bag. I kissed it and fed it to the birds which were surging from the bushes beyond. I know you would have liked it that way . . .

They are telling us to put out the lights now, Margaret, so I must close. I will write again before the boat sails away.

So goodbye until tomorrow.

You are always in my heart forever.
My body and soul are yours to cherish for ever
and ever.
Goodnight my sweetheart.
Jim xxxxxxxxxxxxxxxxxxxxxxxxxx

That night, after reading his three letters, I lay in bed
and imagined Jim boarding the ship, pausing to look back
as he climbed the gangway, thinking of me here in
Blackburn, thinking of him. By now he would be ever
farther away at sea. If I knew where he was I could plot
it in Jeffrey's school atlas.

It wasn't till the next day that I found out where he
was, when another three letters arrived from Jim. The first
of these began with an explanation:

Transit Camp, Southampton
Thursday morning, 10 a.m.

My dearest Macushla,
I have just returned from the Parade Ground.
Many of the soldiers were taken to the Boat, but
we were told to wait for another Boat, as that one
was full. I don't know when I shall go. Everything
is so uncertain. I do wish I could have you down
here, but I might have left by the time you arrive.
I should die if that were to happen . . .

The second letter, written at 2.30 that afternoon, began
by saying:

*I am glad more than ever now that I did not catch
the boat. I can write you a nice, long letter whilst
I am still in England . . . I am alone in the
barrack room, with all your photos spread around
me. You fill the room, Margaret, and tears come to
my eyes when I think of the happy times we have
spent together and will spend together. Remember
when we cooked our meal over the open fire? And
I dropped the egg on the grass. Clumsy of me.
When I saw you leaning over the fire frying the
eggs and you kissed me for being successful with
the fire? That fire is still burning, only a different
type of fire, Margaret, the fire of our love which
will never die . . .*

In the third letter of that batch Jim explained that, not
knowing when the next ship would come, he had been
trying to get leave, but unsuccessfully so far. It was so
hard for both of us still to be in the same country, only
200 miles apart, and unable to be together.

On the following Monday, 13 May, I arrived home from
work to the surprise of my life. I let myself in as usual
and walked into the living room to find Jim sitting on the
sofa, talking to my mother.

'What are you doing here?'

'What do you think?' He stood and we embraced – a
wonderful warm feeling.

'Don't you want me, then?'

'Of course I do. It's great to see you here, but how . . .

did they give you some leave after all? Or have you absconded?' I smiled, sitting down next to him.

'The second ship didn't come, so they're sending me to London to fly me and some others out to India instead, once they've arranged everything. I pleaded with my lieutenant to let me come here before London and he managed to fix it for me. I didn't hesitate. I didn't even have time to send you a telegram. I just packed my kitbag, caught the first train to Blackburn . . . and here I am!'

'That's marvellous. How long is your leave?'

'Only forty-eight hours, but we can do a lot in that time. Can you get the day off tomorrow . . . and maybe the next day?'

'I'll certainly try, but I won't know till tomorrow morning.'

Mother had cooked plenty, so we all had tea together.

'As it's my first evening, let's spend it here with your mother, if that's all right with her,' he said. 'It's already my second home and it's so cosy being here with you.'

Mother had come through into the living room again and nodded her head.

'That will be fine, Jim,' she agreed with a smile.

As it happened, I had told Kathleen and Jenny that I would meet them at Tony's that night to have some fun. So when I saw Jim there, looking so pleased to have surprised me and, I suppose, assuming I would drop everything to be with him, well, yes, I was delighted . . . but I wasn't going to let my friends down.

So I told him, 'I've arranged to go to the dance tonight, at Tony's, with my friends.'

'Well, you didn't know I was coming. I'm sure they'll understand your change of plans, now that I have come home on such a short leave.'

'But I don't want to cancel the dancing. You could come with me?'

'I don't want to go dancing. I don't like going to Tony's and I don't much want to be with your friends tonight either. I just want to be with you.' That's how Jim was. He wanted his entire life to be just the two of us. But I had other plans, and I felt like being awkward, just so that he knew I was the independent type.

'I don't want to go dancing,' he repeated.

'Well, I don't want to be engaged,' I replied, in a mock huff, and flounced out of the room. I went upstairs to change and went to the dance.

I had a lovely evening with my friends. Much later, when I arrived back home, I was amazed and very relieved to find Jim was still there, with Mother and Jeffrey, waiting for my return. As I came into the room, he stood up from the sofa and said: 'Do you want to get engaged again, now?'

'Oh, well,' I replied. 'Might as well.' And it was back on again.

I took the next day off and we explored more of the country lanes together, dreading the moment we would have to say goodbye again.

The time went far too quickly, and early in the morning of Wednesday, 15 May, I went with him to the station. We embraced and he boarded the train bound for London. It was so packed with troops and travellers that he had to stand in the corridor and, as it wasn't quite time for it to go yet, he opened the door again so that we could continue talking and kissing. He didn't want to go and I didn't want him to go. I had tears pouring down my face and the guard was trying to get me to stand back, away from the train, but I didn't want to. Jim pretended to close the door. Then the guard turned round and blew his whistle, just as Jim and I were locked in a kiss.

'Stand back,' called the guard along the platform as he waved his flag and I was about to obey, when Jim took hold of me and lifted me up right into the train with him, slamming the door closed behind me, just as the train started to pull away.

As I realized what was happening, I gathered myself together and said, 'I'll just get the train back from the next stop.' I hadn't realized there were no stops till at least halfway to London, and by that time I had decided I didn't want to go back.

All the compartments were full so we sat on Jim's kitbag in the corridor, giggling together most of the way, then standing when the train became more crowded as it approached London. I had nothing with me except my handbag. I was expecting to go straight to work after I'd seen Jim off, and to go home as usual at the end of the day, working through my lunch hour to catch up on the hour I would have lost earlier . . . but I couldn't do any of that now, and I couldn't even let them know till I found a phone kiosk.

When we arrived in London, it didn't seem that easy to leave again, so I decided to stay. The first thing was for Jim to sign in at his London HQ in the Hotel Grand

Central in Marylebone. So we found the place and he did the paperwork. They expected him to sleep there, but they didn't allow women, now that it had been taken over by the army, so I couldn't stay there with him. And it was too late for me to get a train back home that day.

We didn't know what to do. We were still in the hotel reception area, so we asked where the nearest Girls' Friendly Society or YWCA were, but nobody seemed to know. Not surprising really, since they were all men.

So we left the hotel and bumped into an army pal of Jim's. He was a Londoner and knew this area well, so that was a lucky break. We all went back into the Hotel Grand Central and his pal used the hotel phone and found us a place to go. Jim came back to where I was sitting and told me he had rented a room for the night.

'I can't,' I said in alarm. 'I haven't got a nightie.'

I had my ration book with me, in my handbag, so off we went to find a shop selling nightdresses. I felt really bad about this, as Mother usually made all my nighties. I had to use six precious clothing coupons out of my ration book for the nightie I chose. It was a long, thick, granny-type thing that I'd picked, with long sleeves and a high neck with a neat collar and a ribbon bow. I was already thinking of what Clarry had said: 'No touching of flesh,' and 'No crossing the line.' I still had no idea what that meant, but I had the feeling it was something to do with Jim and me sharing a room in London together.

'I have to phone them at work,' I said. 'Or I'll lose my job.'

'Well, we'd better find a phone box, then,' he agreed. 'And what about your mother?'

We found the familiar red kiosk and I got my pennies out to make the call.

'The General Post Office switchboard please, in Blackburn,' I told the operator, and soon got through. I was relieved to hear a friendly voice at the other end. It was Margaret Abbott, a good friend of mine. She sounded quite excited at the intrigue, but went to get the supervisor, who was anything but excited.

I explained the situation: 'The train pulled away while I was still on it, saying goodbye to my army sweetheart. So I'm afraid I couldn't get back to Blackburn in time for work this morning,' I said.

'This isn't good enough, Margaret. Everyone has had more work to do because we didn't know you would be absent. If I'd known, I could have got a temporary replacement for you.'

I talked her round to letting me keep my job.

'Well, all right, Margaret. You are a good worker and we wouldn't want to lose you. When do you think you will be back?'

'We-e-ll . . .' I told her about Jim's flight leaving soon for India and asked if I could use up all the rest of my holiday allocation to stay in London for the rest of the week.

Gradually, I gained her sympathy and her reluctant agreement.

Next I somehow needed to let my mother know. I had the idea of calling the phone box at the end of Robinson

Street and hoping someone would answer it and go to fetch her to the phone, but that might not work. I was just about to put the phone down from calling the GPO, when:

'Hello, you're back to me now,' came Margaret Abbott's cheery voice. 'Would you like me to go round to your house after work and give your mother a message?'

'Oh, would you? That would be a great help.'

I knew she might be tempted to spread the news, so I tried to be careful. I told her the simple truth: that I was stuck in London with a friend and wouldn't be back till the weekend. I'm sure that must have set her wondering, but at least Mother would know I was safe.

Jim was waiting outside the kiosk, holding a scrap of paper with the address of our lodgings on it, so we went off to find where we would be staying. We soon found it – an ordinary house, with a small, sparse room and one bed in it. I started praying as soon as I saw it. I'd never slept with anybody in the same bed. I was the only daughter, the only granddaughter.

'I can see you praying,' Jim said with a grin. Then he took on a more concerned expression. 'Perhaps I'd better sleep on the floor?'

'No, I can't let you do that,' I replied. But from then on I was a nervous wreck.

We stayed together in that room, with its one bed, for all five nights and I felt confused, hovering between heaven and hell. It was a wonderful time and also a fearful time. Without quite realizing it, we crossed the line . . . and I can't begin to describe how I felt. It was marvellous –

great. But I went through a whole range of emotions. It was a cross between terrified and gloriously happy, I suppose, but also with a lot of guilt. Clarry's words kept coming back to me; his warnings plagued me. My expectations got all mixed up. I didn't know what to think. Clarry had said: *once you've crossed the line, there is no going back*. Would I always be haunted by that? Jim went and told his senior officer what we had done and asked whether that would make a baby. We didn't have a clue. I was very worried about it, so was glad when he asked, but there wasn't a clear answer.

During the days we went walking and out to eat together. Jim had to sign in at the Grand Central Hotel every morning, and we could never go too far from there in case he was needed, either for his plane to India or, as on one day, to take part in a parade. But the rest of the time was ours. We strolled in the parks and we walked around the shops, looking in their huge windows, choosing what furniture we might like to have in our first home, after we were married. We started to make plans for our future life together.

Finally the time came – the heartbreaking time of going to the station, having to leave him and come home alone. When I got back to Blackburn, I was still confused about what we'd done together. I couldn't talk to any of my friends about it and especially not to Mother.

In fact, I thought Mother would blow a fuse when I got back but she seemed her usual calm self. 'I'm sorry if you were worried about me,' I said.

'I didn't know you had gone. I assumed you were at work all day, as usual, until Margaret came round to tell me.'

'She gave you my message, then?'

'Yes, and I got Jim's too.'

'Jim's?' I was incredulous.

'Yes, didn't you know? He wrote a letter to tell me what had happened with the train moving before you could get off.' She paused. 'And he said he would look after you, and I trusted him . . . and here you are, safely back home again.'

I didn't know what to say . . . I was so proud of Jim for doing such a caring thing. It was just like him.

Jim continued writing to me morning, noon and night, so that his letters poured though our letter box, two or three a day. He had little else to occupy him while he waited for his transport to India, other than to revisit all the places we had been during those wonderful five days in London.

Despite my employers being cross with me for taking leave without notice or permission, I somehow convinced them that it would never happen again. But I had to work even harder and longer than before, to show them I meant it. So I could only write once a day back to Jim, except at weekends.

While we were in London we had talked about our future life together, even down to what kind of clock we would have on the mantelpiece. Jim wrote in one of his letters that his preference was for 'a Westminster chimer, which will give a peal every quarter.' I hated the things myself!

A few letters later, he wrote to paint a word picture of what our lives would be like:

> *I can picture us now, Margaret, me getting up first to light the fire and getting ready for work, looking forward to my breakfast, cooked by you, because I can't for the life of me cook bacon and eggs, as you already know. Then I can picture me returning home to you at night after work is done, to sit down to tea, just you and me to be together until the following morning. I think I shall enjoy looking after the chickens and the small garden. We can't help but be the happiest couple in the whole wide world.*

When I read this paragraph, I naturally assumed it meant that Jim would leave the army before our wedding. After all, everything we had talked about in London depended on that, so we carried on with planning how we would have our house.

On 27 May, I spent my twentieth birthday without Jim. It was a subdued celebration with my friends at Tony's, and nearly all the boys danced with me, including possessive Joe – I couldn't say no as I worried about his reaction, but it was difficult for me and even more so for him. I could see the pain in his eyes as I did my usual flirting with everyone. He clearly hadn't got over me yet. But none of the other boys were special to me now. I only had that real spark with Jim and he would be gone, maybe, for a very long time.

At the end of the evening, Joe came up to me with a small, slim gift-wrapped box. I didn't know what to do or say, other than, 'Thank you very much.'

'Open it when you get home,' he said.

I did, and it was a very pretty box with a bottle of perfume inside called Elle Elle. When I dabbed a spot of it on my wrist, it gave off a beautiful scent. I know it seems strange, but it immediately became my favourite perfume and I used it for a long time, until it ran out. A couple of years later, when I was throwing out some rubbish and started tearing up the pretty box that Joe had given me the perfume in, I found a little groove under where the perfume bottle had been and under that was a note: *I love you. I always have and I always will. Joe 1946.*

Can you imagine how I felt? Even now, I still feel guilty that I'd let him down so badly.

Jim's time finally came on 3 June to fly off to India, by way of Cairo.

I have now left England, flying over the English Channel. I did experience some sort of thrill when the plane left the ground and I knew I was on my way, but the thrill I am living to experience is the one when I hold you in my arms again, never to be parted . . .

With every thrust of the propeller, with every

beat of my heart, with every second that passes,
my love for you is growing within me . . .

By the time I received this letter, he would be settled
into his new barracks, with half the world dividing us.
He'd never felt so far away before.

21

A World Apart

1946–1947

Almost as soon as Jim had gone, in June 1946, Bobby wrote to tell us that he would be coming back to Britain for good in early August. Normally I would have been very glad to see him after all his time away, but I feared having to tell him about my engagement to Jim. How would he react? Not well, I was sure, especially if he ever found out about my five days in London with him. Should I tell him myself, or wait till someone else did?

As the weeks passed and a particularly rainy summer gripped the town, I longed for Jim to come back and felt as if some essential part of me was missing. Every day, except when the situation in India held up the post, I had his loving letters to maintain the thread between us. They were our lifeline. Reading his latest letter, I could tell he yearned to be back in Blackburn as he wrote of trying to cope with his new living conditions:

They have dumped us here, right in the middle of a hot, dusty desert – a fitting introduction to the

*land of torment . . . It is very hot here and
sweaty and I am very uncomfortable. The sun is
glaring down and the dust almost obscures it.
Boy would I love a cup of tea made by your
mother. We used to drink a lot of tea, didn't we?
That is the only thing you can drink here. Beer is
unknown. The water is always putrid and
warm . . .*

At night, when he finally arrived in his new barracks,
he described as much of his surroundings as he was allowed
to:

*The incessant racket made by the bullfrogs and
mosquitoes is enough to drive anybody off his
head. I have had enough of this place . . . dirt,
bad smells and discomforts. At night, when
everyone is in bed under their mosquito nets, as if
by a signal, all the jackals and hyenas begin their
incessant howling and shrieking. As soon as I get
into my bed, I shall hear the big rats nosing
around the room in search of food. Heaven knows
what I shall do if any of them jump into bed with
me.*

At the letter's close, his thoughts turned, as they always
did, to home and our future, where his heart was:

*Each time I write your address on the envelope,
my mind fills with cherished memories of the many*

times I have come down to your house to call on you. Remember when I used to stumble down the high step at the corner of the back street, and how many times have I come round the corner to find you playing with Alan and the children? I can picture it now, as I came down one Sunday after dinner and you were giving Alan a donkey ride on your back. You were wearing a green dress and afterwards we walked to Hurst Green. That was a marvellous day, Macushla. I would give anything just to relive any one of those hours of gladness . . . It reminds me of the poem, which I'm sure must be about the Ribble Valley and Hurst Green:

There is not in the wide world a valley so sweet,
As that vale in whose bosom the bright waters meet.

(From 'The Meeting of the Waters' by Thomas Moore)

On 23 August 1946, only two and a half months into his posting, Jim wrote a scrawling letter to say that he was in the camp hospital, down with malaria for the fifth time. He had it very badly this time and had to be injected with all sorts of things. Although he underplayed how ill he felt, I was worried. I knew it could be life-threatening and was always relieved when another letter arrived. Within a few days of starting treatment, though, he began to rally and was soon back to his duties again.

In early September, however, I was even more anxious:

My own darling Macushla,

You must excuse the terrible writing as the place where I am now isn't what you would call an ideal writing desk – namely the street cart. You see, there is trouble again in Bombay and we are here on the outskirts of the city in case the military is called in. I am browned off . . . I have been wet through all day, the place stinks and I have no bed to go back to tonight.

To make matters worse, I haven't had a letter from you for nine days . . . I keep wondering if you are ill and I am worried to death . . . To be without mail from you is almost driving me crazy . . . You mean everything to me . . .

Gosh, but I'll be glad when I am away out of this hole, back in England where everything is clean and the air is pure, where everybody isn't waiting around the next corner to stick a knife in your back . . .

I was always fearful of his being killed, just as so many others had been before him. As I read his description of men with knives standing round corners ready to attack, I wondered whether he had even survived that day. Fortunately, his letter the next day showed him back on form again, having received three of my letters at once.

As Bobby's return loomed closer, I felt more and more anxious about how to tell him and what he would say. I tried to think of various ways to start the conversation . . .

but almost as soon as he entered the house, Bobby demanded to know everything about Jim. Somebody must have told him already!

It was as tricky as I feared. He was not happy that I had got engaged to a man I'd spent so little time with (as far as he knew) and that it was someone he had never even met.

'I expect you have met him,' I said.

'Oh yes? When?'

'When we were children, he used to come and play at the Tanners'.'

'Well, that's not exactly a recommendation, is it? Lots of children came to play at the Tanners'. The whole of Blackburn probably came there at one time or another, but you don't have to marry one of them.'

I bit my lip. He was clearly worried about me.

'And what about Joe? Aren't you still supposed to be engaged to him?'

'No, I told you, remember, on your last leave, that it was already over then.'

'Well, that's not what Joe told me. You still had his ring, so you were still engaged to him the last time I was here. You can't be engaged to two people at once.'

'I've tried several times to give him back his ring, but he won't take it.'

'If you want to get married,' continued Bobby, 'how can you possibly not want to marry Joe? He's handsome, he's a good dancer, he's generous . . . and he loves you. At least if you marry Joe, I get on with him well and I will make sure he looks after you properly.'

'But I don't love Joe,' I said, trying to stay calm. 'I like him as a friend, but I don't love him.'

'I don't want you marrying a stranger,' he continued.

'Jim's not a stranger. Mother likes him.'

'Huh! Mother likes everybody. And anyway, it's you I'm worried about.'

'Well, I love Jim,' I said, defiantly. 'He's a good, kind man. We're a couple and we love each other, so I am going to marry him.'

'You're too young to know what love is. I'm the head of this household and you have to have my permission to marry anyone. So I say you can't marry Jim.'

'Not yet, maybe,' I said, trying to stand my ground. 'But I can after I'm twenty-one.'

'Well, that's not going to happen. You'll probably have a few more engagements yet before then, knowing you!' he sneered.

I decided not to take the bait and kept my mouth shut. One step at a time.

It had been an uncomfortable conversation, and others followed over the next few days and weeks. I didn't dare mention anything about my trips to Southampton . . . and especially my week in London with Jim.

While Jim was away I had continued with all my favourite activities, including the regular evenings I spent at the George and Dragon with some of my old friends, Kathleen and Peggy, plus some new ones from the GPO and Tony's, including Margaret Abbott, Frank Best and Bob Tyson, who was courting Doris Smith, so she came too. None of us had a lot of money; none of us drank much, but we would often all get together to sing. Well, I didn't sing, because I was terrible! Joe was a good singer, though, and he had now been demobbed, so he joined us. I continued to be friends with him, in a reserved way, but made sure I was never alone with him.

'If you haven't got anything better to do,' I suggested to Bobby as I was leaving for work a few days later, 'why don't you come and join us down at the George and Dragon tonight?'

'Well, I might,' he said with a shrug.

About halfway through the evening, in walked Bobby. He ordered a pint at the bar and came over. As luck would have it, the only empty seat was next to my friend Margaret Abbott from the Post Office, so Bobby sat there and they started chatting. They hit it off really well, which led to them going out together and soon they were courting. Bobby stayed in the RAF and was posted to Stornaway, from where they continued their courtship, writing letters to each other. I was relieved he had something else to think about, to take his mind off my engagement to Jim.

Jim's letters kept coming, all of them full of ardent love, expressed in every way he could think of. He said he understood about me carrying on a social life as before with my friends, both girls and boys. But I was beginning to feel that our relationship was becoming too intense, especially as we might not see each other for many months and India wasn't the safest place for him to be. I suggested to him that we should think of our relationship as more of a friendship while he was away. I suppose I was protecting myself in case he came back in a coffin. I'd been there before with Ray and Les – committing myself, only for it to end in tragedy.

'I'm young,' I wrote to him in one of my letters. 'And I think it's getting too serious. I think we should give it a rest for a while.'

Jim wrote back to say that, for 'whatever happiness we have, we will have to pay a high price.' We had talked about this before, when we had been in London. But we both agreed that this didn't mean we should avoid being happy, as long as we accepted there might be some kind of payment laid at our door.

But now, that's what I was afraid of: we'll have to pay for this. I'd been this happy before and I'd been hurt. I didn't want to rush into it again. I wrote to him that evening to explain how I was feeling.

But Jim's response in his next letter was, 'I could not live without you,' and, 'You are my life, my heart and soul. Without you, I could not continue.'

Was he insinuating something? Was this emotional blackmail? Or was I imagining it? I couldn't be sure, but he wrote similar phrases in several letters, so I didn't dare mention my concerns again. In my head, I stopped planning our future home and life together. Jim carried on with all his suggestions, but it seemed so far ahead of us that I didn't have the enthusiasm to do anything tangible about all that yet. I was uncertain in some ways, but not in others. I still had that spark for him. In some ways, Jim was still an unknown quantity and yet not one of the men coming back from the war measured up to him. He

was everything right to me, and he showered his love on
me through his letters. I had made a promise to him and
I didn't intend to go back on a promise, especially when
he was halfway across the world. I just didn't know what
to do.

Jim was still firmly on my mind the next day as I walked
to meet Mother at the cinema. As I was crossing Darwen
Street, outside the Post Office, I suddenly caught sight of
a figure I recognized. It was my father. I was so shocked
– I had no idea he was living locally. I could hardly believe
it. I hadn't seen him for more than ten years, not since
the night he left with his blonde, who I noticed was walking
slowly behind him. I ran over to speak to him and when
she saw me she stayed well back, out of the way.

'Hello, Father,' I said, stepping in front of him.

'Hello, love,' he replied, looking as surprised as me.
Perhaps more so. I was a little girl the last time he saw
me, so I wasn't sure he even recognized me immediately.
He looked puzzled for a few seconds, then realized. 'Hello,
Margaret,' he said, without even a smile.

'How are you?' I asked him.

'Fair,' he replied. 'Well enough.'

I waited for him to ask me, but he didn't, so I told him
my news. 'I'm going to get married in a few months' time,'
I explained.

'Oh no, you're not!' he growled. 'Who is he?'

'Jim Ford' I said, dismayed at his reaction.

'Never heard of him. Where does he live?'

'Mary Street.'

'Never heard of it.'

'It's in Eanam, and they're a good Catholic family,' I added, hoping that would please him. 'Will you come to the wedding and give me away?'

'No. You're not marrying him,' he repeated. 'So I won't give you away . . . and that's that.' Without another word, he turned and walked off down the street. He'd barely been involved in my life and he'd still managed to make me feel ashamed and upset.

When I got to the cinema, I told Mother what had happened.

'So I don't really feel like watching a film this evening,' I explained.

'We'd better go home,' she nodded. 'You never know what he's going to do.' So off we went, back to Robinson Street, to the safety of our house, in the knowledge that he didn't even know where we lived.

I never saw him again.

Jim had asked me before he left for India to go and visit his mother while he was away. He wanted us to get to know each other better. Jim's parents were always welcoming, especially his mother, but his brothers were still not happy about our engagement, particularly the eldest, Jack, so he and Louis would always make themselves scarce when I came. In fact, I rarely saw any of them, so we never actually talked to each other. It was only Jim who got it in the neck from Jack for being too young to marry, and he took no notice. It seems the brothers were not that close and, in temperament and looks, Jim was the

odd one out. As Christmas 1946 approached, I reflected
on the long seven and a half months Jim and I had been
apart already and how much I missed sharing such occasions with him. If only he could come back again soon.

Christmas in India for Jim was very different in some
ways, but alike in others. On 24 December he wrote:

*I'm afraid that nothing exciting has happened for
me this Christmas Eve. There has been a kind of
party in the Mess, with singing, etc., the beer being
finished by nine o'clock, as there were only three
bottles per man . . . We are having turkey and
goose for dinner tomorrow, so I hope the cook
makes a good job of it. We will only have a light
snack at lunchtime, then the big feed at seven p.m.
The food is the only reminder of Christmas around
here. The weather is so warm one could fry eggs
on the pavement (if there was a pavement) . . .
Gosh, they could have all the turkeys and geese
and good cheer in the world, if I could be sitting
down somewhere with you, eating some of your
mother's chips . . .*

*I can picture the dance halls and the parties of
crowds and merrymakers. Still, if they enjoyed
themselves a million times more than they are
doing now, they would still be unhappy, compared
to how happy we two will be from that heavenly
and glorious moment when we meet again. Every
day will be Christmas Day, every second complete
with love and happiness . . .*

New Year 1947 heralded much soul-searching for me as I once again felt insecure about what this year would bring. Would Bobby come to accept my engagement with Jim? Would Jim survive to leave the army and come home this year? If he did, would we be married?

Jim was looking ahead too. Despite 'crossing the line' in London, we were both still very hazy about how things worked. I knew that my two younger brothers were both born in my mother's bedroom, but how did they get there? Nobody ever told me. Jim was equally confused, as he wrote in one of his letters: 'How wonderful it will be if, when we are married, we wake up one morning to find our own little baby at the bottom of our bed.'

The months passed and my twenty-first birthday approached. Uncle George arranged for me to have my party in the posh ballroom at the Conservative Club, with a small band playing my favourite music. My mother had the invitations printed and I gave them to all my friends and relations. I also invited Jim's family. Bobby, still stationed in Stornoway, managed to get leave to come home for the party. All my aunts and uncles were there, and my Harrison grandparents, Jim's parents and all my friends came. Some of the boys came in uniform, which was lovely for me. It seemed so much brighter – just like during the war.

Sadly, I couldn't help noticing a slight sense of discomfort amongst the older generations, between my Grandma and Grandad Harrison, who were both staunchly Protestant, and some of the older Catholic guests on both sides. They sat apart from each other in the hall and avoided talking to one another where they could. I was worried that Jim's parents might hear a whisper or notice any tension there might be. But if they did, they certainly didn't show it, smiling and enjoying the evening, to my great relief.

The party itself went very well and I had a great time with everyone, despite Jim's absence. There was one particularly awkward moment, however, when Uncle Eddie's wife Jenny came over to speak to me.

'Happy twenty-first birthday, Margaret,' she began, in a loud voice. 'How do you like your jewellery?'

'What jewellery?' I asked. I noticed that the guests around us had suddenly gone quiet and there were some loud intakes of breath nearby.

'Grandma Holden's jewellery,' she said. 'Do you remember, when you were little and played with all of Grandma's gold jewellery?'

I nodded, but was too surprised to speak, uncertain as to why she had asked me. I was just about to say that her jewels hadn't been in her cupboard any more after she died, but then I realized that might suggest I was accusing someone of taking them.

Just then I caught Mother giving Jenny a black look.

'He got rid of that years ago,' Mother said, then turned away.

Somebody must have told the band to play something loud and this incident was soon forgotten. In bed that night, I began to puzzle out what had happened from my mother's reaction. Why had nobody told me that Grandma had left me her jewellery? How come Jenny knew about it and I didn't? And who had got rid of it? My father, perhaps? Surely he hadn't thrown it all away? I assumed he must have sold it when he was losing at cards.

When the party was over, some of us went back to our house, more or less across the road, where Kathleen, Peggy, Jenny, Margaret Abbott, Bert, my brother Bobby and I stayed up and talked the night away. Bobby was now quite serious with Margaret so he was in a good mood that night. It was a flash of the old Bobby who always wanted the best for me and took that thrashing for me when I was little. But how long would it last?

Sure enough, the next day he asked me: 'Are you still carrying on your correspondence with Jim?'

'Yes.' I was going to say more, but something told me the least said the better.

'Well, you needn't think you are going to marry him if he ever comes back here.'

'Why not?'

'Because I won't give my permission.'

'But I don't need your permission,' I said. 'Now that I'm twenty-one.'

'I'm head of this household, the man of the house, so I have to make the decisions.'

Not my decisions, I thought . . . not any more.

In fact, I was feeling rather disillusioned. It was more than a year since Jim had gone to India, and there was no sign of him being allowed to come home. In the weeks following my birthday I made a confusing discovery when

Jim let a clue slip in one of his letters. Instead of working out the last few months of his army service and coming home to start a new life in our own home, as we had planned, he had actually signed on, from the start, for a term of nine years in the regular army, plus another three in the Reserves. Through all our letters, he had somehow neglected to tell me this. Whether he forgot or preferred not to tell me, I don't know. But it made a charade of all this planning for how we wanted our own house to look and what to have in it. We would have to live in married quarters wherever we were sent, with no home to call our own, or else live separately. This was not the life I had planned.

I knew he still loved me very much, and I loved him too, but I felt unsettled and insecure. Disappointed because the excitement had gone out of my life, I was restless and felt it was time for me to make some sort of decision of my own. I needed to feel as if I was taking back control of my life.

Because I worked with Bobby's girlfriend, Margaret, I knew she was also feeling at a bit of a crossroads as things were heating up between them. Bobby was becoming too possessive, so she wanted out of the relationship.

With both Jim and Bobby away, Margaret and I talked it through and we decided, on a whim, that we would both give up our Post Office jobs to go and join the WAAF (the Women's Auxiliary Air Force).

I wrote and told Jim our plan, thinking he would be pleased for me, so I was very disappointed to read his response:

Naturally I have been shaken by what you told me
as regards joining the WAAF . . . You want my
honest feelings – here they are. I know you want
to be doing something to pass the time away. In
that respect, it will favour us admirably. You won't
be in long enough for your number to dry (army
wisecrack to young soldiers). I hope that you have
found out that you will definitely get your
discharge when we are married. So you see, sweet
darling, you will only be wearing uniform for a
few months at the most.

Despite Jim's lukewarm reply, I was determined to do
this for myself. So off we went to sign up, but first we
had to have medicals. Margaret passed hers, but sadly I
didn't. I had to go back twice for further investigation
into an old hearing problem I'd had.

Meanwhile, Bobby found out what we'd done. I don't
know what he said to Margaret to dissuade her, but he
made it very clear what he had in mind for me.

'As I'm in the RAF, if you join the WAAF, I can claim
you, as my sister, to come to be with me on my base.'

Well, I didn't know whether that was true or if he was
making it up, but the thought of being stuck with Bobby
on an island in the North Atlantic put me off completely.
So, all in all, the whole idea just fizzled out.

Jim was very pleased with that outcome and in his
letters he seemed optimistic that he might, at last, be able
to have some leave. Though it was exciting for both of
us, I didn't dare get my hopes up.

22

Ship Ahoy!

1947

On 27 August 1947, from New Delhi, Jim wrote the best letter yet:

> *I have been told that I will be 'standing by' to move out from the 3rd September . . . I only hope the fact that so many troops and civilians are leaving India, due to independence, doesn't make shipping scarce. I am like a cat on hot bricks. I do want to see you so very much and to be with you . . .*
>
> *I have all my clothing ready now, darling . . . just this afternoon I bought some dark brown corduroy slacks, which will be just the thing for going on our long hikes together – they won't wear out due to lying on the grass so many times!!!*

With Jim's return in sight, I realized just how much I had to do. However, the major stumbling block remained:

how could I arrange a wedding, without knowing when it would be? Even so, I began to feel excited again, and started to organize what I could at this stage.

I loved my bedroom at Robinson Street. But now I needed to think about it from Jim's point of view, as we didn't know where or when he would be posted after his leave so we might be staying in it for a while. I needed a new bed anyway, so the first thing I did was go out and buy a new double bed, which was duly installed. It wasn't just a mattress, like so many of our friends were using in those days, after the war. It was a proper bed and it had to be double for after we got married, though of course when Jim first came home he would sleep at his parents' house.

Next, one night, I wrote out a list of all the people we would like to invite to the wedding. It was a long list of more than fifty, so it might have to be shortened to about thirty. I would have to consult Jim about that.

Meanwhile, an idea formed itself in my mind. I had been saving money ever since I started work at thirteen, and more regularly after we had that week in London, sixteen months ago – I wanted us to have enough to buy our own little house in Blackburn. When I checked with the bank, it looked as if I'd saved quite a healthy amount, but it was nowhere near enough.

Mother had moved into our house, with Bobby, Jeffrey and me, when she was a newly abandoned single mother, scrimping and scraping, sewing and mending to pay the rent as well as keep and feed her hungry young family, soon increased with the arrival of Alan. It had been a tremendous struggle for her, with no help from anyone, especially not our father. It was only when first Bobby and then I felt obliged to leave education and start work to help pay the bills that she could breathe a little more easily. Bobby and I had paid the rent between us for years. But Bobby was still in the RAF, so was only home for a few days occasionally. I might soon be leaving as well, to goodness knows where, so now this idea came to the fore. Instead of leaving the money in the bank, doing nothing, I could perhaps buy our house for Mother to live in, so that she would never have to worry again. We might even need to live in it ourselves sometimes, between postings, or when Jim left the army, so it seemed the sensible thing to do.

I went to see the bank manager and asked about a mortgage. I didn't really know much about such things, so he explained it all for me. I found that, with the deposit I had saved and my good income from the GPO, as well as Jim's army income, the bank would agree to provide me with a mortgage on Mother's house.

I had to persuade a friend and neighbour, Albert Bennett, to come with me to see the landlord, who had once followed me round and round the table when he came to collect the rent and I was alone in the house. (Dear Ray had appeared at just the right moment to save me that day.) I didn't trust him without a chaperone, and Albert was the perfect person. He owned the shuttle factory and he was in the Home Guard throughout the war, so he was well known and wouldn't stand any nonsense.

I had a plan up my sleeve. Our house needed a lot of

work doing to it, so I started with a long list of repairs that were needed. The landlord looked very shifty, trying to get out it.

'I can't afford all that,' he complained.

'I could go to the council and get someone round.'

'They wouldn't be interested!'

'Oh, I think they would,' I insisted. 'My Uncle George is a councillor and an alderman . . .'

He looked as if he was starting to take me a bit more seriously now.

'Of course, if you can't afford the repairs . . . I'll tell you what,' I continued. 'I'll not report you to the council for being a bad landlord, if you let me buy the house.'

I was very determined and I could see Albert nodding his approval. The landlord thought about it but not for long.

'All right,' he said with a shrug. 'But I'll want the full price. It must be worth at least £800.'

'The *market* price,' I emphasized. 'I've had it valued, by Harrison's.' (This was my grandfather's company, but I didn't tell him that.) 'And they've said it's worth £500 in the current market,' I said.

He looked surprised, not so much at the value, but at my daring to do all this.

'£650,' he said. 'And not a penny less.'

'We have to leave a margin for the repairs,' I replied. 'And the builders have estimated at least £100 for those.' I paused to give him a few seconds to think. 'So I won't pay a penny more than £550. That's my absolute maximum.'

He cleared his throat, looking distinctly uncomfortable.

'£550 and it's a deal, or I go home and we forget about it.'

Now both the men looked surprised.

The landlord looked cornered. He swallowed hard. 'You drive a hard bargain,' he said in a whining voice.

'Yes. I like everything to be fair.'

'Right,' he mumbled. 'You win. You can have it for £550.'

With great reluctance, he shook hands with me and we left.

I was quietly pleased at how this meeting had gone. I didn't tell him, but I would have gone up to £650 if I'd had to.

Next I went to a solicitor to sort out all the paperwork. I didn't want to mention it to Mother until it was all finalized and the house was in Jim's and my names. I just assumed she would be pleased that she would never again have to worry about paying the rent.

A few weeks later, when it had been completed, I explained to Mother what I had done.

'I wanted to have a chat with you about the house,' I began.

'This house?'

I nodded.

'What about it?'

'Well, you know there is a lot of work and repairs needed?'

'Yes, love, that's all been building up since before the

war, since we first moved in. I've asked the landlord to get going with some of the most urgent repairs, but he said he can't afford it. He's always been a right miser.'

'He said the same to me,' I agreed with a smile.

'When did you see him?' she asked, rather alarmed. 'The rent's not due till next week.'

'Yes, I know it would be . . . but now it's not due any more.'

'What do you mean?' she interrupted.

I took a deep breath. 'I had a letter from the solicitor this morning and he said that the house is now ours, mine and Jim's, so you never need to pay rent again.'

Her normally placid face showed a mixture of shock and confusion. Her mouth opened to speak, but nothing came out.

'I'm sorry to take you by surprise, but I didn't want to tell you till it was done and completed. You see, Jim and I have been wondering where to live when we are married. Of course, we will mostly have to live in married quarters, away from home, but when he's on leave and if he gets posted abroad again, we need a house that is our base, here in Blackburn. It struck me that if I went to see the landlord, he might sell it to me.'

'How?' she asked. 'Where will the money come from?'

'Well, it's all been arranged. I used some of my savings as a deposit . . . and the bank manager kindly gave me and Jim a mortgage, based on both our salaries, so we managed it. It's paid for and, from today, it's our house – your house, for you and the boys too. Nothing will change, except for Jim sometimes living here with us. And we'll gradually do the repairs as well.' I smiled nervously as she rocked her chair to and fro in thoughtful silence. I suppose she was trying to take it all in.

After a few seconds I asked her, 'What do you think, Mother? It will help you because we'll still contribute to the food and bills.'

'Well,' she said, giving me a curious look. 'Does this mean you are now my landlord?'

I laughed. 'I would be,' I replied, 'if you were paying rent, but you won't be.'

'You always were a clever girl, Margaret, but how you've done all this without me knowing about it . . . well . . . I don't know what to think.'

Mother sat back and said nothing more, but she seemed happy enough.

When I woke up early the next morning, however, I sat up with a jolt at the realization that I had forgotten one very important detail. I should have consulted Bobby, or at least told him my plans early on. The house was Bobby's home too and he expected to come back and live in it again himself when he left the RAF, which he would shortly do. So, quite rightly, he was entitled to know and have his say before I went ahead. But I never even mentioned it to him. I just went ahead regardless. Talk about single-minded! I'd forged ahead with my plan and left him out of it completely. Now I was in fear of his reaction, but I would have to tell him, somehow.

So, on his next leave, I tried to tell him and explain, but he was in no mood to listen. He was furious.

'How dare you go ahead without even consulting me? This is MY house you are talking about. I am the head of this household . . . and now you try to make your pathetic excuses.'

'I'm very sorry, Bobby.' I took a gulp of air. 'It was foolish of me, I know, but it's done now and all I can do is apologize.'

'How dare you decide to take over like that? How dare you do anything without my permission?' His face was bright red and he was marching up and down the living room, berating me with a continuous flow of invective.

I had clearly misjudged the whole situation. But I had no idea that he would be quite so angry. I had assumed he would be pleased at no longer having to contribute to Mother's rent, but how wrong I was!

'How could you even think of making such an important decision behind my back? I'm sure it will all go wrong. And are you telling me that Jim is going to come and live in MY house? No, I can't allow it. I am the man of this house and I make the decisions round here.'

I didn't necessarily go along with that, but I did accept that I'd gone about it all wrong.

'I'm sorry, Bobby,' I apologized again. 'I can see now that I should have discussed it with you. It's your home too. I just thought you would be pleased that—'

'Well, I'm not,' he interrupted. 'How could I be? You've gone completely over my head and now it's too late to put things right. You should never have done this, Margaret. I blame it all on Jim. I expect he put you up to it, pushing me out of my own house so that you two

can have it to yourselves. Well, that's not going to happen!'
He paused, his face reddened. 'I will not let it. This is my
home and it always will be.'

'Yes, I agree that it's your home – the home of all our
family. But don't blame Jim. He had nothing to do with
it. It was all my idea . . . and my fault.'

He looked very cross and, if I hadn't known he loved
me, I might have been frightened at that moment but I
knew him well enough to know that his anger hid his
disappointment. He was more upset than he would ever
show, and I couldn't blame him for that. But I did have
to stick up for Jim.

'I know you are upset . . .'

'And it's all your so-called fiancé's fault.'

'No, Bobby, it's all my fault. Jim had nothing to do
with it. He's still in India and took no part in it. So I must
take the blame. Nobody else.'

'Well then, YOU should have asked my permission to
do this. And MY name is the one that should be on the
deeds, not yours.'

I wanted so much to explain to Bobby that I'd done it
for Mother, and for all of us, but he refused to listen to
anything I could say. I had to get away from his ranting,
so I put my head down and left the room. I went outside
to try and calm down, watching Alan play airplane
hopscotch with his friends in the street, just as Ray and
I had done all those years ago. As I tried to hide my tears,
I went over and over what Bobby had said.

I don't know what had made me cry most. Bobby's
fury, of course – the strength of his reaction and all that

shouting at me – but also a great sense of frustration. I had tried to do everyone a good turn; it had all seemed such a good idea, but now I wished I'd never thought of it.

As I sat there on the edge of the pavement, I suddenly realized that the thing that had probably hurt Bobby the most was the prospect of having to share his house with Jim, whom he'd never even met.

Of course, Jim was the last person Bobby wanted in his house. Although Bobby was a few years older than Jim and they had both gained campaign medals in the war, Jim was senior in rank and he had the Burma Star. Jim was taller than Bobby too. He had been to the top school for boys in the area and, cruellest of all, he was generally admired for having fought in Burma, the fiercest and most dangerous theatre of war, where fighting was often hand-to-hand. Bobby, meanwhile, had travelled from one airfield to another, in Britain, Italy or in African war zones, building Mosquitoes and repairing their war-damaged fuselages. It was very important work, and nobody ever reproached Bobby for it, because it wasn't his choice, but I'm sure he was hurt that he couldn't be the pilot he dreamed of being. I began to realize that he probably knew some of these things about Jim and that he was perhaps a little in awe and maybe jealous of him, which might have played its part in his dislike of the whole idea of my marrying Jim.

He was obviously affronted too that his role as 'man of the house' might be threatened, or at the least shared, which Bobby wouldn't like at all. Whoever's name was on the deeds, to him, it would always be Bobby's house. I did understand.

Finally, Jim had a date for his return, 15 December, so at last we could set a date for our wedding. I booked the church for Boxing Day, 26 December 1947. Now I had to arrange everything else – flowers, reception, invitations. Mother offered to make my wedding dress, so I did a drawing of what I wanted it to look like. She had a length of beautiful white crêpe de Chine, under which she would make a slip out of unused blackout material which she had bleached white. Every now and then she needed me for another fitting and I could see her finest stitching and the shape of the dress developing into a perfect fit. It was going to look beautiful.

I was desperate to be there, on the dockside, to meet Jim as soon as he touched English soil. I wouldn't miss that for anything . . . and he would have been bitterly disappointed if I wasn't there, waiting. So on 14 December I took the train down to Southampton, arriving the night before Jim's ship was due to dock. I stayed at the Girls' Friendly Society hostel and got up very early, so excited to see him, as if arriving early would bring his ship in sooner. I took a taxi down to the dockyard and showed my papers before being allowed through. I thought it would be packed with people meeting their loved ones. Perhaps they were already there, lining the dockside.

I found my way to the correct quay. Not having seen

a large troop ship coming in before, I expected it to be anchored in the harbour, with the men being ferried ashore in small boats. But I was wrong. As I rushed round the last corner I nearly ran too far. One more step and I'd have fallen in.

There was a vast steel wall alongside the empty quay. I looked up and there was the side of the ship right in front of me, so tall and wide that I had to stand back to see it properly. As I did so, all I could hear was a loud chorus of shouts and wolf whistles. I'd never heard anything like it. The troop ship had three long tiers of uniformed soldiers, all hanging out and waving. I looked around . . . but I was the only person there. Were they all waving at me? I waved back. There must have been hundreds of them, perhaps thousands, all cheering and whistling at me.

As I waved, I ran my eyes along each tier, trying to look at all the faces, but it was an almost impossible task. I thought I saw Jim on the top deck and directed my waves and smiles at him. I was the only girl on the quay, so I had whistles, cheers, everything. It was an amazing, exhilarating experience. I kept on waving at the soldier I thought was Jim, and all those around him were patting him on the back and shaking his hand. Then, as I waved, something made me turn to my right and there was Jim, running along the quay towards me!

He picked me up, swung me around and kissed me . . . to the sound of even louder cheers and whistles. We were still locked together in our first embrace for nineteen long months when two policemen appeared and tried to pull us away behind some huge cargo crates.

'If you carry on like that,' said one of them with a gruff voice and a wide grin, 'we'll have a riot on our hands.'

'Yes,' said the other. 'Keep out of sight.'

So, still entwined, we sat down behind the crates and talked and talked, while the policemen kept guard.

'I'll have to go back to join the others,' said Jim.

'Why?' I asked, incredulous. 'We've waited long enough to be together, I don't want to lose you after just ten minutes!'

'You can't go back now, sir. You'll be killed by the crush. You'll have to stay here, out of the way, till the majority of them have disembarked. Then we'll escort you back and explain why we made you wait.'

'Yes, officer,' said Jim and we kissed again.

I thought we would just go straight to the station and back to Blackburn. But no.

'We'll have to sign out first,' explained Jim. 'Then we have to get a train to London and change to another train going to Scotland. I have to report to the depot at Buchanan Castle to sign for my new orders, passes and money for my leave.'

By the time we'd got out of the dockyard, onto the train and arrived in London, it was mid afternoon, so we decided to go to the pictures at a cinema in Tottenham Court Road that we had been to before. Then it had been a new American film – *Gilda*, with Rita Hayworth and Glenn Ford. This time they were showing a Marlene Dietrich and Charles Boyer film – something about a garden, I think it was. We didn't see much of the film. We were just locked in each other's arms. Then we went to

King's Cross and got tickets on the overnight train to Stirling, then a taxi to the castle. I had to stand and wait outside, looking at this amazing building with its tall, round turrets, while Jim went in and completed his paperwork. He came out with his money and passes and we then had to make our way back to Stirling. We walked out of the grounds and must have looked rather lost and forlorn by the side of the road. Jim was still in uniform, which is perhaps why a lorry stopped.

'Do you want a lift?' asked the driver.

We were so tired by then that we would have gone with anyone. So we got in and the driver talked to us as he drove us all the way to the station in Stirling – probably well out of his way. He was a cheery, helpful soul and dropped us off by the station entrance. We gathered ourselves and walked in. It wasn't until we got to the ticket office to buy a train ticket to Blackburn for me that Jim made the awful discovery.

'Oh no!' he said, his tanned face turning pale. We looked at each other in alarm.

'What is it?' I asked.

'My money is gone. Everything – money, passes, the lot!'

'But you only just collected it all. I saw them in your hand when you came out of the castle. Then you put them in your pocket.'

'I know, but they're not in my pocket now.' He frantically checked all his pockets. 'No, not in any of my pockets.'

'What are we going to do?' I asked. 'I've got *some* money.'

'Yes, but we need to find . . .'

Just then, who should come running towards us but the lorry driver, with the whole package held triumphantly aloft in his hand.

'Here, you left these in my cab,' he said with a cheery grin. 'Lucky I spotted them on my way out. They must have fallen out of your pocket when you got in. I'm glad I caught you.'

'Thank you so much,' we chorused.

'It was very kind of you to bring them back here for us,' I added. 'We are so grateful.'

'Yes, pal,' said Jim. 'You're one in a million.'

We were very lucky that morning and desperately tired. At last we were going home to Blackburn and our plans to start our new life together.

We had talked it through on the train and decided to split up when we got back, so that Jim could go and see his family while I dealt with the upset I was sure I would have to face when I got home.

In fact, I was right. All hell was let loose in both our houses. Jim's parents welcomed him home as if he were the Prodigal Son. But his two older brothers were furious with him for wanting to get married so young, they told him, and would barely talk to him. I think they steered clear of him as much as possible. I couldn't understand why at the time, but I wonder now whether it was something to do with me and where we lived – two different areas of Blackburn. People could be quite sensitive about that in those days.

Meanwhile, at my house, Mother was suspicious about how I'd spent my extra night and day away. I could understand that and I tried to explain. But Bobby was furious. I know my delay had made him think the worst and he therefore didn't believe me.

'You're too young to get married,' he said later that day. 'I want you to cancel this fiasco of a wedding. I've always promised myself that I would take you travelling with me all around the world. Now is the time. I'm leaving the RAF and you can leave the GPO, then we'll set off on our travels. Won't that be wonderful? We'll see all the sights and do lots of new things in every country we visit.'

'No, Bobby,' I interrupted him. 'I'm sorry, really I am, but I can't come with you round the world. I hate travelling. I thought you knew that. Anyway, I love Jim and I am going to marry him. Nothing will make me change my mind.'

At this point Bobby stormed out of the house and I sat down in the living room, my head in my hands.

Within half an hour, the last person I wanted to see, Joe, was knocking at our door.

'I'm back for good now,' he said. 'So let's get married.' He stepped forward to kiss me, but I moved to the side. Had Bobby sent him? Or was it a coincidence? Either way, I knew where my heart lay.

'I'm sorry, Joe, but I thought you would have realized by now – I am not going to marry you. I hope you have a happy life, but I will not be a part of it. I am engaged to marry Jim Ford and we will soon be wed. So please leave now.'

He looked shocked and confused.

'But . . .' He tried to step inside.

'No. Goodbye, Joe.' I firmly closed the front door.

When Jim and I were comparing notes, later that afternoon, out for a walk in the fast-fading light, he told me about his brothers' reaction against him marrying and asked me what Bobby had said about our wedding.

'Was Bobby happy for us?'

'I'm afraid not. He was angry too because I am disobeying him to get married.' I didn't want to say how furious he really was, as it would have worried Jim. 'I expect he'll come round to it.'

We were both glad to be walking together, wrapped up well on this cold winter's day. We kept on the move as I told him more details of our wedding plans and who I'd sent invitations to. He described the suit he'd had made in New Delhi to wear at our wedding, but admitted he wasn't sure whether to wear that or his uniform.

'Definitely your uniform,' I said.

We discussed what would happen after his two and a half weeks off, just after New Year, when he would be based at Chester, with married quarters for us both to live in.

'But what about my job?' I asked.

'You can give your notice in now,' he replied. 'There's no need for you ever to work again.'

I stopped in my tracks. 'But I want to work. I love working. I know I'll have to leave this job, but I can find a new one in Chester.'

'Why?' he asked, with a hurt look. 'Isn't it enough for you to look after our home and me?'

'No!' I replied, rather too sharply. 'I don't want to sit around all day, doing not very much. I'd be bored to death.'

He was clearly disappointed in me. He had been building up his dreams and hopes over all those nineteen months, and me working wasn't in his picture of our happy domestic future together. But it was in mine.

There were only a few days left until the wedding now and I still hadn't found anybody willing to give me away. Bobby had downright refused.

'I'm not giving you away to anyone but Joe,' he said. 'In fact, I don't even want to come to your fiasco of a wedding.'

'All right, then. I won't invite you,' I replied.

My father had already refused when I had met him by chance that day in Darwen Street. He probably didn't want to meet any of the relatives. Next I asked my mother's brother, Uncle George, but he said no, because the wedding was going to be in a Catholic church. Well, of course, both Jim and I were Catholics, so that was also a black mark to some of my family and that was why Grandad Harrison also declined to give me away. I wondered about Jeffrey, but Mother said no, he was too young at fifteen.

I was unsure what to do next. Bobby was visibly pleased that I'd failed so far. Then, however, I had a brainwave and asked Uncle John, my father's older brother. I had never liked him, but he did agree, so that was a relief.

Now the wedding could go ahead and we had only the last-minute things to sort out.

Meanwhile, Jim and I spent as much time together as we could, out walking in all weathers in the daytime to get away from our families and just be the two of us, making up for lost time. We spent some of our evenings at Tony's so that I could dance, and Jim even occasionally joined in too, with a bit of tutoring from me.

Sometimes in the evenings we went to the cinema and a couple of times we joined the group in the George and Dragon. One night, though, Jim and I went to the Jubilee Inn, just across the road from the George and Dragon. Peggy must have seen us go in, because the next thing was that we could hear the sound of singing, wafting across the road and coming closer. Then in through the door of the Jubilee Inn came the choir, all of them, including Joe, all filing in and lining up right in front of us, singing, 'With someone like you, a pal good and true . . .'

It was as if they were saying goodbye to me. I suppose they were. I looked along the line, all of them smiling – even Joe, who looked directly at me as he sang. Of course, he could have meant that this was what he wanted himself, but that night I thought he was saying through this song that he now accepted the situation, that he really meant it for me. Was that wishful thinking?

When they finished the song, some of them bought drinks and they all came to join us in a large group. Knowing how volatile Joe could be, I suddenly felt nervous and was on the brink of suggesting we leave, when the strangest thing happened.

I had told Jim everything about all my old boyfriends. This naturally included my engagement with Joe and his refusal to let me go. So Jim knew all about Joe, but Joe didn't know that he did. Jim went straight over to where Joe was sitting. I dreaded to think what he would do, but I needn't have worried. Jim put out his hand to Joe and he took it. They shook hands.

'Thank you for taking such good care of Margaret while I was away,' said Jim, with a genuine smile.

I held my breath and waited, fearing the worst, but I was amazed to see that Joe was a real gentleman about it and took what Jim said at face value, though I thought I detected a slightly quizzical expression on his face afterwards.

It was a brave and caring gesture of Jim's, but would it make any difference? I could only wait and see.

23

Best Laid Plans

December 1947

Boxing Day 1947 dawned with thick snow on the ground, the rooftops and the trees. Jim and I had been to midnight Mass together to hear our banns being read for the final time. Now everything had been done and it was time to get ready for our special day.

This day was the culmination of all of Jim's dreams – everything he had written in his letters and all that he wanted in life. My fervent hope early that morning was that it would all go to plan, with no upsets, so that it could be a wedding day to remember.

Mother came in with the wedding dress she had lovingly made for me and laid it out on my bed. First I helped her to get ready. Then I went back to my bedroom, put on some make-up and brushed my hair. Normally I put it up, but not today. Jim had especially asked me to wear it loose for our wedding, as he always preferred it that way, with my natural curls down to my shoulders.

I put on my dress, with Mother's help, as it fitted perfectly to my shape. It had quite a high stand-up collar, puff-topped sleeves tapering down to a point at each wrist, a full skirt down to my feet and a frilly bit draped from the point at the back, right around.

Jim had once written to me from India, saying he'd seen the most beautiful white material for my wedding dress . . . but then he'd remembered Ray and his white lace, and Jim thought he'd better not buy it for me, in case it upset me. In those days of rationing, it would have been sensible to bring material from India, but I think Jim was right. I probably would have refused it. Anyway, as always, Mother had done a brilliant job of the dress with what she had.

When I went downstairs in my wedding dress, Bobby was nowhere to be seen.

Oh dear, I thought. Where was he? I knew he had refused to come to 'this fiasco of a wedding'. But I had hoped he would be there to see me in my wedding dress. I just prayed that his absence at this moment was not something I should be anxious about. Perhaps it was his way of showing he loved me by finally accepting the situation and refraining from marring my happiness. I hoped so. I knew that, deep down, Bobby would not have wanted to hurt me. He had always been my protective big brother because he loved me and he knew I thought the world of him. We were very, very close – too close, I suppose.

It was Joe's unpredictability that I feared the most. What if he decided to crash the wedding and tried to halt it? If only Bobby could be there to prevent him. I couldn't bear it if anything happened to scupper Jim's dreams.

*

Fifteen-year-old Jeffrey came to join us, looking very smart, with his hair brushed as flat as he could make it. Mother decided that, at seven, Alan was too young to come to a wedding, so he was spending the day with a neighbour but would join us afterwards.

Uncle John arrived, smartly dressed. 'You look nice, Margaret. I'll wait in the car for you. Don't be long.' Mother adjusted my dress.

'You look lovely,' she said with a smile. 'I'm sure Jim will be proud of you.' She and Jeffrey went off to the church, so I locked up and went out to the hired car.

'Are you ready to go?' asked the driver.

I nodded. 'Yes, I think so,' and off we went, at a stately pace, through the snow. Uncle John didn't speak so as we drove along there was nothing to distract me from the conflicting thoughts chasing round my brain. I knew I loved Jim, but was I really ready to settle down with a regular soldier, to move from place to place like a nomad, to give up my job, to lose my independence? By the time we reached the turning for St Alban's Church, I was wracked with doubt. My hands were sweating inside my gloves, but my throat was dry and my heart was racing.

The driver turned into the drive and continued slowly upwards towards the church entrance. Outside, stamping their feet in the snow to keep their circulation going, stood Jim and his younger brother, David.

I don't know why, but on the spur of the moment I decided.

'Stop and turn round,' I told the driver in a resolute voice, though I certainly didn't feel resolute. 'I can't go in.'

The driver looked surprised, but attempted to turn the car – more tricky than usual on the carpet of snow, trying not to let his wheels spin. Uncle John said nothing.

'Back out and go round again,' I said to the driver.

As we receded backwards down the drive, I glanced at the two figures, expectantly waiting for us to stop. I saw Jim's beaming face as it crumpled into disbelief. That's an image I shall always remember.

The driver took us on a tour of the nearby roads, while I imagined Jim being distraught. Why had I done this to him? I didn't know the answer myself.

'Are you ready to go back now?' the driver asked in a kindly voice.

'Yes please,' I said, fearful that I'd ruined the whole day. Would Jim still be there? Would everyone have gone home? What could I say to them?

Our lovely driver turned in towards the church again. I shifted forward on my seat to get a better look and, to my great relief, Jim and David were still there, looking baffled as we approached. A huge smile spread across Jim's face before they dashed into the church. Now I knew it would all be all right.

Jim's Uncle Nicholas married us in St Alban's Church – a beautiful building with a special atmosphere. Yes, it was Roman Catholic. It was a nuptial mass; the whole congregation was there as well as all our guests and the church was packed. My parish priest attended too. He knelt, holding the big black Bible on his head for Father Ford, alias Uncle Nicholas, to read from. The marriage ceremony went well, up to the part where the priest asked whether there were any objections. This was the bit I was dreading. What if Joe had crept in at the back of the church, ready to shout out at this moment? I looked round at my mother and she looked at me, knowing what I was thinking, and we both held our breath. I'm sure Jim did too. The seconds seemed like minutes but the silence certainly was golden that day. With huge relief and no interruptions or hitches, we were pronounced man and wife.

We smiled at each other and kissed, then went to sign the register. We came back out and stood for a few seconds as the organist started to play. Instead of some classical anthem or hymn, the melody that came out was 'The Bells of St Mary's' – a Bing Crosby song. I tried my best not to laugh. The organist, I discovered later, was from St Mary's College, where Jim had gone to school and where Jeffrey was now a pupil. He obviously had the same impish sense of humour as Jim, whose idea it was to depart from tradition as a kind of joke for my benefit. Everybody loved it, except perhaps one or two of the older members of the congregation who may have muttered their displeasure to each other.

Jim and I went in the wedding car and everyone waved us off before coming to join us at the Grosvenor Hotel in Blackburn, where our wedding breakfast would take place.

The hotel itself looked absolutely beautiful, with white ribbons draped from the picture rails, starched white linen tablecloths, silver cruets and cutlery, crystal glasses and gold-rimmed plates. All of Jim's family were there, except for Jack and Louis, his older brothers. All of my usual family members were there too, except for Auntie Elsie, who said she had a cold. I didn't understand that, as one of the uncles or cousins would have given her a lift, I'm sure, and she needn't have stayed all day.

Of course, my father and Bobby were obvious by their absence, for different reasons. I had nurtured this little hope that Bobby might change his mind at the last minute and come. But he didn't. I refused to be sad on my wedding day so I didn't dwell on it and neither did Jim.

Nearly all our close friends were there to help us celebrate and everyone seemed to be in a good mood when they arrived, though if there was any slight nuance of tension, it could only have been the old sore point of religion. After all, the wedding had been a Catholic service in a Catholic church, led by a Catholic priest. I expect that might have been hard for the Protestants to swallow.

We all found our places at the table for the sit-down meal. Grandad Harrison had supplied the Grosvenor Hotel with a dozen chickens and they cooked them a special way, which was delicious in that time of rations and shortages. The speeches passed me by in a whirl. We had a pianist who played all the popular tunes of the day while a lot of the younger guests danced. It was all very celebratory. This was our day – Jim and me. We had been separated for so long and we were very happy to be wed at last.

Ever since Ray's father came round to our house that day, to tell me Ray had been killed by a bomb sinking his submarine, I had kept in touch with his parents. I used to go and have a cup of tea with them every now and then. I had invited them to my twenty-first birthday party the previous year, but I wasn't sure whether they would come to the wedding, as to them I suppose it should have been Ray's wedding to me. But I sent them an invitation anyway and they accepted. I was so pleased to see them there.

I know that, without a body to bury or a grave to visit, nor any irrefutable proof of their son's death, they still nurtured some tiny germ of hope that it was all a mistake, and Ray would come back one day. His father could not shake this notion and often told me he felt he was still alive. Meanwhile, Ray's mother had been to several seances and she always used to come round to our house to tell me what the spiritualist had said. It was always just a bit more each time, to keep her going back, I suppose.

'Ray's alive!' she said the last time. 'He's alive and living on an island, but he's gone blind – he can't see at all.'

Every time I had tried to be sympathetic, but it was all very unsettling for me, as I had accepted Ray must be dead. I'm sure she told me with the hope that maybe I would not marry Jim, or anyone else, but wait for Ray to come home. I didn't know what to do to stop her, so finally I had written to Jim about it and he wrote to Ray's father, asking him to stop his wife coming round to me with all this. He put it very well, saying how much I loved to see them – they had been part of my life for so long.

On the day I married Jim, Ray's father came over and hugged me, as if it was Ray I was marrying. But Mr Nash knew Jim too, as Jim and Ray were the same age when they joined the Home Guard together, where Mr Nash was their sergeant. Ray and Jim even went to join up for the war together as they both wanted to be in the navy, though Jim soon after changed his mind in favour of the army.

Both Ray's parents were very good about me marrying Jim. As well as the warm hugs, they gave me a wedding present.

'Open it,' suggested Ray's father, with a tear in his eye.

I unwrapped it to find a lovely photograph frame.

'Look,' he said. 'You can swing it like this,' and he showed me how it swivelled.

'It takes two photos,' said Ray's mother. 'You could put Raymond's photo in that if you like. I'm sure Jim wouldn't mind.'

At the end of the wedding reception, we had the hired car again to take us back to my house to change and go away. We'd booked to stay in Ireland for a few days. I can still remember the address: Clontarf Street, Dublin.

'Are you really looking forward to this honeymoon trip?' I asked Jim as we sat in the back of the car, going home.

'Yes,' he beamed, then gave me a look of concern. 'Why? Aren't you?'

'We-e-ell.' I hesitated. 'It's so cold – just imagine how freezing it will be on that ferry to Ireland this afternoon.' I shivered. 'I'm not sure I want to go anywhere today.'

'I hadn't thought of that,' he said. 'The ferries might not even run in this weather.'

'As long as we're together,' I continued, 'wouldn't it be cosier just to stay at home and be warm? Then we can go out for lots of walks, just like we used to do, to all the places we love.'

So that's what we decided. We arrived back in Robinson Street, where all our relatives were also converging. The hotel had been marvellous in giving us all the uneaten food to take away with us – very useful, with so much still rationed in the shops. I had been bottling peaches for weeks, so I got those down from the pantry shelf and I started preparing a splendid tea for all the family. But as I was doing the finishing touches . . . oh, the horrible aunts! Like gannets on sparse feeding grounds, they rebelled against so many years of short rations, brazenly uploaded various amounts of food and went off home.

I had invited our next-door neighbours to come round, so now they sat down at our table tucking into everything that was left.

'Who is going to help me with the washing-up?' I asked, as they moved off, back to their house.

'I'll help you,' offered Jim.

'No, it's all right,' I whispered. 'What I'd really like you to do is to take Mother and Alice out somewhere.'

'Where?'

'I don't mind; anywhere will do,' I replied. 'As long as you give me enough time to have a huge wash-up and to clear away all this mess.'

Dear Jim. I have no idea to this day where he took them, but they were out for quite a while and by the time they got back, it was all clean and tidy. So that was our wedding day, right down to the bride doing all the washing-up!

There was one disturbing footnote to the day. When Jim came back with Mother and Alice, they told me what they had heard from a man down the street, who was on his way home from a lunchtime drink.

'Apparently, Bobby and Joe smashed all the glasses in the George and Dragon,' said Mother.

'Oh no!' My heart sank. 'What, both of them?'

'Yes,' said Alice. 'We heard they made a real mess of the pub, so it will be the talk of the town!'

'It's such a shame,' added Mother. 'Two nice young men, good boys, both of them. I know our Bobby was against the wedding,' she said. 'But I can hardly believe he did that.'

'I think they were both cross with me,' I explained. 'Joe would probably have gone into one of his rages because I wouldn't marry him. If he couldn't marry me, he couldn't stand the thought of anyone else having me . . . and Bobby didn't want me to get married at all, and especially not to Jim. I know he didn't like that.'

Everyone was silent as we all took it in.

'It wasn't how I dreamed our wedding would be,' muttered Jim. Then he turned to me. 'But we've had a lovely day and I've married the best girl in the world, so that's all that really matters.'

The way my beloved brother Bobby behaved on my wedding day caused a rift between us that sadly didn't heal fully for many years. Indeed, it was another sixty years before Bobby wrote me a letter out of the blue that told me a lot of family secrets and explanations I had never known or understood, including the real reason why he didn't come to the wedding. He said it was so that he could stop Joe's plans to ruin everything, to burst into the church and object to the marriage, to start something, perhaps a fire, so that the church would have to be evacuated. Joe had been determined to stop the service before we were officially wed. Although Bobby succeeded in preventing him from ruining our wedding, he did it by steering him into making his protest in the pub instead. Bobby couldn't stop him smashing the glasses in his fury and frustration. Joe had started it and goaded Bobby into joining in.

Finally, after a long day of ups and downs that saw us married at last, we could relax and warm ourselves in front of the sitting-room fire before bed. In so many of his letters, Jim had written about how he couldn't wait to get into our bed together on our wedding night. At last it was really happening.

The following morning, we got up and dressed, feeling rather embarrassed about going downstairs to see everyone. I opened our bedroom door a little, just as someone knocked at the front door.

'Is Margaret in?' asked the voice.

It must have been Alan who opened the door, as I heard him say, 'She's in bed with Jim. I don't know what they're doing.'

We cracked up laughing. Now we really didn't know

how to get out of the bedroom! In the end, we just had to walk down the stairs as if it were any normal day.

Despite the snow, we had several idyllic days of being together and knowing that nothing could part us for a long time now. Jim would be posted to Chester after New Year, where we could start our new life together in married quarters. We hadn't seen the place yet, but I already had ideas about how we could make it our own.

As midnight struck on New Year's Eve, Jim opened a bottle of champagne. I never drink alcohol – well, hardly ever – but this was a special occasion: the beginning of what we hoped would be our bright future, together at last. When the chimes finished and it was the first minute of 1948, Jim proposed a toast:

'To us, to our future together – long life, love and happiness, looking forward to travels with the army to foreign lands, new friends and starting our own family. You never need to work again.'

We clinked glasses and I sipped that first fizzling taste.

Smiling at Jim, I silently added my own personal wish: that whatever Jim thinks and wherever we go, I will have a good job of my own . . . and I will carry on dancing.

Epilogue

We never did have our honeymoon, but our lives were packed with travels and adventures; highs and lows in equal measure. When Jim was posted to Chester, soon after our wedding, there were no married quarters available, so I had to stay behind in Blackburn. Mother and the boys went down to Southsea on the south coast to stay with an uncle, so I was all alone in our house in Robinson Street. I carried on my job at the Post Office and started on much-needed repairs to the house. Here I was, newly married, yet living apart and lonely. I had serious doubts whether I had done the right thing.

But things did get better and I soon joined Jim in Chester, where we had two and a half happy years in army accommodation. From there followed many excitements and challenges as we embarked on a series of postings abroad. We went all over the world, first to Egypt and then to Cyprus and Singapore. I never thought, after growing up in Blackburn, I would get to visit and live in so many exciting and exotic places. We had such adventures together and I have such fond memories of those times. Wherever we were, I always tried to work and get stuck in with the social life. We adopted a stray Alsatian in Egypt, escaped a ship fire on the way to Cyprus and I opened the first two bookshops in the Union Jack Club for all servicemen in Singapore. I was in my element!

In 1974, when I was based back in the UK, something happened during a posting in Northern Ireland that affected Jim badly. When he came home he was very moody and changeable, so I felt I was always walking on eggshells. I never did find out what happened, but I looked after him and tried to do my best for him. Looking back, I know that he must have been suffering from PTSD. But there was no name for it then and no help, so it affected him for the rest of his life.

After Jim left the army, we lived in Morecambe for a while before we finally settled in a small bungalow near Carnforth. We enjoyed sixty-seven happy years together but sadly he died, clinging to me, on 26 November 2013. Despite my grief, I was relieved that after so many years of suffering, Jim was at last free.

Bobby broke his silence three years after my wedding by writing me a letter, in which he apologized for not attending the ceremony. He explained that he only ever wanted to protect me. However, it would be several more decades before he gave me a full explanation of everything – not just his behaviour on my wedding day, but all the mysteries I had never understood about my family. We kept up a lovely correspondence over the years, and there were meetings too, with him, his wife Phyllis and their four sons. It brought Bobby and me close again through the rest of our lives.

Just after writing this book, I saw a plea in the *Lancashire Telegraph* for anyone who might have known Flight Sergeant, Wireless Operator/Air Gunner Leslie Fielding to make contact with a man who lives in France, near the Second World War crash site of Leslie's Lancaster bomber, shot down by the enemy.

Benoit Howson has installed a memorial to all those five men who were killed that night. It included their names, ranks and portraits, but there was no picture for Leslie. Benoit was looking for a family member or anyone else who could give him a photo of Leslie to inlay on the memorial beneath his name.

I contacted Benoit through the newspaper editor and he called me direct from France. He was delighted when I told him that I do have a good photo of Leslie, a copy of which I emailed to him straight away. I was also able to tell him a lot about Leslie and how close we had become during the months leading up to his death that fateful night.

Benoit immediately emailed me some pictures of the memorial, now with Leslie's portrait in place. He also posted to me, seventy-four years after the event, some fragments of the very aeroplane itself – the Lancaster bomber shot down that night.

It all came back to me again, as vivid as if it was now – that evening when he told me I would not see him again. He knew it was our last embrace and I know now that he was releasing me, not rejecting me, when he said, 'This is the last time.'

I am now aged ninety-two and still live in our bungalow

in a quiet village south of the Lake District, within sight of the sea. Here I still love talking to people, whether it be Kim, my technician nephew who visits to upgrade my computer, or occasional phone calls with nieces. Jim's niece Susanna, who had always written letters to him when he was overseas, now regularly keeps up with me and takes me out for enjoyable lunches and shopping trips from time to time. Sadly, all my old friends have died.

I spend most of my time these days rereading Jim's 630 love letters from all over the world and listening to our favourite music from the Forties; living in the past, when times were harder and people so much friendlier.

Acknowledgements

My husband Jim, for sixty-seven years of love and adventure.

My mother, who never confided or complained.

Raymond and Leslie, for their love.

Jacquie Buttriss, for her interest in writing this story.

Clare Hulton, my literary agent.

Ingrid Connell, Charlotte Wright and everyone at Macmillan.

Mum, Dad and toddler Bobby riding in a landau in Blackpool.

Me with Grandma Harrison.

Aged four playing outside.
Independent as ever!

My older brother Bobby, aged
eighteen. I idolized him.

Our rented house in Robinson Street.

Childhood sweetheart Ray, aged sixteen,
in the Home Guard.

Me, aged eighteen, with a bow in my hair!

Leslie Fielding in his RAF uniform. He really meant a lot to me.

Enjoying a day out with a friend in Blackpool.

Handsome Joe who soon
became too possessive.

Jim in Burma, wearing the bush
hat I love.

Jim and me on
our wedding
day in
December
1947.